# THE ARMY IN THE AIR

## THE HISTORY OF THE ARMY AIR CORPS

Corporal Aircrewman Woods (later sergeant and a pilot) flying 'shotgun' in Northern Ireland operations, *c.* 1971 (*Museum of Army Flying*)

*Best wishes,*

# THE ARMY IN THE AIR

## THE HISTORY OF THE ARMY AIR CORPS

*Anthony Farrar-Hockley*

### GENERAL SIR ANTHONY FARRAR-HOCKLEY

#### WITH A FOREWORD BY
#### HRH THE PRINCE OF WALES

ALAN SUTTON PUBLISHING LIMITED

ARMY AIR CORPS

First published in the United Kingdom in 1994
Alan Sutton Publishing Limited
Phoenix Mill · Far Thrupp · Stroud · Gloucestershire

First published in the United States of America in 1994
Alan Sutton Publishing Inc
83 Washington Street · Dover · NH 03820

Published in association with the Army Air Corps
Regimental Office · Headquarters Director Army Air Corps · Middle Wallop
Stockbridge · Hampshire

British Library Cataloguing-in-Publication Data
A catalogue record for this book is available from the British Library

ISBN 0–7509–0617–0

Library of Congress Cataloging-in-Publication Data applied for

*Endpapers: front: Samuel F. Cody in his British Army Aeroplane No. 1* (MOD (RAE)); *back: Gazelle of 2 Flight exercising with the ACE Mobile Force in Norway, 1991*

Typeset in 10/13 Baskerville.
Typesetting and origination by
Alan Sutton Publishing Limited.
Printed in Great Britain by
The Bath Press, Bath, Avon.

# Contents

**A Fighting Arm**

**Appendices**

**Maps**

ST. JAMES'S PALACE

Having always been fascinated by military flying, I hold the early aviators of the Royal Flying Corps, the Glider Pilot Regiment and the Air Observation Post Squadrons in high esteem. They were ordinary men, blessed with rare skill and courage, who served this country well in time of war. In very basic aircraft and with little or no armament to defend themselves, they fought against both the elements and the enemy. They also contributed significantly to the development of military aviation and laid the foundation of today's Army Air Corps, of which I am enormously proud to be Colonel-in-Chief.

General Farrar-Hockley was a distinguished airborne soldier and is a well known military historian. In this book he has captured the spirit of the early aviators and shown that it is still very much in evidence in the modern Army Air Corps. He traces the development of the Corps, from its humble beginnings in 1957 to its present position as one of the three direct fire arms of the British Army. Above all, it is a fitting tribute to the skill of all those who have been proud to wear the distinctive pale blue beret throughout the history of the Corps.

The Corps has earned a reputation for military professionalism and flexibility which has become the hallmark of Army aviation. I am sure that those who read this book will agree that, with such a fine heritage, the Army Air Corps is well poised to play its full part in whatever lies ahead.

# Acknowledgements

Numerous people have assisted me in the completion of this book. I must first thank Mr Harry Foot for his devotion and patience in producing and annotating documents for me from the Public Record Office and the Museum of Army Flying. In this connection, I must also thank the Director and Curator of the Museum for their help together with the devoted group who give much time to the maintenance of the historical section. Major John Dicksee has been tireless in his help, finding documents, and giving invaluable advice on sections of the typescript; and I have benefitted greatly from his association with the former Royal Artillery Air Observation Post organization and the select band of its pilots. Among them is Lieutenant-Colonel Lionel Wheeler who has freely loaned me his photographs and records of 656 Squadron during security operations in Malaya.

All the Directors of Land/Air Warfare, Army Aviation, and Army Air Corps from inclusive Lieutenant-General Sir Napier Crookenden, have kindly given me their perspective of the events during their respective tours, some of which threatened the demise of the organization. I thank the present Director, Major-General Simon Lytle and his Regimental Colonel, Colonel W.A. McMahon, for their support over the past year.

Lieutenant-Colonel Nigel Thursby was most helpful in the opening stages of research. His place was taken by Lieutenant-Colonel Charles Blount who has shouldered a rising burden of tasks as time for publication shortened. I cannot thank him enough for his responsiveness and good humour.

Colonel Michael Hickey produced material for me and, with Colonel John Everett-Heath, read sections of the typescript and corrected errors of fact. I thank them and all those who have done likewise though, on the event of publication, I must take responsibility for the text as it stands.

Finally, I thank all those who have given me their time and assistance in many ways. They form part of that host whose constituent numbers, whether mentioned specifically in these pages or not, have at one level or another contributed to the establishment, operation and development of the Army's light aircraft in peace and war.

Anthony Farrar-Hockley

# Foundations

CHAPTER ONE

# 'Yea instruments to flie withall . . .'

Aman is standing in some great space – a vast hall, perhaps, or in the open air. A strange
confidence persuades him to move his arms up and down vigorously as a bird flaps its
wings. To his joy, he rises from the ground. He is flying.

This is one of the commonest dreams of humankind, the expression of a longing to move freely
through the air like a bird, climbing, diving, wheeling, turning, floating even on a rising current, at
times motionless except for the occasional lift of a finger tip to maintain balance.

It is a dream we share with the peoples of the earliest civilizations. Man learned to run, they
reasoned, and discovered how to swim; why should he not fly? Though lacking wing structures his
arms and hands were highly adaptable; his breast muscles might be developed to match those of
the birds. A man might fit artificial wings upon his arms and rise into the air. In ancient Greece it
was said that Daedalus, the Athenian craftsman, contrived artificial wings to escape successfully
from Crete and the Minotaur, the feathers on his arms held fast by wax.

Perhaps this myth inspired men to emulate Daedalus. King Bladud perished in an attempt to fly
across London in AD 852, one of many to believe erroneously that feathers or cloth wings
vigorously waved would bear him up in a breeze. They were not dissuaded by expert advice.
Following several mortal failures in the Kingdom of the Two Sicilies, Giovanni Borelli, a
Neapolitan professor of mathematics, observed in 1680 that the relationship between pectoral
muscle and body weight in a human was too low: 'it is impossible that men should be able to fly
craftily by their own strength'.

While this conclusion gradually dissuaded bird emulators from leaping off towers or cliffs, it did
not quench the longing to fly or discourage scientists from one century to the next to seek a
reliable means of taking to the air. Research and progress followed two approaches: heavier-than-
air 'contrivances', the path of aviation; and that of aerostation, lighter-than-air devices. A few of
the pioneers straddled both.

Roger Bacon, a Franciscan monk and noted scientist, was credited in 1270 with the invention of
a flying machine,

. . . yea instruments to flie withall, so that one sitting in the middle of the Instrument, and
turning about an Engine, by which the wings being articially composed may beate the ayre
after the manner of a flying bird.

Leonardo da Vinci, whose interest in flying in the view of Vallentin, his biographer, occasioned
the 'most tremendous, most obsessing, most tyrannical of his dreams', produced aircraft designs
early in the sixteenth century which are celebrated for their technical innovation. Most
importantly they contained suggestions for the use of an airscrew as a means of propelling fixed
wings but, unfortunately, the studies were not circulated until 1797.

For over three hundred years there was virtually no progress in the flight of a craft heavier than air. Successive designs either failed to progress beyond the drawing board or, if built, to take off. The principal reason was the notion that flight required flapping wings. Such machines have been described as 'ornithopters'. Those who believed in this method expected to find an engine to beat the air with sufficient power to overcome gravity. Steam engines were employed in this capacity in 1830 but blew up.

Another approach favoured use of the wind to lift a body from the ground. The Chinese and Japanese had learned to do this by progressive cunning in kitemaking at a time when Englishmen wore woad. Devised as playthings, there came a time when kites were taken into military use in the Orient for signalling and occasionally lifting soldiers; but no attempt was made to advance this form of aerofoil.

A toy was on sale in Europe by 1325 which eventually attracted the interest of aspirant aviators. It was a crude form of helicopter. A spindle turned by string launched a rotating wing or wings into brief flight. Sir George Cayley studied its potential in 1796, incorporating the principle for a model helicopter. He was also investigating the propulsion of fixed-wing aircraft. Pulling an aerofoil into the wind would, he knew, cause it to rise. He had designed a number of surfaces from the kite form, and was then engaged in constructing a wing which would be controlled in flight by rudders and elevators. Beginning with a kite wing model, 5 ft in length, he progressed over the years to a glider in which 'a boy of about ten years of age was floated off the ground for several yards on descending a hill, and also for about the same space by some persons pulling the apparatus against a very slight breeze by a rope'. In June 1853, towards the end of his life, he launched his coachman in a triplane with flapping wing-tips across a small valley on his estate near Scarborough. Sir George's granddaughter recalled that '. . . the coachman had got himself across clear . . . he shouted "Please, Sir George, I wish to give notice. I was hired to drive, and not to fly."'

These experiments, of importance to the advance of aviation, were limited because, as Sir George realized, he lacked the means to move the fixed-wing glider through the air at speed for a sustained period. An airscrew was needed to do that. By 1857, a French naval officer had fitted first a clockwork engine, subsequently a small steam engine, to a propeller on a model 'glider' which took off and landed successfully. By 1874, this same man, Felix de Temple, had built and flown very briefly a powered aircraft, launched down a ramp.

Another school took the view that fitting engines was pointless until a sure means of controlling a glider in flight had been discovered. From 1889, Otto Lilienthal, a German engineer, made 2,500 flights in hang-gliders of his own design, until his death in a crash in the summer of 1896.

These men, British, French, German and American pioneers, were notable among a number engaged in the reasearch and development of a flying machine heavier than air. Meanwhile, man had taken successfully to the air in balloons.

A Jesuit priest demonstrated the lifting power of hot air 'enclosed in a sphere' to the King of Portugal's court in 1709. It was another scientific toy but a considerable innovation nonetheless. Soon the great chemist, Henry Cavendish, had discovered a means of producing hydrogen by adding sulphuric acid to iron filings, offering a superior means of lifting a container from the ground. The Montgolfier brothers, Joseph and Etienne, began to make the containers out of paper.

The Montgolfiers manufactured paper near Lyons and had become interested in what they took to be the tendency of hot gases to rise as they observed the smoke rising from their factory chimneys. For a time they believed that the denser the material used as fuel the greater the lifting power of gaseous smoke, and burned old shoes and decaying meat until they discovered their error. The paper containers were reinforced by silk and sometimes linen. Large models succeeded small ones. Animals were 'elevated' in cages beneath hot air balloons during a demonstration to Louis XVI and his court at Versailles in September 1778. These being successfully recovered by means of a rope tether, men were ready to make ascents.

The first balloon carrying men rose to 84 ft. Soon members of the court joined the Montgolfiers and their supporters, progressing not only in height but in 1783 to free flight. When the ground anchor was released for the first time in that year the balloon travelled at a height of 300 ft for some 5 miles.

Meanwhile, public subscription had financed a competitive venture by the French Academie des Sciences, employing hydrogen as a lifting agent in a sphere of rubberized silk. Following the launching of such a balloon unmanned, a physicist and one of the constructors took off from the Tuileries Gardens in Paris in December 1783 watched by a huge crowd. After a flight of two hours they landed at Nesle, 27 miles away. In 1785, a hydrogen balloon carried two men across the English Channel, though they were obliged to jettison all their equipment and some of their clothes to maintain sufficient height during the journey.

At last, man had discovered a means of flying in the sense of being able to rise at will into the air and land again successfully. Hot air balloons continued to be used, but chiefly by showmen at fairs and as a novelty for the well-to-do. Coal gas, less efficient but cheaper than hydrogen, was taken into use as another lifting agent, and was employed in a journey of 480 miles from London to Weilburg in Germany in 1836.

Getting into the air was one thing; steering to a desired point was another. Untethered, the spherical balloons drifted in accordance with the wind currents, sometimes vertically as well as horizontally. Other limitations were overcome or mitigated in the century following the first manned flight but lack of navigability persisted. On this account, military interest in ballooning was limited: a free balloon might well find itself sailing over enemy territory; a tethered balloon could be useful to observe enemy movement but was prone to spinning in adverse currents, causing acute vertigo among occupants of the basket or cage beneath.

It was soon perceived that elongation and other alterations to the shape of the bag improved stability in direction, but that did not solve the problem of moving on a course contrary to the direction of the wind. A balloon travelling roughly at the same speed as the wind was like a boat moving at the same speed as the sea around it. In both circumstances there was no capacity to steer. Fitting rudders was fruitless. Those engaged in the development of lighter-than-air flying devices found themselves in the same position as those engaged with heavier-than-air machines: they lacked an engine suitable to propel them at a speed greater than that of the wind. Compressed air, steam engines, clockwork engines, an engine drawing on coal gas from the balloon were all tried during the nineteenth century; all failed to provide sufficient power to manoeuvre other than in conditions close to still air until 1884, when a French dirigible with a 9 hp electric motor was able to steer in light airs.

Advances in engine technology had also raised expectations of those engaged with heavier-than-air machines. In 1890 the French engineer Clement Ader succeeded in launching a fixed-wing aircraft into a manned flight of some 50 m using a light steam engine of his own design. He achieved a hop at a height of 8 in above the ground rather than a sustained flight but this success won him the interest and, more importantly, the financial support of the French War Office. Professor Samuel Langley flew steam-powered models in the United States shortly afterwards and similarly attracted financial assistance from the American government. He was probably on the edge of successful flight as he recognized the value to his work of a new source of power, the internal combustion engine fuelled by petrol.

Professor Langley was overtaken by the Wright brothers, Wilbur and Orville. Like so many of their predecessors, the Wrights had become interested in aviation following a boyhood study of bird flight. An account of Otto Lilienthal's work following his death quickened their interest. They had sufficient funds of their own from a small but thriving bicycle factory to build and fly gliders. The designs sprang from considerable reading – they obtained a number of books and papers from the Smithsonian Institution – and discussion. On the advice of the Washington Weather Bureau, they chose Kitty Hawk on the coast of North Carolina as an area in which they would find suitable winds. In 1900 and again in the summer of 1901 they tried their hand at gliding, both as designers and pilots. They were not searching simply for a vehicle which would take off into wind and follow the same course but one which could move at will up, across, and down wind by use of rudders and banking systems, and could rise and descend by means of elevators.

Deliberation and thoroughness characterized the work of the brothers and a small team of employees, including an engine fitter. They discovered that some of the published data on which they drew for their initial work was inaccurate. A wind tunnel was built to test design modifications in the winter of 1901 before returning to the Kitty Hawk area in 1902. In that year their Glider III was flying up to 622 ft.

After further modifications to the design, this model was judged to be ready for powered flight. For want of anything satisfactory on the market, they built a power unit of their own based on a 12 hp car engine to turn twin 'pusher' propellers, also designed by themselves. Twin elevators were fitted in front of the biplane's wings, twin rudders behind. Twisting wing-tips permitted banking during turns. Tests were made on the rig between September and December 1903 at their camp site, the Kill Devil Hills, 4 miles south of Kitty Hawk.

On 14 December Wilbur Wright made the first attempt at take-off using a rail laid down a sand dune. The aircraft stalled, due, as he admitted, to his mishandling of the elevators. The next day, Orville became the pilot. Forty feet of launching rail had been laid on level ground to moderate the pace of acceleration. Pushed forward by the twin propellers driven by the loud, crackling engines, and watched by five witnesses, the machine rose on the rail and, clearing the end of this, rose above the ground, travelling a distance of 120 ft over 12 seconds, a sustained flight rather than a hop. Taking turns, the brothers made three more flights that day, reaching 852 ft in 20 seconds. By 1905 they had increased the distance and duration to 24 miles and 33 minutes.

Reports that men had flown a heavier-than-air machine were doubted for many months. Indeed, scepticism persisted until the Wrights gave public demonstrations in 1908 in the United States and in France. By this time they had secured patent rights and were ready to show their designs to potential customers, notably the military departments of governments on either side of the Atlantic. They were demonstrating an uprated Wright Flyer III, a two-seater biplane powered by a 30 hp four-cylinder engine. Pilot and passenger were sitting upright, whereas, at Kitty Hawk, Wilbur and Orville had been lying prone to operate the controls.

The reaction of other aviation pioneers to the relatively late and rapidly triumphant entry of the Wrights' aeroplane was mixed. Most expressed some form of satisfaction that their expectations had been realized. A few scientists and technicians were unwilling to concede first place to the American brothers, none more so than the arms manufacturer Sir Hiram Maxim, who had turned to aircraft research. He remarked to a sub-committee of the British Cabinet in 1908, 'all machines that raise themselves from the earth are on my lines exactly'. This was the product of an inflated ego and ignorance as to the advances made elsewhere with unmanned machines raised, like his own, within anchored test rigs. French pioneers had come closest to the Wrights in success and remained for some years in the vanguard of aviation not only in the design of airframes but equally, at times pre-eminently, in engines.

Though Sir Hiram Maxim's experimental group had produced remarkably efficient lightweight steam engines at the end of the nineteenth century, the internal combustion engine had overtaken them. Two French names are notable for originality in adopting this form of power for aeroplanes: Levasseur and Seguin.

Leon Levasseur, a former artist, had produced the first of a series of aero-engines before the Wrights had patented their own. He called it the Antoinette, the name of his patron's daughter. It was remarkable for its size relative to power at a time when the quantities of iron, steel, brass and copper required for engine block and fittings, including quantities of water and pipes for cooling, imposed a weight penalty of 10 lb for each horse power developed.

Laurent and Gustav Seguin had a novel idea to solve the problem of reducing weight and size. Instead of adapting engine forms used in road vehicles, they conceived an engine designed specifically for use in the air. It would be air cooled; a rotary engine which would turn with the propeller. By 1908 it was in production, producing 70–80 hp on the basis of 3 lb/hp. They called it the *Gnome*.

The British had not lacked interest in flying during the nineteenth century: enthusiasts had blown themselves up on steam engines or crashed their gliders as frequently as the French and Germans. One of their number, Percy Pilcher, was carrying forward Otto Lilienthal's ideas when he was himself killed in 1899 following the disintegration of the tail section of his glider. Yet, despite the claims of Sir Hiram Maxim, British efforts did not produce an aeroplane capable of sustained flight until July 1909, when A.V. Roe, encouraged by earlier 'hop' flights, took off successfully from the Essex marshes in a triplane of his own design with a 9 hp JAP engine.

British work with balloons had been more productive. Experiments in aerial observation began in 1863 at Aldershot, site of a developing garrison, with 'spheres and other apparatus' hired from the civil market. After fifteen years of intermittent study, enlivened finally by reports from the Franco-Prussian War of 1870–1, a trials unit was formed by the Royal Engineers, the Army's technical arm. The necessary equipment was to be manufactured at Woolwich Arsenal.

On this basis, from 1878, an air arm began to develop within the Army, due principally to the personality of Captain James Templer, a militia officer and noted private balloon pilot. He was engaged initially to pass on his expertise to officers of the Royal Engineers on the basis of 10s for each day of instruction, but he rapidly acquired additional duties, including supervision of balloon manufacture, the site of which shifted in 1882 to the Royal Engineers' base at Chatham. He

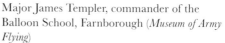

Major James Templer, commander of the Balloon School, Farnborough (*Museum of Army Flying*)

assembled a staff of instructors, scientists and craftsmen – carpenters and joiners, smiths, riggers and engine fitters – to serve the new military arm. Though hired almost entirely on a temporary basis, all became devoted to their work and to Templer's leadership.

Their enthusiasm was not widely shared by officials and officers in the War Office, or indeed by the Army as a whole. Protracted discussions delayed the movement of a balloon detachment to Egypt to support General Wolseley's operations there in 1882. It arrived too late to contribute. Supported by a complaint from Wolseley's headquarters that his force had been denied an important facility – notably in the aerial observation of the Egyptian artillery in Tel-el-Kebir – Templer obtained authority to despatch a detachment to the Bechuanaland campaign in 1884. However, he soon came to regret this decision, for within a matter of months he was ordered to deploy a second detachment with other reinforcements to join General Wolseley's expedition into the Sudan from Suakin on the Red Sea.

All that remained at Aldershot was a small cadre and a number of students. Templer formed a scratch unit of a subaltern and eight other ranks of the Royal Engineers under his own command. They lacked transport and administrative resources, and their hydrogen generation plant was limited. Fortunately, Templer had both an attractive personality and considerable powers of persuasion. Horses and wagons were provided, permitting his small detachment to enter operations with the infantry, sometimes inside their moving squares, sometimes outside them. They were increasingly in demand; the ability of aerial observers to see enemy concentrations heartened the troops on their marches and dismayed those gathering to ambush them. In this early, limited test in the field, one of Templer's many initiatives proved invaluable: British military balloon fabric was made from goldbeater's skin – ox gut – which retained the gas more efficiently than any other material then in service. Demands on the generation plant were thus within its modest supply capabilities.

Anxieties that the balloons would be grounded for lack of hydrogen were overtaken by difficulties concerning manpower and the frequent withdrawal of horses and wagons. The two officers spent the majority of their time arranging transport. When the expeditionary force was withdrawing from Suakin in the summer of 1885, Major Templer discovered three steam tractors lying apart in the port area. He marked them in chalk 'Return to School of Ballooning, Chatham', and thus acquired some transport of his own on the return home.

Over the next few years, Royal Engineer balloons of various types took part in manoeuvres, cooperated with artillery shoots, and engaged in experiments with aerial photography. A wide measure of success won the support of several influential senior officers. In 1887, after almost twenty-five years of discussion and experimentation, the air arm was put on a proper footing as the Balloon Establishment. It comprised:

1 officer in charge
1 instructor in ballooning (Major Templer, who also functioned as superintendent of the factory)

*Balloon Detachment*
1 lieutenant
1 sergeant
15 rank and file (corporals and below)

*The Balloon Factory*
1 military mechanist
1 gas maker          } civil
1 storeman         } staff
1 driver             }
10 balloon-making hands  } including women.

Specialist transport was provided but without horses. The establishment was to draw on the Army Service Corps for draught animals and general service wagons. Fortunately, Templer's tractors were still in operation. Others were borrowed. By 1890 the detachment had become a section numbering three officers, three sergeants and twenty-eight rank and file. Templer was promoted to lieutenant-colonel. The factory was expanded both in numbers and productive capacity of balloons, together with associated equipment. As the Chatham barracks were no longer capable of providing the accommodation required, the entire organization was moved to Aldershot. When the South African war began in 1899, two sections were sent at once to join the Army under General Sir Redvers Buller; a third followed.

All made an important contribution during the initial phase of the war and the subsequent running down of the Boer formations by Lord Roberts. Members of Boer commandos were very ready to testify to the value of balloons as observation platforms. But after Roberts' capture of Pretoria, they were unable to assist in the protracted mobile counter-guerrilla operations.

Royal Engineer observation balloon at Ladysmith, 1900 (*Royal School of Military Engineering*)

However, many commanders, staff and regimental officers in the war who had not previously seen the balloons at work came to value their contribution. Their comments, taken with reports from continental Europe of the German Zeppelin and other dirigibles under power, persuaded the British government to grant additional resources to the Balloon Establishment in 1902. Two thousand pounds were allotted for the construction of a full-scale experimental powered dirigible. But even as design work began, the Wright brothers completed their successful flights at Kitty Hawk and the aeroplane began to compete with lighter-than-air craft for funds.

Lieutenant-Colonel John Capper, Royal Engineers, a former secretary to the Military Aeronautics Committee, took command of the balloon sections in 1903. He then reaped some reward for his advocacy of specialization in air duties within his corps.

For some years officers and men had been posted to other duties after a tour of two or three years with balloons. While this was done with the object of building up numbers trained in this speciality, the policy inhibited progress. For example, in order to meet the desired time of 20 minutes to fly a balloon from the moment of unloading it from its transport, a series of drills had been evolved. To meet emergencies, individuals within each team had to be interchangeable. Much time was thus spent in practice as a consequence. Then, the routine of repair and maintenance of equipment was more speedily and effectively accomplished by experienced hands. By 1903, selected officers and men were being retained for four or five years to raise and broaden the levels of expertise.

These cadres were particularly valuable as Capper increased the number of Royal Artillery officers under training in aerial observation, and extended air to ground signalling systems. In

1904, largely due to Templer's influence, he was able to visit the world fair at St Louis in the United States which contained a section devoted to aeronautics. The event disappointed him but he had permission to visit several sites noted for flying experiments. One of these was to Kitty Hawk.

Until he met the Wright brothers, Capper's prime interest and experience in flying had been with balloons. The sight of their aircraft in flight made him realize that these machines had a far greater scope for development than the powered dirigibles, rigid and non-rigid, under trial. But he was not ready to abandon these forms of vehicle. 'Airships' might offer services beyond the capability of the aeroplane. The captive balloon was cheap, effective, and in service. Even so, he told Templer that the British Army must procure aeroplanes as soon as possible.

Through Colonel Capper, the Wrights opened negotiations with the War Office to supply 'an aerial scouting machine' and manufacturing expertise. These came to nothing. The British authorities wanted to examine the machine and see it fly before making any formal offer. The Wrights had had similar responses from other potential customers. They perceived a danger that their technology would be copied without any return to themselves. They were unwilling to proceed until they held the necessary patents. By 1908, when they completed a contract with France, the British had made other arrangements.

These seemed promising at first. Having been appointed in 1906 to the chief post in air developments, Superintendent of the Balloon Factory, Colonel Capper had employed an American, Samuel F. Cody, who had developed a number of successful kites. These were, basically, hang-gliders, some of which were demonstrated by Cody on the Aldershot military training

A kite balloon designed by Samuel F. Cody (*MOD (RAE)*)

Samuel F. Cody in his British Army Aeroplane No. 1 (*MOD (RAE)*)

grounds at the end of 1905 and early in the following year. Members of the balloon companies made ascents in them.

However, although he had been employed for work with kites, Cody had greater ambitions. He proceeded to flying a glider biplane under power. Although unmanned, it flew successfully on a circular course until the petrol was exhausted, when it glided smoothly to the ground. From this he moved on to the construction of an aeroplane. It was to be powered by an Antoinette engine.

By September 1908, the Cody aeroplane, British Army Aeroplane No. 1, incorporating some of the Wrights' technology, was ready to fly at Farnborough and managed several hops. Adjustments were made to the controls. On 16 October it flew a continuous distance of 1,390 ft over 27 seconds, reaching a height of 30 feet, but crashed when Cody, at the controls, inadvertently dipped a wing on to the ground during a turn. This was the first powered flight under British auspices, albeit principally the work of an American. Further flights and a number of crashes followed in the early months of 1909.

Overlapping these trials, and also funded by Balloon Factory resources, was the swept wing, tailless biplane designed by Lieutenant J.W. Dunne of the Wiltshire Regiment. He had conceived

Army Aeroplane No. 1 in flight (*MOD (RAE)*)

an airframe which was inherently stable, and indeed succeeded during gliding trials in maintaining level flight without recourse to corrective action by the controls. To maintain the secrecy of his work, trials were conducted in Scotland. Funds for the continuation of the project were requested for the financial year 1909/10.

In the latter part of 1908, the War Office was by no means disposed to approve this request. There were, as ever, many competing claims for equipment development and support. Some of those who had opposed the introduction of balloons now doubted the military value of the aeroplane. Proponents and opponents of aerial vehicles argued their cases. Mr H.H. Asquith, the Prime Minister, was advised that the entire matter should be examined by the Committee for Imperial Defence (the CID). He agreed. A sub-committee of enquiry was convened on 23 October 1908 with the following general terms of reference:

Several of the great powers are turning their attention to the question . . . and are spending large sums in the development of dirigible balloons and aeroplanes. It is probable that for countries with land frontiers immediately across which lie potential enemies the development of airships has hitherto been more important than it is for Great Britain, and that we have been justified for this reason in spending less money in experiments than some of our neighbours. The success that has attended recent experiments in France, Germany and America has however created a new situation which appears to render it advisable that the subject of aerial navigation should be investigated.

Lord Esher was appointed chairman. The members were as follows:

Mr D. Lloyd George (Chancellor of the Exchequer)
Mr R.B. Haldane (Secretary of State for War)
Mr R. McKenna (First Lord of the Admiralty)
Captain R.H.S. Bacon RN (Director of Naval Ordnance)
General Sir W. Nicholson (Chief of the Imperial General Staff)
Major-General J.S. Ewart (Director of Military Operations)
Major-General Sir C. Hadden (Master-General of the Ordnance)

Specifically, they were to look into the future dangers from the air, and the naval and military advantages that might accrue from airships or aeroplanes; and to suggest what should be spent on them and by which departments of state. Written evidence was submitted by the War Office, principally concerning balloons and dirigibles, and from four individuals: Sir Hiram Maxim, as noted, Mr Charles Rolls – of Rolls-Royce – who had a private pilot's licence, Lieutenant-Colonel Capper, and Major B.F.S. Baden-Powell.

It was clear that General Nicholson was a considerable sceptic concerning the value of aerial craft of any sort. Balloons would have to ascend to a great height, in his opinion, to be able to observe reverse slopes. They would then be too remote to identify anything of value. Aeroplanes, flying in excess of 40 miles an hour would, he believed, be travelling too fast to permit any useful observation.

Even so, impressed considerably by Count Zeppelin's achievements in Germany, the sub-committee decided that rigid airships, which could remain in the air longer, were capable of making a contribution to naval scouting, and semi- or non-rigid dirigibles to reconnaissance and artillery spotting on land. Conversely, it was accepted that airships might in time be able to strike at the British isles by raiding and bombing.

It was their final opinion that aeroplanes would not be suitable for naval warfare, and were not sufficiently advanced for use over land, though they might in time offer an additional means of reconnaissance. It is possible that the sub-committee was swayed by personal observation; most had seen the Army airship piloted by Colonel Capper which circled over London in October 1907 but were unaware that it had been unable to fly back to Farnborough. None had seen an aeroplane fly.

The sub-committee recommended provision of £35,000 to the Admiralty for construction of an airship, and £10,000 to the War Office for non-rigid dirigibles with the rider that these would replace captive balloons. As for work on aeroplanes, experiments in hand at the Balloon Factory should be discontinued. They recommended that 'advantage should be taken of private enterprise in this form of aviation'. Charles Rolls had, incidentally, offered to make his own Wright model available if the government would provide a suitable airfield. Approving the report on 25 February

1909, the Committee of Imperial Defence accepted the offer 'on the understanding that facilities will be provided by the state . . .'.

Joining the CID in that month, Mr Churchill, as President of the Board of Trade, protested that these proposals were in danger of being considered 'too amateurish . . . we should place ourselves in communication with Mr [Orville] Wright, and avail ourselves of his knowledge'. This was prescient. Numerous designs of aeroplane were taking to the air successfully, among them a Blériot XI monoplane which crossed the Channel on 25 July. H.G. Wells remarked ' . . . in spite of our fleet this is no longer, from the military point of view, an inaccessible island.'

On 26 July the editorial of the *Daily Graphic* noted that,

. . . When Mr [Henri] Farman flew a mile it was possible to say that an ingenious toy had been invented. But a machine which can fly from Calais to Dover is not a toy, but an instrument of warfare of which soldiers and statesmen must take account.

The Parliamentary Aerial Defence Committee had already indicated its dissatisfaction with government measures on 25 April 1909, though this embraced flying devices of all types. Public anxiety grew as newspapers and periodicals carried news of aeroplane developments in Europe

Spherical tethered observation balloon at Farnborough, 1909, by one of two hangars. Right, a powered semi-dirigible, 'Beta', which failed in trials (*MOD (RAE)*)

and America, even in New Zealand. On the initiative of Mr Haldane, at the War Office, an Advisory Committee for Aeronautics was formed. Catching the mood, Mr Asquith told the House of Commons less than three months after endorsing the report by Lord Esher and his colleagues that,

> . . . the work of devising and constructing dirigible airships and aeroplanes has been apportioned between the Navy and the Army. . . . The investigation and provision of aeroplanes are also assigned to the War Office.

There was, however, still no money to finance enterprise in aeroplanes. Flying training continued for a time with Rolls' aeroplane; and when he was killed at the Bournemouth aviation meeting in July 1910, three officers of the Royal Field Artillery, Captains J.D.B. Fulton and Bertram Dickson, and Lieutenant Lancelot Gibbs, used their own.

At the same time, organizational changes were taking place which persuaded government to finance aircraft development. First, the Balloon Factory was separated completely from the School of Ballooning and balloon companies. A civil superintendent was appointed. In the spring of 1910 the CIGS proposed that the companies should be separated from the school and should pass, as operational units, to his direct control. In the summer, Capper advised the Home Ports Defence Committee, investigating the vulnerability of these sites to bombing from airships, that aeroplanes might be the most effective means of defending the ports against such attacks. Haldane was also coming to the view that aeroplanes should not be neglected. He attended a meeting of the Army Council at the end of July 1910 to consider

Bristol monoplane No. 256 launching, Larkhill, 1910 (*Glider Pilot Regiment 182*)

formation of an air battalion which would include among its three companies one containing aeroplanes.

This idea was gradually accepted, and with it a suggestion made earlier in the year that the officers should be drawn 'from any branch of the Army provided they show aptitude for aerial work . . .'. These words were used in a press release from the War Office on 9 October. They affirmed the idea of an Army 'Air Corps'.

The retention of Royal Engineer officers at the school or in balloon companies had certainly raised standards of proficiency and encouraged innovation within them. But by 1910 many of their number complained that they found themselves disadvantaged from a career point of view; preference was given in promotion to those officers with experience in all branches. It was on this basis, rather than any general advantage to the Army of employing cavalry, infantry or artillery officers as pilots, that the change was made.

A Special Army Order was issued on 28 February 1911 establishing the Air Battalion, Royal Engineers, from 1 April that year. 'Royal Engineers' was included in the title because all the other ranks would continue to belong to that corps. The battalion headquarters superseded the disbanded school as the command echelon; its sub-units were one balloon and one aeroplane company, 190 in all, comprising 14 officers, 23 warrant officers and sergeants, and 153 rank and file.

Captain Dickson pilots Boxkite No. 4 during the Army manoeuvres on Salisbury Plain, September 1910 (*Museum of Army Flying*)

In peace, the unit was to occupy itself principally in training and experimentation, including basic flying training for aeroplane pilots. It was soon apparent that this was beyond the battalion's resources, but a simple and relatively cheap solution was soon agreed. Aspirant officers – there were to be no other rank pilots – would make their own arrangements to obtain a proficiency certificate from the Royal Aero Club or any other recognized body in Europe. They would then be eligible for a compensatory payment of £75 (which by no means covered the individual's expenses) subject to their commanding officer's recommendation for flying duties. The other criteria for selection, which bear every sign of having been devised by an informal committee, were:

(c)    previous experience of aeronautics
(d)    rank not above that of captain
(e)    medical fitness for air work
(f)    good eyesight
(g)    good map-reader and field sketcher
(h)    unmarried
(i)    not less than two years' service
(j)    under thirty years of age
(k)    good sailor
(l)    knowledge of foreign languages
(m)   taste for mechanics
(n)    light weight (under 11 stone 7 lb)

Given an opportunity to fly at the government's expense, about forty officers applied to join the Air Battalion. A number failed to pass the Royal Aero Club's proficiency test, which required a successful candidate to fly a circular course of three miles thrice, landing at a designated point on each occasion with engine off. By 1912, however, civil flying schools had trained some twenty officers to pass this test, a number of whom were in the reserve forces.

As a means of increasing the number qualified as pilots and observers – and as an economy – Mr Churchill suggested to the Standing Sub-Committee on 18 December 1911 that non-commissioned officers should be employed in these roles. They were looking towards a contribution to the Expeditionary Force in war of seven aeroplane squadrons with a balloon and kite squadron. All agreed that wastage from accidents and wounds among them would probably be high. The idea was adopted, though it did not produce the results anticipated. The Memorandum on Naval and Military Aviation, 1912, noted that

> . . . The training of the rank and file as pilots has not so far proved successful, only one petty officer having as yet qualified as First Class Pilot; twenty five have qualified as Second Class Pilots during the last twelve months. These men have been slow to learn; and although they make fair aerodrome flyers, they have not so far proved that they possess the qualities to make good cross country pilots. . . .

The problem was not one of potential skill or intelligence but of education. When NCO candidates were coached in subjects unfamiliar to them, the numbers qualifying as pilots quickly increased.

Maurice Farman 'Shorthorn', handled by crews from Naval and Army Wings (*Trustees of the Imperial War Museum, London, Q 67026*)

Two years after its formation, the Air Battalion was ready to take a full part in manoeuvres, but not quite as originally foreseen. Its capability in balloons and dirigibles was declining; the requirement for captive balloons was confined to artillery spotting, the aeroplane was better suited to scouting than the dirigible, and those dirigibles procured were in a sorry state. Its use of kites from which to suspend observers was negligible. On the other hand, notwithstanding airframe and engine limitations, errors and omissions by the pilots, maintenance and repair problems, the potential of the aeroplane to contribute to land battles was manifestly growing.

In May 1912, the battalion had eleven aeroplanes in service with a further eight being modified or rebuilt in the Farnborough workshops. They included a Blériot monoplane, a Breguet biplane, seven biplanes originating from Henri Farman designs, and three Bristol models. Few of these possessed reliable compasses. None had altimeters; crude calculations as to height were made by reference to aneroid barometers tied to a spar adjacent to the pilot. The maximum speed of the aircraft was about 60 mph, often less if the engine was disgruntled, and thus flying training tended to be early in the morning or during the evening when wind speeds dropped.

But the pilots were flying, not just in short runs but considerable distances, sometimes in public competitions, sometimes in military enterprises. In July 1911, a Royal Engineer, Lieutenant R.A. Cammell, flew 110 miles continuously. In the following February, Lieutenant B.H. Barrington-Kennett, Grenadier Guards, set the world record at $249\frac{1}{2}$ miles for a flight with a passenger.

Navigation was advancing, though names on railway stations were still widely used as a means of verifying locations; and night flying was becoming a regular feature of advanced training.

There were, of course, many setbacks, some humorous, some grievous. Lieutenant Cammell was killed in September 1911 flying an unfamiliar aircraft. Lieutenant H.R.P. Reynolds RE discovered the wayward character of winds when his DH Farman type biplane turned upside down before flying backwards during a thunderstorm.

During 1911 the aeroplane company had moved to a tented camp at Larkhill, where several permanent hangars were erected for its use. It was an isolated site; conditions were poor for the other ranks, the officers were living in cramped comfort at The Bustard inn and were in any case too often away in the air or in social pursuits to arrange improvements. In those days officers were more often out of their unit lines than in them, but regimental organization ensured that administration was not neglected. In the aeroplane company this was largely lacking: all were to one degree or another strangers to one another; the pilots tended to be preoccupied with their flying activities. Mounting disciplinary problems brought about a change: pilots were allocated specific responsibilities for groups of soldiers. A barrack block at Bulford was secured for living accommodation in the winter of 1911. More importantly for the longer term, two important organizational changes were in train.

These had been prompted by the crisis of 1911 when, for a brief period, it had seemed that Britain would be at war with Germany. In the immediate aftermath, the Committee for Imperial Defence had come to recognize that its armed forces were unprepared for war with a major European power. Brigadier-General David Henderson, director of military training in the War Office, urged several remedial measures, one of which was the expansion of the Army's air reconnaissance capacity. This was accepted equally by Mr Churchill in the Admiralty. A central flying school for both services was established at Upavon for the training of all future pilots.

Second, the Air Battalion could no longer continue as a nominal unit of the Royal Engineers. Its warrant and non-commissioned officers had all acquired different trades skills in their years with the 'Air Corps', and the same was true for many among the junior ranks. A proper basis for the recruitment and dedicated training of other ranks was required. During April and May 1912, a Royal Flying Corps was formed. For a time, this was also a joint service unit with a naval as well as a military wing, but the former soon drew off within the Royal Naval Air Service. Looking towards an establishment of 131 Army aeroplanes in seven companies – shortly to be renamed squadrons – the War Office ordered 26 new machines in February 1912. Some of these had arrived in time for the annual manoeuvres in the autumn of that year.

Lieutenant-Generals Sir James Grierson and Sir Douglas Haig commanded the respective contestant forces. The latter had remarked in the previous year that '. . . flying can never be of any use to the Army'. Grierson was ready to see what the Royal Flying Corps could do. They were about to save him from a serious error.

Lieutenant Arthur Longmore RN, and Major Hugh Trenchard, from the Central Flying School were attached to the RFC and General Grierson's command for the manoeuvres. They flew over 'enemy' territory at first light on the first morning and observed General Haig's force detraining and deduced the axis of his advance. This news was welcomed ruefully by Grierson and his staff; his cavalry had been sent off on a false scent. Longmore offered to try to find them. Following their route at very low level, he spotted the headquarters, landed close by and delivered a change

Royal Flying Corps 'Concentration' at Netheravon, June 1914. The camp and aircraft seen from the air. The building on the extreme right is still in use as the Warrant Officers' and Sergeants' Mess, 7 Regiment AAC (*Trustees of the Imperial War Museum, London, O 30732*)

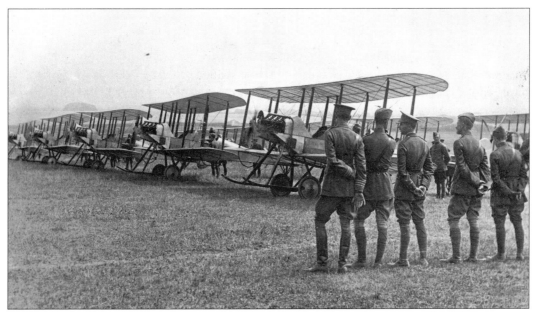

The 'Concentration' at Netheravon during Lord Roberts' inspection. The aircraft shown are BE2s (*Trustees of the Imperial War Museum, London, Q 35204*)

of orders. This combination of reconnaissance and liaison greatly impressed Grierson and many participating officers.

Haig regarded the event as a sort of stunt which would not be practicable in war, even though, in the following year's manoeuvres, aircraft picked up with considerable accuracy the moving columns of his opponent. Still, he was not alone. A majority among the cavalry led a faction which regarded money spent on aeroplanes as wasted.

Money was, however, forthcoming from the War Office. In 1911 the War Office offered prizes for the aircraft most suitable for military use, whether designed as such or adapted. It would have to lift 350 lb in addition to instruments and have sufficient fuel for a sustained flight of four and a half hours. During one hour it would be expected to sustain a height of 4,500 ft and attain a speed of 55 mph. Other stipulations related to pilot facility, ability to operate from ploughed fields, and noise levels. Sums of £500,000 provided in 1912 and 1913 for the winner were doubled to £1 million in the estimates for 1914. The resources were there; common sense was lacking in their application.

The winner was a BE2 designed from a Blériot and developed by the Army Aircraft (formerly the Balloon) Factory at Farnborough. It encouraged the idea that outsiders were not capable of meeting the standards required, and none believed this more than the superintendent of the factory, Mervyn O'Gorman, an established consulting engineer who brought the talents of his profession to this post. But he brought also an excess of self-regard and obstinacy. It was his wish that all aircraft destined for the Army should at least follow the design and development of his establishment both in airframes and engines. This attitude denied to the Royal Flying Corps the considerable expertise and, for a time, the manufacturing capabilities, of the commercial aircraft industry in the United Kingdom. No less, it diminished the potential of the factory (renamed again as the Royal Aircraft Factory in April 1912) to undertake advanced research and development to gain an advantage in the crucible of war.

Immediately, however, the Royal Flying Corps had all the aircraft it could cope with: Blériot and Henri Farman monoplanes, BE2s, Avro 504s, and a number of special models such as the RE5. In 1911 an attempt to hold a military air convention had had to be suspended because most of the aircraft foundered en route. But during the three summers from 1912, these occasions prospered. Individual and squadron tests and exercises were held, lectures and presentations given, and discussions conducted with representatives of other arms.

In June 1914 the greater part of the seven squadrons then formed or forming, together with members of the air reserve, assembled at Netheravon. When they dispersed, many to take summer leave before the autumn manoeuvres, they had in fact completed the last major training programme for the war which began in August that year.

CHAPTER TWO

# Air Power in Action

T he dreadful spectacle of the First World War – the 'Great War' – is familiar to us in black and white photography. These two tones perhaps bring to life more immediately than colours the mood and circumstances of the battlefields in the pictures of men marching, fighting, sheltering, wounded, gassed and dead in a desolate landscape of crater fields, mud and shattered buildings.

Yet the war was not like that in the early stages. Hostilities began at the height of summer; there was still plenty of grass for the horses, trees were in full leaf, grain, vegetables and fruit swelling in field and orchard as the cavalry of each side reconnoitred to and from the course of the River Meuse in Belgium to its source within sight of the Vosges mountains. Somewhat more slowly behind them, the columns of German infantry and guns advanced from railheads at marching pace. The days were hot, the skies generally clear. It was good flying weather.

The Royal Flying Corps prepared to fly the aircraft of four squadrons to France from Dover. The headquarters, the Aircraft Park (the reserve aeroplanes) and the ground apparatus of the squadrons were to travel by road and sea to the concentration area at Maubeuge on the French side of the Belgian frontier.

Brigadier-General Henderson had been chosen to command the 'Army Air Corps', which led him to qualify as a pilot at the age of forty-nine, the act of 'a madman' in the view of his friends and relatives. Major F.H. Sykes, and Major A.D. Carden, pioneers from the period of balloon trials, were respectively Chief of Staff and Officer Commanding the Aircraft Park. Four of the reserve aircraft, crated, moved with the road party; the remainder to a total of twenty were flown by staff officers and supernumeraries. Their first destination was Amiens, whose citizens received them with rapture.

At home, 1 Squadron was required to reinforce 2, 3, 4 and 5, ordered to France. It was then to be built up to operational strength by reserves to defend the homeland against air attack in company with the Royal Naval Air Service. Nos 6 and 7 Squadrons, also retained at home, were to undertake the training of reinforcements.

The aircraft of 2, 3, and 4 Squadrons arrived at Dover by 12 August after several misadventures, including the fatal crash of Lieutenant R.R. Skene and his supporter, Air-Mechanic R.K. Barlow. After a night sleeping in the open with their machines, officers and attendant technicians took off in succession from 6.25 a.m. on the 13th to stage through Amiens, led by Lieutenant H.D. Harvey-Kelly. First off, he aimed to be first to land in France and, having been overtaken by his squadron commander during the flight, he asserted his lead by landing without making a circuit of the field. A faulty engine obliged Lieutenant R.M. Vaughan to land near Boulogne, where he was arrested as a possible spy by the French Territorial Command. In the hiatus of war, a week elapsed before he was released. By this time, 5 Squadron had overcome its own difficulties to move on with the main body to Maubeuge. Two more aircraft crashed during the flight. Even so, by 18 August, 105 officers, 755 other ranks, and 45 aeroplanes were ready to open operations from Maubeuge.

The General Headquarters (GHQ) of the British Expeditionary Force was ready to employ them. The Commander-in-Chief, Field Marshal Sir John French, had orders to advance into Belgium on the left wing of the French Army. His forces were completing concentration on their particular march routes on 19/20 August but there was little reliable intelligence, though many rumours, concerning the enemy. Captain Joubert de la Ferté, flying a Blériot monoplane of 3 Squadron, and Lieutenant G.W. Mapplebeck a BE2 of 4 Squadron, took off at 9.30 a.m. to survey likely enemy approaches. Cloud separated them prematurely but both brought back useful information. Though this was chiefly negative, one had travelled almost 60 miles beyond the foremost Allied forces. This radius was far beyond the capabilities of horsed cavalry in a matter of hours.

From this beginning, the GHQ staff began to realize the extraordinary contribution of the Royal Flying Corps squadrons to operational intelligence. As the field marshal advanced his two corps towards Mons and closure on the French left, aircraft picked up piecemeal and then continuously the German movements which confirmed a huge force ahead of them engaged in a grand outflanking manoeuvre against the allies. Their reports principally persuaded Sir John to draw back, and to go on drawing back in a troublesome situation; the enemy was treading on the coat tails of his rearguards.

During their first week in operations, the four squadrons came rapidly to identify enemy arms on the march, the columns of infantry, horse and field artillery, and the heavier garrison or siege artillery whose gun crews marched on foot. They learned to distinguish the difference between headquarters and supply units along the country roads or in villages. Although the Germans were aware that they were under aerial scrutiny and opened fire on British and French aircraft from time to time – Sergeant-Major D.S. Jillings of 2 Squadron was wounded by a rifle bullet in the leg on 22 August, the first aircrew casualty – they made no effort to conceal themselves when halted.

There were problems in navigation. The Royal Engineer survey branch had brought quantities of large-scale maps of Belgium, with which the British Expeditionary Force was expected to operate. The considerable detail on these confused pilots and observers: 'arrived at a big town', Lieutenant Mapplebeck reported on 19 August, 'but could not place it on map. (On my return I discovered this to have been Brussels.)' They preferred the smaller scale of the French maps, initially road touring sheets obtained by private purchase. These showed the pattern of railways, rivers and roads more readily picked up at heights above 1,000 ft. On the ground, however, the command, technical and administrative elements, moving back from day to day into France to fields judged suitable for landing and take-off, urgently required large-scale maps.

In successive movements back from Maubeuge just ahead of the two British corps, the ground parties were rarely able to provide details of the evening landing site to pilots who had taken off during the afternoon. On occasion, pilots landed at headquarters sites at which they exchanged information for the use of a telephone to discover the latest map reference of their squadron and sometimes, too, it must be admitted, to verify their own position.

On 30 August, one of the hottest days of that hot summer, the field marshal was beginning to lose his nerve. Out of touch with the true state of his divisions, he was developing a plan to pull right out of the Allied line for resupply and reorganization, believing that his force had been severely mauled during its fight to disengage from the Germans as it drew back from the Mons area. Air reports on both the 30th and 31st indicated that the general enemy thrust in the north was beginning to change direction, but the proximity of German forces to the BEF confused attempts to discover their immediate intention. A visit from Lord Kitchener, senior as a field marshal and concurrently Secretary of State for War, reorientated Sir John and ensured that he remained in the Allied line.

He derived some comfort from the consistency of his air reports over the next few days: the Germans were unquestionably shifting away from the British frontage, as the French liaison officer, Colonel A. Huguet, reported to the French Commander-in-Chief, General Joffre, on the evening of 3 September:

> . . . very reliable reports from British airmen, all of which agree, that the whole of the German First Army except the IV Reserve Corps . . . are moving south east across the [River] Marne . . . The heads of columns will without doubt reach the Marne this evening.

This did not, unfortunately, persuade Sir John French to stand and fight the light forces spilling across his Front. If he had done so, his army would have been saved further marches rearward. British and French air reconnaissance were in complete agreement as to the precise location of all the German formations north of the Marne. This intelligence inspired General Joffre to launch a counter-attack from the river.

> I wish to bring particularly to your lordship's notice, [Sir John French wrote to Lord Kitchener on 7 September] the admirable work done by the Royal Flying Corps under Sir David Henderson. They have furnished me with the most complete and accurate information which has been of incalculable value in the conduct of operations.

Yet, as the grand counter-attack proceeded, the limitations of the aeroplane and aircrew were demonstrated. The first was dependence on reasonably clear weather; thunderstorms broke on 9 September, though not before enemy concentrations were seen to be assembling or standing at various sites. In fact, they were getting ready to withdraw but this was not evident to observers in the air. Here was another limitation: on such occasions commanders and staffs had to make their own judgements as to enemy intentions. On the 9th, the most immediately useful information provided to corps and army headquarters was the location of the British advanced guards at a given time. The divisions had no wireless sets and, on the move, information was sent back by runner or horse from battalion to brigade, by horse or car from brigade to division.

On the 10th, morning mist and persistent rain clouds prevented flying until the afternoon, when aircraft were able to confirm a general retirement by the enemy from the Marne; reconnaissance was pressed without difficulty beyond enemy rail-heads. But as the three British corps (the third corps had formed during the long withdrawal) began their struggle to capture the heights above the River Aisne in the second half of September, the contribution of the RFC squadrons changed in character.

During their first month in France and Belgium, they had been engaged almost exclusively in reconnaissance of manoeuvring forces, and their contribution had indeed been of 'incalculable value'. Other activities – exchanging random small arms shots with enemy aircraft, for example, throwing hand grenades on to enemy columns, and occasionally forcing enemy aircraft down – were incidental.

On the Aisne, movement stopped as the Germans fought to hold the ridgelines on the far side. British and French attacks made slow progress. The battleline, which had moved one way and the other swiftly for six weeks, became virtually static.

The urgent demands on Royal Flying Corps Headquarters for tactical reconnaissance thus dropped away. The more deliberate process of strategic surveillance prospered. At the same time the use of aeroplanes for artillery shooting was further explored. The unique 'wireless flight' in 4 Squadron was brought into service. The squadron records the following wireless telegraphy on the afternoon of 25 September to a Royal Artillery battery seeking to destroy enemy guns behind a ridge:

4.02 p.m.   A very little short. Fire Fire.
4.04 p.m.   Fire again. Fire again.
4.12 p.m.   A little short – line OK.
4.15 p.m.   Short, over, over and a little left.
4.20 p.m.   You were just between two batteries.
            Search 200 hundred yards each side of your last shot. Range OK.
4.22 p.m.   You have them.
4.26 p.m.   Hit. Hit. Hit.
4.32 p.m.   About 50 yards short and to the right.
4.37 p.m.   Your last shot in the middle of three batteries in action; search all round within
            300 yards of your last shot and you have them.
4.42 p.m.   I am coming home now.

Though the British Army in France was static along the Aisne, the ground north of the Somme remained empty of troops in late September through Artois into Flanders; the right wing of the German armies had passed that way towards the Marne but left no line of communication behind them. The only concentration of German forces in Belgium was engaged distantly, besieging Antwerp. Reviewing the developing trench lines, German and French supreme headquarters suddenly realized their opportunity to exploit the tract extending to the north coast, and began almost simultaneously a 'race for the sea'.

Each side brought up divisions to march round the opponent's open flank. As fast as one deployed the other opposed. Piecemeal, the line extended northwards to the North Sea. Early in October, General Joffre persuaded Sir John French to join a French advance into Belgium with the aim of entering Germany north of Luxemburg. By 19 October this concentration was accomplished, the BEF holding the frontage between Ypres and La Bassée. Just as the advance began, a considerably greater force of the German Army began to attack from the opposite direction, aiming at least to capture the Channel ports. Belgian, French, and British forces, in that order of distance from the coast, were drawn into an intense and ultimately successful defensive battle lasting five weeks, the First Battle of Ypres. The closely locked lines, intense shell fire, and frequent bad weather offered little scope to aerial enterprise.

'I don't suppose we shall see much of our flying friends until the spring,' a staff officer remarked to others in the operations branch at army headquarters on a late November morning. Low clouds in northern France had again prevented flying that day. This view was to be expressed on a number of occasions during the winter of 1914/15. Sorties were certainly curtailed during winter storms and clouds, but a further assumption that with the spring the Royal Flying Corps would return to operate in much the same way as it had in the previous summer and autumn was greatly mistaken. The experience gained during this period had stimulated considerable enterprise in the expansion of capabilities, in technique and practice, and in organization. Much of this sprang from the enthusiasm of individuals among all ranks within squadrons. Examples abound.

While many pilots and observers were initially delighted with their ability to complement the application of artillery fire, they soon became impatient with the often protracted correction procedures. Lieutenant D.S. Lewis hit upon a simple means of improvement which was so effective that it was soon adopted universally and has continued in use ever since. He drew a grid of vertical and horizontal lines on the maps used in common by gunners and aircrew, and numbered them. The grid reference system was thus brought into use to identify a precise square upon the ground. He further refined references to shellbursts in relation to the target by introducing a notional clock-face, of which the target itself lay in the centre. A burst would then be described, for example, as being at 8 o'clock at a given number of yards from the desired point of strike.

The British maps were based on French and Belgian military survey. They showed the detail of a land at peace. What was needed was a map of the enemy defences, and developments within these from one day to another. Encouraged by Major H.R.M. Brooke-Popham early in 1914, members of 3 Squadron carried forward the experimental work of aerial photography begun by the balloonists. Requests for official funds being denied, Captain Joubert de la Ferté persuaded his brother officers to join him in making private purchases. By the early summer of 1914 they had successfully photographed the defences of the Solent and Isle of Wight by a series of shots, creating a map.

Later assisted by public funds and French expertise, Royal Flying Corps Headquarters in France formed an experimental photographic section under Lieutenant J.T.C. Moore-Brabazon to expand this option. With just one other officer, Lieutenant C.D.M. Campbell, Sergeant F.C.V. Laws, and Second Air-Mechanic W.D. Corse, an extraordinary facility was developed, the continuous trench map, reproduced subsequently in printed form by the Royal Engineers survey branch. No less importantly, their experimentation revealed the value of photographing selected points from one day to another as a means of picking up changes in enemy defences such as the inception or extension of trenches and fortifications. From this work, air photographic intelligence was added to Sir John French's staff. Indeed, the early product of Moore-Brabazon's team was so remarkable that the French general headquarters, GQG, requested copies of everything printed thereafter.

These innovations survived triumphantly in a tide of activities within the corps. Pre-eminent was the expansion of aircraft numbers and men; Lord Kitchener, Secretary of State for War, and Mr Churchill, First Lord of the Admiralty, alike gave strong encouragement to this growth. The RFC took four squadrons to France in August 1914 to support an army of two corps controlling one cavalry and four infantry divisions. By the end of 1914, the British Expeditionary Force contained two armies controlling six corps with four cavalry and ten infantry divisions in the field. In the autumn, two 'wings' had been formed, each comprising two aircraft squadrons, one wing to each corps, with a squadron directly serving General Headquarters. The expansion of the ground force outran this arrangement. The wings were necessarily allotted to the two new armies, First and Second, pending the training and equipment of additional squadrons.

This was partly accomplished by releasing the units left behind for training, such as 6 Squadron. Schools were established to train pilots, observers and tradesmen. These requirements had to be met within an overall claim by the two armed services for arms and equipment, instructors and administrators, and accommodation for the hundreds of thousands of men being mobilized; a claim in part resisted by the managers of industry expected to meet extraordinary production demands on factories and mines.

Demands on the national industrial base included orders for aircraft production; the Royal Aircraft Factory was incapable simply due to its size of meeting these. Arguments between commercial companies and the factory concerning designs delayed the production process. But the superintendent and his staff were at the same time providing an essential clearing house for the host of calls for new equipment and modifications to items in service, pending the establishment of a government ministry to undertake this work. The RFC workshops in France carried out many modifications proposed by squadrons, and occasionally manufactured items designed locally – for example, by the air photographic section – but there was a limit to their capacity.

It may now seem strange that the potential of the aeroplane as a weapons platform was accorded a distinctly lesser status in this tumult of development. The principal reason is that during the first months of the war the requirement for reconnaissance was paramount, and direct participation in the battle was taken up by artillery spotting. Opportunities to strike directly at the enemy became apparent almost incidentally. The mounting of weapons had indeed been considered before the war. Two Lewis guns had been provided for trials, but this light machine-gun had not then been accepted for the Army. In the opening months of the war, aircrew of both sides progressively armed themselves with rifles or carbines and shot at one another, but such action was incidental. The first requirement was for bombs to take the place of hand grenades and, due to work undertaken for bombing from dirigibles, a light 20 lb and a heavy 112 lb bomb came into service, though their use was limited in the absence of a bomb sight. Still, by the end of 1914, both the Royal Flying Corps and the Royal Naval Air Service had requested machine-guns and made various proposals for bombing.

In this connection, the naval air arm had acquired considerable credit and valuable experience in bombing German naval and airship bases. Their raids began in September, somewhat ineffectually, but progressed to the destruction of a Zeppelin and its supporting buildings at Düsseldorf. In November, three of four naval aircraft reached the Zeppelin base on Lake Constance after a flight of 125 miles from Belfort, where they caused severe damage for the loss of a further aircraft, a brilliant feat which alarmed the German government and people.

By the end of the year, too, all British military aeroplanes had adopted the roundel of three colours for identification purposes.

'I am quite sure', Moore-Brabazon remarked later, 'that at least half of our aeroplanes lost to ground fire in those early months were shot down by British soldiers. As regulars, they were better marksmen than the German conscripts and whenever we appeared anywhere near them there was invariably a storm of musketry. We tried to dissuade them by painting Union Jacks on the underside of the wings but at any height the only identifiable bit was the St George's cross in the middle, and this was taken for the German air force cross. So we put on roundels. The French had appropriated the red, white, and blue from the outside inwards so we had to use blue for the outside ring.'

These changes and advances were the outcome of four months in operations. There were changes, no less, at the working level. An old Royal Engineer who had passed into the Royal Flying Corps as a founder-member, but who had once been a groom and then trained by his employer to drive his motor car, recalled:

When the squadron formed up at the beginning, it was like being on a shoot all the time. You got up every day to get the gentlemen on with their sport. When it was finished, you cleared up, had a yarn, and slept anywhere there was room, in the stables often as not. There was always food and often we were left some beer. The officers came up for their flying and then they went off to the local hotel. Manoeuvres started the party again. The officers often had a drink with us when they were over.

When we went to war it was different. First we had to keep on moving, but we also had to keep the aeroplanes going. Soon as they came down, the fitters and riggers got on to them. We had no proper hangars at first – it didn't matter, the weather was mostly good. Very quickly, they got the aerodrome under control, where you could drive, where you could walk, which way the planes were taking off and coming in. The pilots had to report in as soon as they came down, not after they'd been to the mess like they did when we were on the [Salisbury] Plain. The major, he got very strict about the lines, making sure we all had proper places to sleep, and the canteen running. Everyone formed their own family, in a flight or in the [squadron] headquarters. And you knew which squadron you were in – didn't know too many in other squadrons. By the time that first winter came, when we had canvas hangars, some of us were in billets in the village, others were in tents. It was cold in the tents but the serjeant-major used to say, 'Better in the tents, lads, than in the trenches'.

.    .    .    .    .    .    .    .

For different reasons, the Germans, French, and British had expected that the war would be over in 1914. In 1915 and 1916, their illusions drained finally away.

By the beginning of 1915, Lieutenant Lewis's system of target coordination was widely in operation. Ground response was improved when the snow melted, by the use of white cloth strips indicating intentions to engage following registration or otherwise.

The first major ground operation was an attack to capture the village of Neuve Chapelle, a step to the occupation of high ground overlooking the city of Lille. This task fell to the First Army under Lieutenant-General Sir Douglas Haig. His Chief Staff Officer, Brigadier-General John Gough, was a rising star in the Army. He had drawn the Royal Flying Corps into the operation with the full approval of his commander.

Haig had modified his peacetime views about the value of aeroplanes in war. While he maintained his opinion that horsed cavalry were indispensable in reconnaissance, he accepted that flying machines could range more deeply into enemy territory and at considerably greater speed. He concluded that there was a place for both arms. He was also much impressed by the use of aerial observation both for artillery spotting and photography.

He studied closely the photographic map of the enemy positions at and around Neuve Chapelle to a depth of three-quarters of a mile. Gough went further. After some discussion with the Army's 'wing commander', routes along which reserves might move to the Front, assembly sites and headquarters were identified for aerial bombing.

Visiting the line on 20 February, Gough was mortally wounded. The plans he had prepared for Haig, however, were carried through on the morning of 10 March. Neuve Chapelle was taken by the infantry and held against counter-attacks, but attempts to exploit the higher ground beyond were unsuccessful. While the air photographs had revealed the whole of the enemy's local defence system, they were unable to disclose points crucial to its possession. This pointed to a conclusion from ground and air interaction in the previous year: however useful a report or a picture, judgements as to their import had to be made by commanders and staff.

Reconnaissance and interdiction were undertaken despite the massing of rain clouds on the 10th. German troop movement behind the Front was kept under observation, and low-level bombing hit a communications centre – believed to be a divisional headquarters – a troop train at Courtrai, and cut the railway at Menin. Three aircraft were lost in these operations.

As attempts to advance beyond the village were abandoned, an aircraft was sent to identify the precise run of the British line in the area; telephone lines to those in the forward trenches had been destroyed.

Similar support was provided for an attack to capture Hill 60, just south of Ypres, in mid-April. A second assault was assisted by air attacks on enemy artillery positions. As the area was temporarily subsiding, Captain L.A. Strange of 6 Squadron observed about 5 p.m. on the evening of 22 April a dense cloud 'yellow-green' in colour issuing from the German lines. It was chlorine gas drifting into the trenches of the French 45th Division where its effect was devastating. A prisoner of war had earlier warned that something of the sort was impending. Uncertain as to its value, the Germans failed to make immediate use of the opportunity it offered. The French division was effectively put out of action: its sector was open to exploitation.

Belatedly, the Germans attempted again to break through in the Second Battle of Ypres. The struggle continued into May. But on the 12th there was some hope of a reduction in the German onslaught as aircraft reported considerable movement southwards from the Ypres salient towards Douai and Lens.

In this sector Lieutenant-General Haig's First Army had begun to attack in cooperation with the French Tenth, the latter towards Vimy Ridge, the British once more towards Aubers Ridge overlooking Lille. A thrust at Neuve Chapelle having failed on 9 May – due much to a shortage among the Royal Artillery of high explosive shells – the frontage of attack was shifted a little to the south round the village of Festubert.

French artillery was attached to the British force. They brought with them a kite balloon for observation. The Royal Flying Corps continued their own work of artillery spotting and the supply of air photographs daily. But before the infantry assaults began, air-to-ground cooperation was carried further. Three Maurice Farman biplanes with 'pusher' engines of 16 Squadron were fitted with wireless sets specifically to report on the progress of the infantry, sending back their observations to corps and army headquarters. For their part, the infantry carried panels of white cloth to be laid out on each objective as it was reached. But this was an additional measure; the aircrew were briefed to report all infantry movement whether panels were displayed or not.

On the first morning, 9 May, when the attack was renewed from Neuve Chapelle, visibility was excellent. Unfortunately, the repulse of the British infantry prevented any panel displays and their movement was too limited to be apparent to aerial observers. The experiment was repeated at Festubert over the ten days of fighting from 15 May. In this period, however, there was a good deal of ground mist; reports were consequently few and patchy. The formation staffs considered the experiment a failure. Thus, when the RFC discussed ways of developing their contribution to the ground battle during the summer months, close cooperation with the infantry was not considered.

Yet of all the problems thrown up by the extension of trench warfare, none was greater than communication of their movements to the higher staffs and the artillery. In 1915 there were no mobile ground wireless sets, and even if carrying parties had been allotted to advance the heavy and bulky equipment with selected units, they would have been vulnerable to shell and machine-gun fire. Telephone cable run out with infantry assaults was invariably cut by shellfire at an early stage. Time and again following an assault, the infantry were isolated in the enemy trenches either lacking artillery support or, worse, subjected to the fire of their own batteries following a plan which had gone awry.

Since success depended ultimately on the success of infantry offensives, the scope of aircraft to resolve this problem by what was becoming known as a 'contact patrol' should have been explored exhaustively. The Maurice Farmans used at Neuve Chapelle and Festubert operated at speeds of between 40 and 50 mph, by no means too fast to observe effectively. One reason for their inadequacy was that they flew too high to see movements in detail. Another was that their briefing as to what the infantry were seeking to do was insufficient to inspire the initiative of the aircrews. Then, pilots and observers from arms other than infantry did not comprehend the nature of their operations. All these deficiencies could have been remedied.

Poor visibility was another matter, a problem beyond the control of all. But the fact that aircraft would not be able to operate on some days was not a good reason for abandoning their use on others. The artillery, for example, lost air cooperation when the battlefield was obscured by mist or low clouds but recovered it when these lifted. Royal Artillery and Flying Corps representatives discussed their joint work during June 1915 which led, among several enhancements, to a greater degree of standardization in procedure, set out in a working manual.

In August there was a conference betwen aviators, British and French. Intelligence studies had revealed that of 141 bombing sorties between March and June 1915, only three had affected the run of battle; and this despite considerable losses of aircrew and machines in such operations. The German anti-aircraft guns had greatly increased in numbers, and the enemy's ability to camouflage targets contributed to this unsatisfactory outcome. No less was the problem of inaccuracy: there were no bomb sights; bombs were being dropped by rule of thumb.

A makeshift sight using nails and wire had been invented by Second-Lieutenant R.B. Bourdillon. This was sufficiently promising to engage the resources of the Central Flying School. Assisted by Second-Lieutenant J.M. Dobson, Bourdillon produced an improved version which took some account of the throw of the bomb in relation to an aircraft's speed in combination with its height, local wind speed and direction. But the art of delivery continued to rely much on aircrew experience and instinct.

This sight was in service when the Battle of Loos began on 21 September 1915. To what extent it was responsible for important successes in the joint bombing plan with the French is not apparent; certainly, the Allied view that railway sidings and trains were productive targets was vindicated. The range of such attacks extended to 36 miles behind the enemy trenches.

Artillery spotting, which engaged also two kite balloon sections of the Royal Naval Air Service, was widespread and effective even after the weather began to break. But 'contact patrols' were again ineffective. Their use was readopted by formation commanders but without benefit of any improvements in the ideas and methods used at Festubert, and they were largely valueless as a consequence. The penalty was greater on this occasion. The British infantry gained an early success, opening a mile or so of the German line to the north of Loos village, but by the time this was evident the opportunity to exploit it was passing, and was finally lost when Sir John French delayed in passing his reserve to Lieutenant-General Haig's command.

During the second half of 1915, Royal Flying Corps operations were inhibited by the appearance of a dangerous foe in the air:

> . . . I was flying towards Lille when I saw a Fokker scout approaching me, so directly it seemed after a minute or so that I half wondered whether he was going to ram. Seconds later, a stream of bullets passed very close overhead and I turned sharply away. We began manoeuvring round each other. What I couldn't understand was how he was firing at me – as we passed and repassed it was clear that there was no machine-gun on his upper wing. Then I realised that the weapon was just in front of his cockpit. He was firing through the propeller . . .

This was the reaction of a subaltern with almost six months' experience as a pilot, shortly to be severely wounded. He had heard of the French Lieutenant Roland Garros who fired his Hotchkiss machine-gun through an armoured propeller but was unaware that the German air service had improved on this idea. The Dutch aircraft designer Anton Fokker had taken up a pre-war idea, an interruptor device which permitted a belt-fed Maxim mounted just behind engine and airscrew to fire when the blade had passed the vertical position. The aircraft selected to be the 'weapon platform' was the M5 monoplane – *Eindecker* – itself a derivative of the French Morane-Saulnier scout. The M5K scout was thus transformed into the E.I. fighter.

By July 1915 eleven German pilots were flying this aeroplane on the Western Front. Two, Oswald Bölcke and Max Immelman, were to become 'aces'. But the advantage of being able to fire simply by pointing at an opponent and pressing a button did not immediately secure an ascendancy over the Royal Flying Corps. Their 'pusher' aircraft, notably the Vickers FB5 'Gunbus', were able to fire forward from the unrestricted nose of the fuselage. Aerial combat was fast becoming a daily event, but so long as the E.I.s were flying singly they could be contained. During the winter months, however, they began to operate in groups. It became necessary to escort deep reconnaissance aircraft and to cover artillery observation sorties. The kite balloons were frequently attacked.

> . . . the squadron has had very heavy losses this week, seven in all [an RFC officer noted in his diary in January 1916]. Five were new pilots who had hardly got the hang of our work. Harold is among the other two, greatly missed, he was one of the best in every sense.

On another airfield, an armourer recalled,

> . . . terrible to have to take one of our people out of the cockpit when he was half cut to pieces and plainly dying. How some of them got the machines back I don't know. Those days

everyone in the squadron felt low but particularly the men working in the flight lines. Getting the machine ready to fly again was something we all did with a will but cleaning up the cockpit wasn't funny. Our flight serjeant got us on to it straight away – no leaving it till next day.

Two new types of British aircraft were brought into service early in 1916 to counter the Fokker E.I.: the FE2 B two seater and the single seat De Havilland 2 scout. Both had pusher airscrews permitting forward firing by their Lewis guns; the FE2 had a second Lewis covering other arcs. Both had greater power and at once proved capable of fighting the Fokkers on equal terms, despite the disadvantage for the British of having to change frequently the 30 round magazine of the Lewis gun while the enemy enjoyed the advantage of a Maxim fed by a 250 round belt.

New equipment was not the only means of recovering air superiority, however. Major-General H.M. Trenchard, who had assumed command of the Royal Flying Corps in France and Flanders, reorganized his swelling command of thirty squadrons early in 1916. On arrival in France in 1914, squadrons had consisted of several types of aeroplane. Gradually, as the work of the air arm had extended beyond reconnaissance, some degree of specialization had followed but on an irregular basis. Wings were now to be formed into air brigades, one brigade to each of the four armies of British and Empire forces in the theatre. Each army commander would have a close support wing to provide artillery observation, photography and close reconnaissance, and a second for distant reconnaissance and bombing. This wing would also contain all the aircraft designated for fighting the enemy in the air and carrying the attack to the enemy airfields. The scheme was the product of Anglo-French discussions. It was fully implemented as the British forces began to prepare for their part in the Battle of the Somme.

Sir Douglas Haig replaced Sir John French as Commander-in-Chief in December 1915. He was immediately drawn into strategic planning for the approaching year. Offensives were to be mounted more or less simultaneously during the summer by the Russians on the Eastern Front, from Italy, and by the French and British in the west. Action against the Turks in the Middle East and Dardanelles would continue. By this means, the Germans and their Austro-Hungarian allies would be prevented from moving reserves from one Front to another.

The Franco-British offensive was to break open the German defences north and south of the Somme river. The enemy pre-empted this plan. The German Crown Prince's army attacked at Verdun on 21 February with the aim of 'bleeding France white' in defence of an area of historic importance.

For a time it seemed that the operation might be successful. Week by week French troops were engaged in intense fighting to hold the forts and connecting trenches round the city. Exhausted divisions were relieved by others sent from quiet sectors. The British were obliged to extend their line in this connection. By May it was apparent that what had been planned as a Franco-British offensive in the summer would be in effect a British venture which the French would support. Sir Douglas Haig wished to postpone the opening until August, but this sent the French Commander-in-Chief General Joffre into a frenzy of protest: 'the French Army would cease to exist if we did nothing till then'. The opening date was thus to be 1 July.

It was impossible to conceal the huge preparation behind the British Fourth Army, responsible for the operation, over the late spring and early summer months. The first task of the Royal Flying Corps was to prevent German aircraft or observation balloons from approaching the area; and

FE2 B 'pusher' aircraft rigged for aerial photography (see right forward mounting), 1916. Three Lewis machine-guns are mounted with the ammunition drums clearly visible (*Trustees of the Imperial War Museum, London, Q 69649*)

Example of Royal Flying Corps aerial photography – an oblique shot of the Hindenburg Line under construction by the Germans in preparation for withdrawal from the Somme line early in 1917 (*Museum of Army Flying*)

this they did successfully despite the arrival of the Halberstadt scout and an uprated version of the Albatros C series. The enemy air force was driven back 25 miles behind the contact line.

The second task was to record in detail the German defences, including the accession of fire support, as the enemy high command became aware from ground intelligence that an offensive was impending in the Somme sector. In this they were largely successful, though they were unable to pick up batteries brought in by night and skilfully camouflaged, lying silent thereafter.

General Sir Henry Rawlinson, commander of the Fourth Army, his staff, and all his subordinate commanders were thus able to plan with an extensive knowledge of the enemy positions on the ridge of high ground from Thiepval to Guillemont and the flanking features round Serre in the north and Montauban in the south. Observation of the entire ground was also maintained by Royal Flying Corps kite balloons.

As preparations moved to completion, the demands on the RFC for artillery spotting grew. The system of calls for a variety of tasks and changes of location had been considerably enhanced, aided by the experience of Loos. The 'clapperbreak' had been introduced to reduce interference between friendly aircraft attempting to transmit wireless messages simultaneously. It was thus possible to operate one spotter aircraft over each 2,000 yards of the line.

Four hundred and twenty-one aircraft and fourteen balloons of the RFC were committed to the opening of the battle on 1 July. Many of those flying or mounting them from the ground were temporary soldiers, men who had volunteered for the duration of the war. Their character was mirrored by the ground forces engaged, the 'new armies' raised by Lord Kitchener in 1914 and 1915.

A mist covered much of the battlefield as the night passed. A number of bombing missions were launched but most aircraft remained on the ground until it cleared from 6 a.m. Meantime, the British and French artillery bombardment continued. The German guns responded at some points. Smoke was released in places to assist the attacking infantry but in many sectors the attempts to break in to the enemy line were observed by RFC pilots.

Most of these were engaged in artillery observation but each corps had been allotted a number of contact patrols to follow and assist the infantry's progress. Lamps and shutter boards had been brought into service on the ground to pass messages. Some infantry units wore metal plates to make them readily visible from the air but these were of no value; the men carrying them were cut down or repulsed in no man's land. A few battalions were able to light flares to show their position to aircrew but, as before, all the measures were based on general assumptions and none had been the subject of trials. Of particular importance, there were no arrangements to support the infantry held up at crucial points by direct attack on the enemy trenches. One brigade commander who tentatively suggested such cooperation was told that this 'would be too dangerous. Mistakes might kill or wound our own men.' In view of what happened, the soldiers on the ground might have been willing to take this risk.

For the only success along the Fourth Army Front was confined to the right flank, and that was limited. Much of the enemy wire was not cut. On the left the artillery support was grossly mismanaged. The enemy had deep trenches in which to escape much of the preliminary bombardment, and the concealed German batteries opened fire with considerable effect on the advancing British infantry. Where battalions broke in successfully they lacked communication to the rear to report their situation. Captain C.A.A. Hatt, flying some 600 ft above Thiepval, was able to report that infantry parties – of the 36th Ulster Division – had occupied one strongpoint. A squadron of aircraft brought in to attack this area might have enabled ground reinforcements to reach this group. A German field battery shelling infantry in Bernafay Wood was effectively silenced by the machine-gun of a single aircraft from 9 Squadron. Others followed the struggles round Ovillers and La Boiselle, Fricour, Mametz and Montauban. Of some thirty-three low-flying contact sorties, many obscured by smoke, none were lost to enemy fire.

General Haig now subordinated his Front to two armies, the newly created Fifth controlling the two corps on the left, the Fourth the remainder. Attacks continued at selected points throughout the next two weeks. Aircraft reported on them all, occasionally encouraging continuance unwittingly where the odds were overwhelmingly against success. Then, as the British offensive seemed to be doomed, the Fourth carried through a brilliantly conceived silent night attack on 14 July, breaking open the enemy line. This advance was confirmed by contact patrols and two balloon observation posts early in the day. In the rear, the enemy corps headquarters began to withdraw, expecting an imminent breakthrough by the attackers' cavalry.

Too little thought had been given, however, to the cavalry movement. Hours passed before they appeared; the local corps commanders were irresolute. The Germans were given time to reoccupy ground they had abandoned, including an important minor feature on the Bazentin ridge, High Wood.

The Commander-in-Chief ordered the Fourth and Fifth Armies to engage in a series of 'wearing down' operations during August in preparation for a renewed general offensive in mid-September. The RFC was drawn closely into all of these, and took the initiative in urging greater cooperation with the infantry.

As the aviators saw it, the infantry were failing to use adequately their aids to identification, particularly flares which were readily seen through much of the smoke and dust from shellfire. Some contact aeroplanes had carried klaxon horns on 1 July to notify the men on the ground that they were searching for them, but often with little result. The reason for this was that the majority of the groups which had penetrated the enemy positions were so fragmented, and often so immediately engaged in a desperate struggle to hold on to their gains, that they were unaware of aircraft involvement. There was also a widespread apprehension among regimental officers that flares might attract enemy fire. What was needed was a theatre conference of regimental infantry representatives with aircrew to thrash out options to improve cooperation. None was arranged. On the personal initiative of a few divisional and brigade commanders reciprocated by squadron commanders or individual aircrew, views were exchanged briefly with infantry officers. Otherwise, attempts to develop options and procedures for the line of contact were confined to occasional pamphlets written without regard to unit capabilities, often received by commanding officers distracted by a host of demands on their time. Still, the message that klaxons were sounded by pilots looking for forward positions began to percolate down to company level; and the infantry themselves began to recognize that putting out flares was on balance beneficial to themselves.

During the wearing down operations of the summer, a greater number of sorties were allotted to close reconnaissance of the enemy trench lines to be attacked. An observer hastened into III Corps headquarters on 22 July, for example, to warn of new positions linking High Wood and the village of Bazentin le Petit, information which occasioned considerable revision of the impending plan of attack. Yet if these contributions were important, they were random in nature. Instructions for RFC cooperation in tactical assaults tended to be of a general nature, as distinct from the detailed demands on aircraft for artillery cooperation and the provision of air photographs. Nonetheless, the value of air support was becoming widely recognized by those on the ground. When summer mists or rainclouds shrouded the battlefield, headquarters and artillery war diaries contained such remarks as, 'Weather hampered flying this morning, limiting operations'.

The high tempo of air operations on the Somme and other parts of the British Front, in distant bombing and reconnaissance, was costly in aircrew and aeroplanes. Major-General Trenchard was again obliged as the summer passed to review the value of bombing relative to losses. Bombing involved also escorts and reconnaissance sorties. A second aircraft park had been added to his equipment support facilities, sufficient pilots and observers were being selected and trained to replace his casualties, but he was anxious that sufficient numbers of experienced aircrew should be available to lead flights and develop newcomers to squadrons. He had also to husband resources for the September offensive.

Just at this time the German air service was preparing its own challenge to his capabilities. Limitation of numbers of aircraft due to the demands of several Fronts, and a flawed concept of

Bristol F2 fighter; primary Army Cooperation aircraft from 1917 to 1929 (*Trustees of the Imperial War Museum, London, Q 60547*)

wholesale screening on the Western Front had inhibited German air operations through 1916. A general reorganization led to a new air plan for France and Flanders, the core of which was the deployment of pursuit squadrons – *Jagdstaffeln*. These were equipped either with the high-powered Albatros D series, or the Halberstadt scout, firing Maxim or Spandau machine-guns through the propellers. Operating in complete half squadrons or full squadrons of fifteen aircraft, they overcame the Allied air superiority, permitting raiding and photography over British and French lines. British losses increased alarmingly. Major-General Trenchard secured Sir Douglas Haig's support for the doubling of his numbers and the acceleration of new types of fighter aircraft to France.

Royal Naval Air Service and RFC squadrons were sent from various sites including the United Kingdom. Fighters were needed to defend the home base against German air attack, but the introduction of balloon barrages round London permitted some diversion of aircraft to the Continent. Sixty of the light but highly manoeuvrable Nieuport Scouts were purchased from France to add to the number in service with 1 Squadron. The Sopwith Pup joined the British Expeditionary Force in December. With a forward firing machine-gun, its performance matched that of the Albatros and outmatched the Halberstadt.

By then the Somme offensive had closed. The green battlefield of 1 July, its villages and roads largely undamaged, had become a morass of churned earth and rubble. This was to be the condition of the ground over which the Royal Flying Corps continued its operations through the years 1917 and 1918. The battles for Arras and Vimy Ridge, the Third Battle of Ypres ending on the Paschendaele Ridge, and the offensive and counter-offensive beginning in March 1918 and ending with the defeat of the German Army in the field laid waste a continuous swathe of Belgian Flanders and north-eastern France.

The British and Empire squadrons were drawn into costly battles over many months to secure local air superiority and, finally, to regain superiority. From 4 to 9 April 1917, for example, 75 of their aircraft were lost and 105 aircrew became casualties principally in driving enemy aircraft back from the line round Arras. In this same period, fifty-six aircraft were destroyed or similarly damaged in flying accidents, many due to mishandling by replacement pilots converting from training to operational machines. Many had less than fifteen hours solo flying experience when they were posted to the BEF. The dilution of experience in squadrons became critical for several months. The supply of new aeroplanes, the Sopwith Pups followed by Triplanes, and later from this stable, the Camels, and the SE5, improved fighting capability overall, including the ability of replacement pilots to survive early encounters with the Albatros and Halberstadt.

The final phase of the struggle for air mastery took place in 1918. The Germans launched even greater numbers of fighters in single formations – the 'circuses' of Albatros and Fokker triplanes

The RE8 – 'Harry Tate' – highly effective specialized reconnaissance and artillery spotting aircraft during 1917–18 (*Trustees of the Imperial War Museum, London, Q 67107*)

RE8 about to take off. Note that the officers wore their badges of rank on the cuff (*Trustees of the Imperial War Museum, London, Q 12169*)

led by such men as Manfred von Richthofen – which aimed to destroy Allied reconnaissance and bomber aircraft encountered en route to the battlelines and to swamp fighter groups sent up to oppose them. They had some success, but not enough. In a series of engagements over many weeks, the Germans lost more heavily than their opponents. During these clashes, the German Army launched a final offensive in March 1918, principally striking the British Fifth Army.

In this huge battle, ground-to-air cooperation broke down. Batteries forced to withdraw rapidly lost their wireless equipment. Lacking this means of communication, the artillery observation aircraft were unable to function, though they had numerous targets to offer. Observers took to dropping details of these directly to batteries in message bags. The infantry lines were fragmented. Contact patrols found groups of various sizes from time to time but by the time their locations were reported to corps they were out of date. They engaged the enemy with considerable success, however, attacking troops, batteries and transport with machine-guns from the first day. British and French bomber sorties were coordinated. In March and April, critical months in the air as on the ground, 528 fighters were lost out of a total of 1,032.

This was the peak of air operations in France and Flanders and, coincidentally, in the

Mediterranean and Middle East where the RFC and RNAS contributed jointly to operations. For while the numbers of sorties would continue to rise, the German capability to renew offensive action was spent. Moreover, an early end to the war was assured by the arrival of United States ground and air forces in France.

The British air services were in the process of developing an independent bombing force among a number of measures to destroy the enemy's air power, while simultaneously supporting the armies in the field. But these operations were not to engage the Royal Flying Corps. From 1 April 1918, an independent air force was established embodying the Army's air corps and the air service of the Royal Navy. It was entitled the Royal Air Force, a service in its own right.

The change had been brought about by the submission of studies which purported to show that the damage inflicted on the enemy by bombing operations was so great as to require a discrete organization. They embraced attacks on railways and war industries as well as immediate military targets such as aerodromes. They were supplemented by statistics for similar raids undertaken by the French Air Service. Examined by a committee, the conclusion was accepted: the potential of air power was so great that its use should be separated from the strategies of the seas and the battlefields.

After the war, however, Royal Air Force field teams were sent to inspect chosen areas to report further on the extent of bomb damage. These proved,

> upon inspection to have been considerably less devastating than the photographs had led to believe. Similarly, bursts on aerodromes are difficult to gauge. A group of bombs close to a permanent hangar at Hagenau were found to have caused much less damage than reports and photographs had seemed to indicate.

Thus ran the report of Major H.W.M. Paul to the Air Ministry in 1919. It confirmed the impression of the commander of the Independent Force, who had already observed on 18 August 1918 that,

> I am certain that the damage done to both buildings and personnel is very small compared to any other form of war and energy expended. . . .

Indeed, as investigations widened after the war and were taken up by Canadian and United States teams, the grounds on which the independent air service had been founded were found to be at the very least insubstantial. They may well have been presented to government in good faith. However, the report containing the findings of the field teams and connected studies relating to the strategic bombing of Germany, published by the Air Ministry in January 1920, shows every sign of a rigged document.

But the deed was done. Newly fledged, the Royal Air Force rapidly became jealous of its prerogative to procure, man, operate according to its convictions, and administer every flying machine disposed for duty in the armed forces of the Crown. With this outlook, it celebrated victory over the Central Powers on 11 November 1918.

CHAPTER THREE

# Out of the Air

Haaving begun the war with two armed services, the British and imperial forces ended with three. The Admiralty never accepted the decision to create a separate Royal Air Force, and from the end of the war began a long campaign to recover its own air service. But the Army, committed to a huge range of tasks across the world with rapidly dwindling manpower, was readier to accept the change and the assurances from RAF senior officers – the greater number of whom had belonged to its regiments and corps – that its air requirements in the field would continue to be provided in full. Besides, it had enough problems in finding funds to develop new weapons and equipment devised during hostilities, of which the tank seemed to some to offer the greatest potential. While the cavalry had other ideas, all agreed on one point: they must never accept a return to trench warfare.

The universal view among the peoples who had been at war went further: war should never be used again to settle differences between nations. Politicians and people were caught up in a mass movement to disarm all field forces, retaining at most national gendarmeries. War chests were squeezed among the former Allies and forbidden to the defeated states.

Major-General Trenchard was reinstated as Chief of the Air Staff, determined to fight for the preservation of the Royal Air Force. Convinced that air power, exerted independently by bombers, would be essential to victory in any future conflict – perhaps the principal means of winning it – he preserved a framework on which to build this capability as opportunity offered, and sought to honour his promises to the Royal Navy and Army by maintaining squadrons dedicated to their support. Some of the sympathy in parliament for the Admiralty's case was drawn by opening aircrew posts to secondment from the Royal Navy and Army.

Still, survival of the RAF was by no means assured. From time to time, the Army, desperate to escape further cuts in its funds, joined the naval wrecking tactics. These apart, reductions in the air budget made it likely that the maintenance of basic facilities – training and administration of aircrew and ground specialists – would further constrain the limited number of squadrons authorized. Some relief was secured by demonstrating the economies to be found in air policing.

During and immediately after the war, aircraft on the north-west frontier of India were used effectively against raiding tribes. In that area of precipitous mountains, the movement of Army punitive expeditions was slow and expensive. An aircraft was able to attack the villages of the raiders in a matter of hours, destroying buildings and setting grain stores on fire. In Egypt and the Sudan there had been successful air and ground expeditions against the Senussi and the Sultan of Darfur; warring tribesmen on camels or horses were rapidly seen by reconnaissance aeroplanes. Some dissidence was brought to an end simply by the dropping of a cautionary message to the warriors concerned, despite the report of one observer that 'there was much shaking of rifles and lances as we drew away . . .'.

In 1919 the use of aircraft to bomb the forts of the 'Mad Mullah', Mohammed bin Abdullah

Hassan, in British Somaliland broke the power of a local tyrant and rebel operating since 1895. In the following year, among similar forays into bandit country, aircraft intervened alone along the Euphrates just as Britain took up the mandate to protect the emerging kingdom of Iraq. This territory had been removed from Turkey, Germany's ally during the war, and the Istanbul government was fostering tribal action to destabilize the border region. The British political agent's house at Shatrah on the Euphrates was surrounded by raiders from which he was rescued by two DH9a light bombers. Elsewhere, rebel attempts to break the railway line were driven away by attacks from the air. If Biggles was not among the pilots in person, he was surely there in spirit.

These accomplishments supported a proposal by Major-General Trenchard that the Royal Air Force should assume responsibility for order among the more remote local factions and discourage raiders from outside. In Iraq there was a requirement to patrol extensive deserts in baking temperatures. Desert and mountains inhibited ground movement in the Aden protectorate.

The Royal Air Force proposed to meet the requirement with a modest number of aeroplanes able to reach any part of the territory within a few hours. They would cooperate with a small ground force carried in armoured cars and trucks under RAF command. The Army would be required only to maintain a general reserve against any serious insurrection. It was later proposed to move a part of this by air as necessary.

The first major step was taken towards the policy at Cairo in March 1921. Mr Churchill, recently appointed Colonial Secretary, was anxious to cut the large sums required to garrison Iraq. Major-General Trenchard proposed to use eight squadrons of aircraft, six armoured car companies, two armoured trains and three or four river gunboats. He proposed that a main road should be run from Egypt to Iraq through Palestine. Along the route,

> . . . dumps of petrol and landmarks should be entrusted to the local Shaikhs who would be paid for the services of personnel employed for their safekeeping and efficient maintenance. . . .

The garrison of twenty-three infantry battalions would be reduced to twelve and the overall military cost to less than £6 million a year. Further savings were to be had by using Arab levies in place of airmen in the ground forces. The British and Indian Army garrisons and the Royal Air Force complement would each number two thousand all ranks. Although local political circumstances, and resentment in the War Office that the Army was being displaced, threatened implementation of this scheme, it was approved by the British government on 1 October 1922.

It was thus as an agent for savings as much as anything that the Royal Air Force was preserved through almost twenty years of reduction and constraint within the armed forces. But this triumph was not sufficient to secure the resources to build up the fifty-two squadron force accepted as the requirement for British security against continental air attack. The fact that the air estimates were actually increased marginally in all but one of the budgets between 1925 and 1928 was not of much comfort to Trenchard or his successor, Air Chief Marshal Sir John Salmond. The Ten Year Rule, put on a rolling base in 1928 by Mr Churchill as Chancellor of the Exchequer, assumed that in,

> framing . . . estimates, the British Empire will not be engaged in any great war during the next ten years, and that no Expeditionary Force is required for this purpose.

The international financial crisis at the end of the decade and the following years of recession further inhibited the development of armed forces capable of meeting the commitments of successive governments.

Yet withal, the forces maintained a capacity for active service in imperial policing. Army and Air Force cooperated on the north-west frontier of India, in Iraq, and Aden into the mid-1930s, though aircrew were finding that their primitive foes were no longer overawed by their presence, and were positively challenging below 3,000 ft. A Royal Air Force officer engaged against tribesmen raiding near Shaiba in 1928 wrote home to say that,

> . . . This show is really nasty. [Ed Dowish] runs a gang of 2,500 well-trained raiders, all very good shots. So far he has shot down three people with three direct hits in the radiator. Sqn Ldr Vincent was the first and *he* got away with it. Jackson was the next. He was hit in the radiator and came down in the middle of them. Tried to scrap them with his revolver, but was killed – one in the head, the other in the heart. He was found later, stripped but not mutilated. Next young Kellett was shot down the same way, but landed over a ridge out of sight. He got away with both locks and bolts out of his guns, and collected all his ammunition before they appeared. . . .

Royal Air Force aircrew were pioneers in opening trunk routes to Africa and the Far East, and highly successful in international flying competitions. Their bases, all constructed since the end of the First World War, were the envy of the other two services.

Gradually, as the first dreadful possibility of another war began to take shape with the rise of German militarism, the Army began to question how it should be supported from the air in large-scale land operations involving other major powers. Ideas on the subject were poorly informed. Discussion brought no conclusions, principally because there was no settled strategic concept for the conduct of such operations. New tanks, light and medium, armoured cars and tracked carriers were passing from trials into service, but most senior officers regarded this process as 'mechanization', an improvement in the mobility of field forces. They did not see that the options of mobility and tank weapons opened an extraordinary potential for striking power in manoeuvre. This lack of perception was due in part to a widespread conviction among many in the British military establishment that the British Army must never again be drawn into armed struggle on the Continent. Numbers of RAF officers agreed with this, motivated by the view that a land expeditionary force would require a substantial air component, diminishing the resources available for other, more important tasks.

Still, on the rare occasions when Army and Air Force cooperation was discussed, the Royal Air Force reminded the War Office that it had kept its promises. It maintained Army cooperation squadrons to provide reconnaissance, photography, and artillery observation. The Hawker Audax and Hector had been developed to that end, and were in service in imperial policing. These were to be replaced by the Westland Lysander in 1938, capable of taking off and landing over short distances and of flying at slow speeds.

These provisions did not altogether satisfy the Army. Mechanized forces seemed likely to be vulnerable to air attack. The use of the German Ju 87 or 'Stuka' in the Spanish Civil War as an integral support element of the ground forces confirmed the ability of the modern aeroplane to intervene with devastating effect in the ground battle. Sir Cyril Newall, Chief of the Air Staff in 1937 viewed this as a 'gross misuse of air forces'. He believed that air power should be aggressive and projected by the strategic bomber, arguably a weapon capable of winning a war without significant intervention by sea and land forces. Some of his officers held that fighters were a better investment, providing a deterrent to air attack on the homeland. The inception of radar would enhance their efficiency. When the Royal Navy finally won in 1937 its battle to recover its own Fleet Air Arm, there was even greater determination in the air staff to restrict funds for Army cooperation.

Within the Army, the Royal Artillery maintained a persistent demand for aerial observation posts manned by their officers to direct artillery in the contact zone. Writing in the *Journal of the Royal United Services Institution* in 1933, Captain J.H. Parham remarked that,

> . . . The battery commander, wishing to see a target out of sight behind a hill, is compelled to call upon a unit operating from a distant landing ground when five minutes up in the air above his own battery position – even a thousand feet up – would meet all his needs.

This made the point that when the local artillery commander needed to use aircraft he needed it at once; it would be in every way more efficient to task and brief one of his own officers rather than a pilot of another service who had first to be made available by a headquarters in rear and briefed at third hand by an air liaison officer on an airfield. The solution was to provide aerial Forward Observation Posts – FOPs – adjacent to the artillery positions and piloted by Royal Artillery officers. The argument that the existing system had been effective in the First World War suggested that a future conflict would involve permanently entrenched lines where speed of reaction was not a prime requirement. The Army was determined to avoid a resumption of trench warfare.

Other arguments were adduced, such as the requirement to act swiftly to dodge enemy fighter sweeps, and to use an aircraft so light and manoeuvrable that it could evade fighters. The gunners continued to develop their case year by year. In the early stages, the autogiro seemed a suitable aircraft. In 1930 the A.V. Roe aircraft company built a model designed earlier by the Spanish rotary wing designer, de la Cierva. One of these, the C19 Mark IV, was used during the Army manoeuvres in 1933, and was sufficiently promising as a liaison vehicle and artillery observation post to win an order from the Air Ministry for twelve to permit further trials. Captain Parham learned to fly one. The armed forces were on the edge of a new aerial option, a light aircraft which could manoeuvre and hover, but the technology eluded them. Despite promising developments, the autogiro of the day was rejected because there were doubts concerning its stability, and while it seemed likely that this might be remedied it later became apparent that its ratio of maintenance to flying hours was excessive.

The Royal Artillery were not defeated. A number of officers had learned to fly light aircraft at their own expense, inspired perhaps by the initiative of their predecessors between 1907 and 1910. From 1934, they congregated in the Royal Artillery Flying Club. Some had flown or now became seconded as pilots to the Royal Air Force, including Captain H.C. Bazeley, the club secretary. His aim was to study the system from within. In 1938 he proposed a series of measures which would complement the expertise and equipment of the Royal Air Force and the Army in artillery observation and tactical reconnaissance from the air. For example,

> . . . The method of controlling fire from the air has changed little since the Great War. Nor can it be readily altered, because the control has to be exercised by a pilot . . . the pilot, not being a gunner and being out of touch with the conditions existing at the moment on the

ground, cannot be expected to select targets according to their tactical importance. . . . the observer and pilot must be one and the same person as only the pilot can ensure that the aircraft is in a suitable position at the crucial moment.

On ninety days out of a hundred when it is possible to fly at all it is possible to rise to 1,000 feet. On seven days out of ten when it is possible to rise to 1,000 feet it is possible to see six or seven miles horizontally. Such conditions would satisfy most gunners. . . .

In sum, the Army should cover territory within 3 or 4 miles of the contact line, the remainder falling to the Royal Air Force.

Meanwhile, Brigadier H.R.S. Massey, senior Royal Artillery officer in Southern Command and president of the flying club, pressed these and associated ideas on the general officer commanding-in-chief. There was the further consideration that 'wireless' capabilities now offered the radio telephone – RT – as distinct from wireless telegraphy – WT – facilitating communication between a light aircraft and the battery concerned.

The Air Council responded on 23 July 1938 with assurances that it was only too ready to review 'any unsatisfactory features of the system of cooperation at present in use'. But they pointed out by way of preliminary contention that the methods in use had been developed and tested during the First World War. The majority of the senior and middle ranking officers of the Royal Air Force considering the proposal had served as pilots in operations with the Royal Flying Corps in France and Flanders between 1914 and 1918. Twenty years had passed since the armistice but their impressions of those dangerous years remained strong and, in their view, informed their judgements.

This was an error. The gunners had come close to being drawn into it initially by illustrating their case with examples based on fixed lines in conditions applicable to 1916–18. They had, however, seen the dangers in time. Thereafter, they looked to the support of an army manoeuvring as an entity in the field, sometimes in defence or withdrawal, at others on the offensive, but mobile, controlled widely by wireless communications, and employing weapons of greater accuracy and striking power.

Enthused by Major-General Massey, promoted to become Director of Military Training in the War Office, the Army Council pressed the case. To their great credit and despite huge problems arising from the prospect of becoming involved in a war in continental Europe, the Air Council agreed on 23 December 1938 to engage in a trial of the Flying Observation Post. This was to be undertaken 'as a matter of arrangement between the Air Officer Commanding 22 (Army Cooperation) Group and the Commandant, School of Artillery, Larkhill'. Captain Bazeley and three other Royal Artillery officers seconded to the RAF were detailed to test the concept using the Audax and Lysander. These proved to be too fast and insufficiently manoeuvrable for the task. Various light aircraft and the latest mark of autogiro were then tried.

Flying at considerably lower speeds and thus enjoying the ability to make tight turns, the pilots were able to pick up targets regularly up to 3,000 yards, up to 4 miles in optimum weather conditions. Spitfires were employed to simulate attacks which the light aircraft, turning on their tails, evaded. For all that, the Royal Air Force regarded the results with less enthusiasm than the Army; they did not accept, for example, the viability of a light aircraft flying above anti-aircraft weapons in the contact line. Overall, they doubted whether the system would stand the test of war.

This was now opened to them; for the trials were still in progress when the Second World War began in September 1939.

# Gunners in the Air

## I – Growing Pains

CHAPTER FOUR

# Launching the Air Observation Post

Some three weeks after the outbreak of war, while the Expeditionary Force and Air Component were still in the process of deploying into France, the Army Council felt in need of governmental advice as to what sort of war they were to fight on the Continent. While this was pondered, the matter of air cooperation was raised, specifically the provision of ground attack aircraft for employment in and immediately behind the line of contact. The Lysander was no more fitted for this role than artillery spotting. The Army was looking for a 'small cheap bomber', something on the lines of the German Stuka dive-bomber. Two hundred and fifty of these were subsequently to be demanded by the Army, dedicated to the support of Army formations, manned initially by the Royal Air Force in the air and on the ground, but, from 1940, the responsibility of a resuscitated Army air force. The Secretary of State for War agreed to put the proposal to the Cabinet.

This precipitate decision at the outset of war threatened to overshadow acceptance of the Flying Observation Post. Major-General Massey was determined that, whatever the outcome of the bomber proposal, the FOP should remain in full view. As a result of his influence, the paper for the Cabinet of 6 October 1939 stated,

> . . . The first need is the provision of a new type of light aeroplane to improve the application of artillery fire to be piloted by Army officers. . . . I should like to be assured by the Secretary of State for Air that this matter is being pressed forward. The second and infinitely greater need is that of aircraft for what I may call direct support of the Army. . . .

Unwittingly, the bid by the Army for its own close support aircraft advanced the case for a Flying Observation Post. The Royal Air Force was understandably astonished by the Army's claim for a ground attack force of its own, and no less dismayed by the idea that it should dispose 250 bombers immediately from its front-line aircraft. The RAF was short of production capacity to meet its needs in fighter, bomber, and maritime squadrons just as the Air Component in France with a call on home-based squadrons had drawn heavily on its resources. They were already concerned that early carrier losses would add weight to the demands of the Fleet Air Arm on the national aircraft manufacturing base.

A senior member of the Air Staff remarked that 'it will be much cheaper to show our goodwill to the Army by finding them a cabin version of the [Gypsy] Moth than conceding them a homegrown Stuka'.

Further trials on Salisbury Plain in December failed to convince the RAF members of the joint trials team that any light aeroplane would be viable within range of enemy anti-aircraft weapons or under attack by fighters. Still, 22 Group headquarters conceded in January 1940 that,

. . . if artillery observation of the type envisaged proves to be practicable, it would obviously revolutionise present methods of Army Cooperation, and probably merit the development of a specific type of aircraft for the purpose with the consequent saving in our expensive types of Army Cooperation aeroplanes and highly trained [RAF] crew.

To test the concept, trials were to continue in France. Air Marshal A.S. Barratt, AOC-in-C Army Cooperation Command, commented,

There is nothing new about this. An old horse resuscitated at War Office request. As long as they provide the bodies to be shot down I do not mind. . . .

This stage of the trials had three objectives: 'to determine in the light of practical experience obtained under war conditions' the possibility and limitations of light aircraft as FOPs; the most suitable type of aircraft; and the organization most suited to the operation and maintenance of that aircraft.

The trials unit, D Flight, Royal Air Force, under Captain Bazeley (shortly to be promoted in secondment to the rank of squadron leader) was to work up at Old Sarum, move to France to engage in range work with British and French artillery, and finally to operate an Air Observation Post – a change of title more accurately describing the function – over the line with the French Army in the Saar sector.

Unfortunately, it had no suitable aircraft. The French were experimenting with the autogiro and

Major Charles Bazeley, RA (*Museum of Army Flying*)

American Stinson aircraft taken to France in 1940 for trials by Major Bazeley. Long favoured by AOP pilots, production models obtained after a long delay proved unacceptably heavy on arrival and the model was abandoned (*Museum of Army Flying*)

this was re-examined and again discarded. Weeks passed in the process of selection, for none of those tested met requirements fully. Other options, including pusher types, were not delivered by the manufacturers.

The pilots, Bazeley and two other artillery officers with a Royal Air Force pilot, grew desperate. In the circumstances, two of the American models used in the trials – the Taylorcraft and the Stinson Voyager, both high-wing monoplanes – began to recommend themselves. A manufacturer at Leicester, Mr A.L. Wykes, had a licence to manufacture the former. A fourth mark, Model D, was produced by the company to meet minimum military requirements. Three flew to France with the Stinson. Just as the range work concluded, the German Army struck into France and the Low Countries. Major Bazeley (he had shrugged off his Royal Air Force rank) was at once ordered to return to Old Sarum and disband.

He disregarded this instruction. 'We haven't come this far to give it up now,' he remarked privately to his three pilots. But they had to find a hiding place distant from close RAF scrutiny while representations were made within the Army to rescind the disbandment order. After a visit to the Commandant of the School of Artillery at Larkhill, the flight moved to that area.

More than anything else it was Bazeley's lobbying throughout the summer of 1940 that maintained the survival of the British artillery Air Observation Post. The odds were against him.

The offensive which caused D Flight to be ordered out of France successively separated the Allied forces, leading to the expulsion of the British Expeditionary Force and the surrender of French arms. The British Isles were then threatened with invasion by the German Army. Shortly, the German Air Force began its campaign to break the power of the Royal Air Force in the Battle of Britain. Among many measures of defence and defiance, the new Prime Minister, Mr Winston Churchill, ordered the formation of airborne troops to raid enemy targets on the Continent, a requirement which added to the many demands on the Royal Air Force.

The Army, which had lost numerous prisoners and the greater part of the heavy arms and equipment of the Expeditionary Force in the course of withdrawal to the homeland, was involved in extensive reorganization, re-equipment, and training. In these straits, Air Observation Posts, conceived for use with land forces manoeuvring in the field under some assurance of air cover, seemed irrelevant.

The Royal Air Force was struggling to preserve the air defence of Great Britain. If that should be lost, neither the Royal Navy nor the Army could hold off an invasion. At the same time, an air capability had to be mustered to provide a means of striking back at the enemy in Germany, Italy, and the occupied territories in Europe, in the Mediterranean and Middle East.

For all that, Bazeley secured the re-establishment of D Flight, formally accomplished in August 1940 but tolerated in the interim. On this basis he was able to progress the various modifications to improve the pilot's visibility from the Taylorcraft, and to mount or contain various items of equipment. Mr Wykes had produced a full schedule of prices for the two aircraft returned for this work which were unlikely to strain the finances of the war chest. For example:

Changing to service type compass including design and manufacture of approved compass bracket with fitting.
Changing to wireless type T.R.9. – involving design, mock up and production of special radio racks, controller brackets, etc. Redesign of fairing, supplying and fitting

£36 12 shillings 6 pence.

Meanwhile, one hundred Stinson Vigilants had been ordered from the United States. Delivery was expected in March 1941. The Royal Air Force agreed to train Royal Artillery officers as pilots, offering fifty places at Elementary Flying Training Schools from 9 September 1940 and further vacancies during 1941 and 1942. If there were any dissenters at this stage they were muted when it became known that a powerful figure had spoken strongly in favour of completing AOP trials; General Sir Alan Brooke, Commander-in-Chief Home Forces and the most senior serving officer of the Royal Artillery, called for a joint report as early as possible. It may be thought that the idea of an Air Observation Post had gone somewhat beyond the trials stage with the ordering of one hundred Stinson aircraft and the training of fifty pilots, but the Army had carried the Royal Air Force to trials completion and no further.

By the end of September the School of Artillery reported further favourable progress; but in March 1941, Air Marshal Sir Arthur Barratt suggested that 'the case against the Air O.P. would seem probably conclusive . . . it is recommended that the War Office should be approached as to the possibility of developing man-lifting kites as a substitute. . . .' The Air Ministry was able to show that its own requirements for aircrew and ground support staff, particularly technicians among the latter, precluded supply of officers and other ranks to units dedicated to Army support.

General Brooke returned to the lists. Lysander losses in France in 1940 had been high because they had neither the speed nor agility to escape enemy fighters. The Tomahawk, suggested as a replacement, was not promising. Lack of means to field the full number of AOP squadrons required did not suggest that the whole scheme should be discarded. In March and again in April, the commander-in-chief pressed acceptance of the case, concluding,

> . . . I shall therefore be glad if the Air Ministry may be clearly informed that the Army considers [the AOP] essential, and may be pressed to provide the necessary aircraft at the earliest possible date.

The main order of Stinson aircraft from the United States had not arrived. Four sent in advance for training suggested that they were too big for the task. When at last the first Air Observation Post unit was formed on 1 August 1941 from D Flight, entering the Royal Air Force order of battle as 651 Squadron, it contained a variety of aircraft, mostly Taylorcraft. Two more squadrons were authorized, of which 652 was to be equipped temporarily with Tiger Moths. The complement of each unit was 18 Royal Artillery officers, 18 soldiers, with an adjutant and an engineering officer, and 112 other ranks, from the Royal Air Force. At the same time, 1425 (Army Cooperation Flight) was formed at Larkhill for trials and training.

In conceding agreement to the raising of such units, the Air Ministry insisted that, while operating wholly for the Army, procurement of aircraft and equipment, custom and practice in all matters of procedure, and command overall should remain with the RAF. The Army was not going to be allowed to form its own air force.

Nevertheless, the Army was engaged at that time in raising an Army Air Corps.

# An Airborne Force

CHAPTER FIVE

# Raising an Army Air Corps

In June 1940 there were strong reasons for believing that the United Kingdom was going to be defeated on its own soil and suffer, like much of northern and western Europe, a cruel occupation. The fact that there were substantial British naval, land, and air forces in the Near and Middle East, reinforced by Australia and New Zealand, in India, Burma and the Far East was in a sense irrelevant. They were far from home and, in many ways, tied to their locations. The greater part of the German armed forces was available to crush the under-equipped British home defence forces.

Yet, almost from the moment of becoming Prime Minister on 10 May, Mr Churchill was not only active in the organization of a dynamic defence of the kingdom but insistent on the preparation of an offensive capability. For the medium term the War Office was instructed to lay the foundations of a force to return to the Continent. More immediately, as noted, special raiding forces were to be raised to harry the enemy in occupied territories, the policy of 'butcher and bolt'. The latter were to include an airborne force: Mr Churchill personally proposed 'at least 5,000 parachute troops'.

The Chiefs of Staff, and no less those concerned with shipping and the expansion of war industries, were dismayed by such instructions. They were burdened with the task of simply holding off the enemy, if that were possible. Further tasks, in their view, would certainly detract from this vital responsibility. Still, the Chiefs of Staff set inceptory arrangements in hand obediently. But they were determined to have value for money; the Army and Air Councils were not going to commit anything beyond a token of their scarce means until it was clear that the scheme was practicable and would contribute directly to the war effort.

Within the Army, unit and formation commanders were already apprehensive that the recruitment of commandos would draw off the best of their officers and men. The provision of parachutists was expected to have the same effect. Although instructions calling for volunteers required that 'no applications will be withheld' from the War Office, ways and means of circumventing this were found by commanding officers.

It was thought that air landing – glider-borne – forces would be easier to provide. Infantry battalions in service might be converted for this purpose together with other arms, thus avoiding the creation of 'special' units. At the same time, when not training periodically for the aerial function, they would be available for home defence.

The Air Ministry's conclusions were put to the Prime Minister on 31 August 1940:

(a) We cannot afford to have squadrons of aircraft solely for dropping parachute troops. The heavy bomber must therefore be used.
(b) The aircraft which is to be employed in operations must be used for training.
(c) After examination of all types of aircraft, the Whitley, and later possibly the Stirling, appear to be suitable.

(d) The Air Staff are beginning to think that gliders have much greater potentialities than parachutes. . . .

. . . the Air Ministry do not think it wise at present to divert aircraft and pilots in order to increase the rate of production of parachute troops, unless, and until, some definite operation for which they must be used is in view. Nor does there seem any object in training more than 500 parachutists until there is a likelihood of obtaining sufficient aircraft to operate them.

In a verbal briefing to the Prime Minister it was made clear that the diversion of aircraft to parachute training would inevitably reduce bomber operations against Germany. On this account principally, Mr Churchill accepted a reduced programme of selection and training. In so far as glider-borne troops were concerned he remarked to the Chiefs of Staff on 1 September 1940:

Of course, if the Glider scheme is better than parachutes we should pursue it, but is it being seriously taken up? Are we not in danger of being fobbed off with one doubtful and experimental policy and losing the other which has already been proved? Let me have a full report of what is being done.

'Out of the frying pan into the glider' the Vice-Chief of the Air Staff commented on reading this. But it was possible to show that this option had not been neglected: the specification for a glider capable of carrying eight troops with full personal equipment had made considerable progress. Mr F.F. Crocombe, Chief Designer for the General Aircraft Company at Feltham, Middlesex, had drawn its lineaments in late June 1940. It was expected that the first production model would fly at the end of October. So it proved.

This remarkable accomplishment was due to several factors. Numerous gliders had been produced for sport in the 1930s; their flying characteristics were well known, and it was estimated that several hundred pilots would be found among gliding clubs. Construction was largely a matter of screwing and gluing timber frames and plywood panels into place. Although the first models were contracted to a firm in Yorkshire, Slingsby Sailplanes in Kirkbymoorside, the greater number were subsequently made by sub-contracting to furniture and coach manufacturers.

The first model was called the Hotspur. The initial mark flew adequately unladen to meet the requirement for release at high altitude and a gradual descent to the landing zone or LZ. It could not fly with the specified load. Modification had also to take account of a new consideration: to avoid enemy fire or attack during a long descent, the glider would be released at low altitude, from which it would descend steeply. The underside of the fuselage required strengthening.

The Hotspur was a mid-wing glider. While the prototypes were being produced, Mr A.E. Ellison of Airspeed was designing a considerably larger high-wing transport, later to be named the Horsa. It was to carry twenty-five fully armed troops. Constructed principally of laminated spruce and plywood beneath a cover of doped fabric, the Horsa was manufactured initially at Fairey's Hendon airfield in thirty sections. RAF maintenance units assembled them at various storage sites.

F.N. Slingsby – of Slingsby Sailplanes – was next commissioned to design a glider to carry fifteen troops, the Hengist. But the Horsa was so successful both as a troop and light vehicle carrier that it rapidly became the standard glider for airborne assault: 3,655 were constructed in all. The

Hotspur gliders flying from Weston-on-the-Green, Oxfordshire, late 1941 (*Museum of Army Flying*)

Troops from 52nd Light Infantry emplaned in Horsa fuselage (*Trustees of the Imperial War Museum, London, CH 10208*)

Hotspur was relegated to the role of basic trainer. One requirement remained: a glider which could carry heavier loads such as a 25 lb field gun and towing vehicle, or a light tank weighing up to 8 tons; for the weakness of airborne troops on landing was seen to lie in a lack of heavy mobile weapons. A specification was issued by the Ministry of Aircraft Production in mid-1941 to General Aircraft Limited, and the prototype flew for the first time at Snaith, an RAF bomber airfield, on 27 March 1942.

Despite other enterprises in design, the air landing, as distinct from the parachute, element of airborne forces would be carried into battle by the British Horsa and the Hamilcar, augmented by the American Waco CG4-A later in the war.

While glider production was set in hand, the War Office grappled with the organization of airborne troops. The difficulty was that no one had a clear idea as to how they would be used. As a basis for planning, the Chief of the Imperial General Staff, General Sir John Dill, decided on 11 November 1940 that, 'butcher and bolt' operations apart, two Aerodrome Capture Groups should be formed, one apiece for the corps being earmarked at home and in the Mediterranean to invade Europe during or after 1943. On this basis, a group was to consist of a headquarters, two battalions with ten Bren carriers and five trucks, one squadron of eighteen light tanks, two 3.7 inch howitzers sections, eight howitzers, two light anti-aircraft troops, a signal section, a medical detachment and a supply detachment, in all, 1,730 troops, principally in gliders, an airlift of about 600 tons.

Some 350 aircraft would be required to deliver this force simultaneously, a considerable slice of the bomber force. When it became apparent that there were insufficient pilots, actual or potential, in the RAF to fly gliders in the numbers then conceived, the Army said that it would find them. The War Office was just then preparing a plan to transfer men suited to aircrew duties to swell the Royal Air Force commands. Those required for gliders, believed then to be six hundred over the first year, would be raised from this scheme but retained in the Army. This notion caused the Deputy Chief of the Air Staff to wonder on 11 December 1940 whether the magnitude of the commitment was recognized.

The idea that semi-skilled, unpicked personnel (infantry corporals have, I believe, even been suggested) could with a maximum of training be entrusted with the piloting of these troop carriers is fantastic. Their operation is equivalent to forced landing the largest sized aircraft without engine aid – than which there is no higher test of piloting skill.

This challenge notwithstanding, the air staff continued to hold the view that air-landing forces would be more effective than parachutists because they could be put down precisely on their targets while parachute troops were likely to be widely scattered. Glider forces would also be more economic; it was then thought that a single bomber would be able to tow two or three gliders one behind another. The provision of pilots continued to be one of numerous points of difference between khaki and blue from January to May 1941.

Months might have followed in this way but for two events. The first was that on 26 April 1941 Mr Churchill visited the Central Landing Establishment at Ringway, Manchester, established to train parachutists, air landed troops and glider pilots. He found eight hundred of the former and little more than a cadre of the latter under training there and elsewhere. The second was the successful if costly German capture of Crete by airborne assault begun on 20 May 1941.

Visit of Mr Churchill to the Central Landing Establishment, Ringway, 1941. Air Marshal Barratt is on Mr Churchill's left. Wing-Commander Sir Nigel Norman is on extreme right of picture (*Museum of Army Flying*)

This is a sad story [Mr Churchill wrote on 26 May], and I feel myself greatly to blame for allowing myself to be overborne by the resistances which were offered. One can see how wrongly based these resistances were . . . in the light of what is happening in Crete, and may soon be happening in Cyprus and Syria.

. . . Thus we are always found behindhand by the enemy. We ought to have 5,000 parachutists and an Airborne Division on the German model, with any improvements which might suggest themselves from experience. . . . These will all be necessary in the Mediterranean fighting of 1942, or earlier if possible. We shall have to try to retake some of these Islands which are now being so easily occupied by the enemy. . . . I now invite the Chiefs of Staff to make proposals, as far as is possible, to repair the misfortune.

These admonitions hastened settlement of disputes between the two services, action within the Army and Royal Air Force individually, and revived the attention of the Ministry of Aircraft Production. Major John Rock, the Army representative at the Central Landing Establishment, recalled that, 'We passed suddenly from having to beg, borrow or steal everything to being overwhelmed with staff, vehicles, equipment, another airfield – even flying training'.

This impression was relative. Airborne forces were passing from a gross to a lesser state of neglect. Still, important changes were evolving. It was agreed on 22 August 1941, without recourse to the chiefs' committee, that the Army would provide glider pilots but the RAF would qualify them. Recruitment began to this end.

The Vice-Adjutant-General then raised the question,

> Who is going to administer these glider pilots? They have parent regiments but they are obviously not going back to them. There are enough problems for record offices following the fortunes of men detached across the Army without adding to them.

It was decided to form a new corps to embrace them, a means moreover of fostering a corporate spirit. A title and badge had thus to be chosen. One staff officer suggested reviving 'The Royal Flying Corps' which did not find favour with General Dill. 'That would involve fighting every air marshal in the Air Ministry,' he remarked. After some discussion, the 'Army Air Corps' was adopted on 21 December 1941, though even that, the CIGS warned, might persuade the RAF that the Army was 'still engaged in putting them out of business'. An appropriate badge would be designed.

By this time it was apparent, however, that the new corps should embrace not only the glider pilots but also the infantry forming the parachute battalions. They, too, were drawn from parent regiments and corps across the Army. It was decided that two new regiments should be created, the Glider Regiment and the Parachute Regiment, embraced by the Army Air Corps with its own record and pay offices. All other operational units in airborne forces would continue to belong to their parent bodies and be administered by them. The Glider Regiment (amended shortly to the Glider Pilot Regiment) was formally established in Army orders on 24 February 1942.

Following Mr Churchill's instructions in 1940, pilot training at the Glider Training School, Ringway, had been confined to civil sailplanes, mostly Kirby Kites, loaned or donated by patriotic citizens. These were towed by Tiger Moths, later augmented by Avro 504s to train the first thirty-seven candidates, drawn from 2 Commando, the pioneer airborne unit. They were joined by eighteen from the Royal Air Force. Gliding and parachute training vied for space in the airfield buildings and on the runway and, anticipating an increase in glider pilot trainees, the school began to move to the grass airfield at Royal Air Force, Thame (actually at Haddenham), just after Christmas 1940.

The new site in Oxfordshire provided ample air and ground space for training. Unhappily, there seemed to be no prospect of advancing skills. Glider manufacture was only just beginning; the Ministry of Aircraft Production lacked clear instructions as to targets and priorities. The first six Hotspurs were sent to Ringway for troop trials, using parachute trainees as passengers. None were immediately available for the school. Trainee pilots who had qualified successfully on sailplanes were mostly transferred to the Royal Air Force or sent back to their units during the spring and summer. Only nineteen were left in training in September 1941, in December ten. But the change in circumstances remarked by Major Rock in August was about to improve their prospects.

Joint Air Force/Army boards were assembling to select trainees, using the criteria of the RAF aircrew selection system. Those accepted passed to an Elementary Flying Training School run by the Royal Air Force to qualify over twelve weeks as light aircraft pilots, following the syllabus for all aircrew including Air Observation Post pilots. This was followed by a second phase of twelve weeks in the Glider Training School on Hotspurs to acquire glider techniques, thereafter passing to an operational training unit where, over six weeks, the individual converted to flying the Horsa – when it came into service.

Glider manufacture, now accorded a higher priority on the instructions of the Cabinet Defence Committee, seemed unlikely to match the output of pilots, but the first order for Horsas had been doubled, then trebled. Further urgent orders were to follow.

During the second half of 1941, British airborne forces passed from being a body under trial to one established in the Army's order of battle. The 1st Parachute Brigade was formed in September. On 10 October the War Office converted the 31st Independent Infantry Brigade Group, engaged in mountain warfare training, to the air-landing role. The light scales of weapons and equipment employed in the first were very similar to those required in the second. An overall commander of paratroops and airborne troops was appointed on 29 October, Major-General F.A.M. Browning. His responsibility extended to direct liaison with Air Marshal Barratt, AOC-in-C of the Royal Air Force Army Cooperation Command and the training and trials establishments. An air adviser, Wing-Commander Sir Nigel Norman, was appointed to assist Major-General Browning in this relationship, joining his headquarters at Bulford on Salisbury Plain, an invaluable reinforcement to a slender staff. But from an early stage it was agreed that the headquarters would be developed to a full airborne divisional staff. Shortly, a complement of supporting and administrative arms, tentatively agreed earlier, was established. All these would require gliders to carry vehicles and equipment essential to the full range of their operational capabilities. But, 'Although agreement has been given to the raising of two battalions of glider pilots,' the Director of Military Operations remarked to the VCIGS in September 1941, 'we do not appear to have made arrangements to bring them into being.' This advice almost certainly set in hand the process of finding a commanding officer. The War Office did not have to look far.

By the summer of 1941, Major Rock's work as the Army representative in the Airborne Establishment at Ringway had narrowed principally to glider trials and training. Enthusiastic, experienced, an exemplar and leader, he had become the *de facto* controlling authority of these activities. This situation was recognized by his appointment to raise and command what was then described as the '1st Glider Regiment', from November, in advance of the official formation in the following year. But, as he told Major-General Browning, it was essential that he learned to fly. He was given permission to join the first party of forty officers and men entering 16 Elementary Flying Training School on 2 January 1942. In his absence, the assembly of potential pilots, technical and administrative staffs, weapons, equipment and stores was left to Major G.J.S. Chatterton.

Major Chatterton did not need flying training; he had been a RAF pilot before the war but had left the service as a result of a flying accident. Recalled from the reserve in 1939 to ground duties, he transferred to the Queen's Regiment from which he passed to airborne forces.

Interviewed by Major-General Browning, George Chatterton was at once appointed second-in-command to Rock. Enterprising and highly self-confident, he recognized that the Glider Pilot Regiment was precisely the organization to which he could devote his abilities in the war. It was his early perception that if glider pilots were to survive after landing – more, to make a contribution to local operations pending their recovery to an airfield – they must be highly trained

George Chatterton shortly after rejoining the Queen's Regiment in 1940 (*Museum of Army Flying*)

and disciplined as infantry soldiers. He saw also that in recruiting intelligent young men as flying specialists that training would be all the more necessary to prevent them from becoming self-regarding.

Chatterton decided to create a training centre and depot in the hutted camp provided as temporary accommodation for the regiment at Tilshead, a village to the west of Larkhill. This included two warrant officers, Company Sergeant-Majors Cowie and Briody, 'temporarily attached' respectively from the Coldstream and Irish Guards, an arrangement which became a permanency, not least for Mick Briody who spent the remainder of his service with airborne forces as a pilot, regimental sergeant-major, and later as a paymaster. These two, with weapons and physical training instructors, put newcomers through an intensive infantry course – many were from arms other than infantry – while they awaited vacancies on flying courses. Morse code instruction using buzzer and lamp, and elementary mathematics were added to the curriculum later. A second syllabus was prepared to give continuation infantry training to pilots when they returned.

By the time Colonel Rock returned as a glider pilot in the spring of 1942, the organization which had begun to form during the previous December had been filled out. It was as follows:

*Under Army command (Major-General Browning)*
The Glider Pilot Regimental Depot located at Tilshead.
The 1st Battalion located in huts on a grass airfield adjacent to the neighbouring village of Shrewton.

*Under RAF command (AOC-in-C Flying Training)*
An Elementary Flying Training School dedicated to the inceptory training of glider pilots.
Two Glider Training Schools.
Two Glider Operational (conversion) Training Units.

*(AOC-in-C Army Cooperation)*
One Glider Exercise Squadron (296 Squadron).

The Whitley twin-engine bombers in the latter unit were gradually arriving as tugs for the gliders to replace the variety of light aircraft. Hotspurs continued to be used as trainers but Horsas were entering the conversion unit, and were soon to reach the companies of the 1st Battalion.

From the moment of his appointment, Major-General Browning had been seeking by personal contacts rather than formal submissions to establish a Royal Air Force headquarters in parallel with his own, but had come to think that this would not materialize. He was thus delighted when the two Whitley squadrons, 296 and 297, allotted for glider and parachute training, were placed under a new headquarters, 38 Wing, on 15 January 1942. Sir Nigel Norman, promoted to group captain, was appointed to command and took it as a matter of professional necessity that he would remain at Bulford. He shared Browning's view that airborne training and operations would now proceed jointly.

This arrangement did not please the Air Ministry. It was made clear that 38 Wing's prime duty was training: using the Whitleys of 296 and 297 Squadrons to best effect for the Airborne Division, and developing the technique of towing gliders and dropping parachutists. Bomber Command insisted that command of specific operations and their immediate preparation should remain with its AOC-in-C as these would be undertaken by his squadrons. To dispel any suggestion of a joint operational headquarters, 38 Wing was moved to Netheravon airfield.

This separation added to the difficulties of joint activities: common problems are more readily solved when those involved share a workplace. The two Whitley squadrons provided nominally twenty-four aircraft each working day, actually about twenty on a day-to-day basis due to servicing and maintenance routine and contingencies. Of this number, one or two were often engaged in training new crews or in special tasks, for example augmenting the slender aircraft resources of the Airborne Forces Experimental Establishment. Eighteen aircraft, then, were available to maintain basic training and conduct exercises for a rising body of glider pilots (exceeding three hundred on 1 April 1942), four parachute battalions with other arm units, and Belgian, Dutch, French, Norwegian and Polish allied contingents. The basic flying requirement for each glider pilot was eight hours a month; for parachutists, one descent a month for each man. The aircraft resources could not meet this target. At best, a glider pilot received five hours flying training a month. One of those who had received his Army 'wings' on completion of initial training about the same time as Colonel Rock, commented,

I originally volunteered for aircrew duties with the RAF. I passed the ASB [Aircrew Selection Board] and was then told that I would be trained as a glider pilot. It was no good protesting that I wanted to fly fighters; that was the only thing on offer. I accepted it and was sent off to the EFTS [Elementary Flying Training School] at Derby. Marvellous, we were flying almost every day. I came back to the Depot at Tilshead but was sent almost immediately to join the 1st Battalion at Shrewton. For weeks after that we were on ground training. Six days a week, that was the way we worked; six days on and one rest day – the whole division was the same. In the first month after I joined [my squadron], I had three hours flying.

Another recalled,

To tell the truth, I gave my name in for flying because I thought it would be an interesting and easy life, no guards or drill or fatigues [domestic chores]. Well, the first thing was the Depot where we were on the square or doing PT or guards or on the ranges all day long – and fatigues. Just as I was thinking of asking to go back to my [original] unit, we went off to EFTS. That was more like it. You didn't mind the ground work there. It was all connected with flying – navigation, instruments, checking the aircraft. You wanted to know everything they told you because you knew you would need it as soon as you got into the air. But when I got to the battalion, they had the gliders – Hotspurs then – but hardly any tugs.

Hawker Hectors mitigated the lack of Whitleys. Nine of these towed Hotspurs in a demonstration which included parachute descents for Mr Churchill on 16 April. He was impressed by the quality of the men he saw but vexed to discover that their capability to take to the air was still very limited. Moreover, 'We still await our operational glider, the Horsa,' he was told. His chief staff officer wrote to Air Chief Marshal Sir Charles Portal the next day as follows:

C.A.S. [Chief of the Air Staff]

In the course of the Prime Minister's visit to the Airborne Division yesterday, the old question of lack of aircraft and gliders came under discussion; and the Prime Minister instructed the Commander of the Division to let him have a short note on the position in order that he might take the necessary steps to have it remedied.

. . . Would you be so good as to have it examined by your Staff and ask them to provide me with material for a note to the Prime Minister.

The air staff had details ready to hand because Army requirements of the Royal Air Force had again been pressed vigorously following the appointment of General Sir Alan Brooke as CIGS. In his former post as Commander-in-Chief [Army] Home Forces, he had come to the view, following major exercises, that air support for British land forces was insufficient in quantity and inadequate in ground attack, reconnaissance, and transport capability. His apprehension had been heightened by the inability of the Royal Air Force to cover the Army in the Far East following the Japanese invasion of Malaya.

The needs of airborne forces were joined to this criticism: 'Events have shown that airborne forces have come to stay and that they must in future be as much a part of the Army as are armoured forces.' Air Observation Posts, still lacking a purpose built aircraft, were considered to have a similar claim. A general staff paper on 7 March 1942 observed,

If the Air Ministry is unable to ensure that in future these requirements will be met, there will be no alternative but for the Army to be given its own Army Air Arm on a basis similar to that of the Fleet Air Arm. . . .

The air staff's position remained substantially that it was expanding as rapidly as circumstances permitted and was trying to meet all reasonable demands. Satisfaction of the Army's demands would severely limit air capabilities at home and abroad.

Reading the exchanges between khaki and blue, Mr Churchill moderated on 7 April. Each side must attempt to meet the difficulties of the other. But his visit to 1st Airborne Division persuaded him that Browning needed help. He wrote to Sir Charles Portal on 27 April,

Chief of the Air Staff

Please make me proposals for increasing the number of discarded Bombers which can be placed rapidly at the disposal of the Airborne Corps. At least 100 should be found within the next three months. We cannot go on with 10,000 keen men and only 32 aircraft at their disposal.

The phrase 'Airborne Corps' may have been used as a general term by the Prime Minister. But during a series of meetings over following weeks, one of which was chaired personally by Mr Churchill, Sir Alan Brooke stated that the War Office planned to raise a second airborne division for use against German forces, and a third in India for operations in Asia. Under pressure, the Chief of the Air Staff conceded the diversion of up to a hundred medium and eight heavy bombers to airborne forces, of which the first increment had already been supplied. Not unimportantly, all heavy bombers in future production would be modified to tow gliders. Bomber squadrons would thus be readily available to meet the contingency requirements of airborne operations, in which it was envisaged a division would require 400 bombers for the two parachute brigades in one lift, 430 bombers for the air-landing brigade and divisional troops in two equal lifts, 700 Horsas and 60 Hamilcars.

Two limitations were noted: they would never have the means to lift more than one division at a time, and timber shortages made it unlikely that sufficient gliders would be produced to lift a second air-landing brigade. All ideas of designing and constructing a British transport plane which, among other roles, would replace the makeshift bomber transports, were shelved. For that, as in the easement of so many of the British operational difficulties in the spring and summer of 1942, they would have to look to the Americans.

An American parachute battalion was indeed attached to the division during June. With it came the first of the C–47 Dakota transport aircraft but none were immediately available for glider training. However, the inflow of Whitleys into 296 and 297 Squadrons, a new squadron, 295, and shortly a fourth, 298, together with the approach of the Horsas, stimulated a sense of progress among all members of 1st Airborne Division. At squadron level in the early summer of 1942, the glider pilots

received news about the Horsa from time to time from battalion headquarters, but never enough to satisfy them [Sergeant-Major Mick Briody later recalled]. The main topic of conversation was 'When are they coming?' After Mr Churchill's visit [on 16 April] an American general [George Marshall] visited and there were hot rumours that we were going to be supplied with American gliders, towed by their aircraft. But shortly afterwards the [air-landing] brigade headquarters said the loading trials on the Horsa were coming to an end. Then we heard that six Horsas had actually arrived at Netheravon – we forgot about the Americans!

'Loading trials' – seeing what could be fitted into a Horsa in one combination or another – begun at Ringway in March with Messrs Airspeed had been transferred to the company's factory at Portsmouth. This was mainly due to the Army's assumption that any load offered would be accepted provided there was space for it inside the hull. For example, a new American light truck, the 'Jeep', on order for the British Army, was offered by the goodwill of the United States Army attaché in London, but was at first refused by Airspeed's representatives at Ringway. They pointed to the manufacturing specification which expected the heaviest equipment load to be a motor-cycle combination. They had not constructed a floor to bear relatively high weights, or anchor points of sufficient strength to secure dense loads in a diving glider.

These objections were overcome: the jeep fitted snugly in the Horsa, leaving room for a 75 mm gun as well, and the floor was discovered to be sturdier than at first supposed, no less the anchor points. Even so, it was clear to Brigadier G.F. Hopkinson, Commander of the 1st Air Landing Brigade, and his brigade major, that they must investigate every conceivable permutation of fitment – men, weapons and equipment. Airspeed provided a 'mock up' – a basic fuselage – for this purpose. Lieutenant-Colonel Rock was drawn into the trials. An early discovery was that, when the interior was packed to capacity with light and bulky items the pilot could not get into his seat in the nose. The latter was modified to swing open on a hinge, providing an independent means of entry.

The six Horsas assembled at Netheravon on 6 July 1942 began flying to test a variety of lashing patterns and load balances. These progressed until 11 August when, during taxi trials behind a Whitley, a dreadful discovery was made: the Whitley lacked sufficient power to tow a fully laden Horsa. During the remainder of the month and into September, further checks were made by Airspeed and the Royal Aircraft Establishment, but the first conclusion stood. There were then two options: operating the Horsa half empty behind a Whitley with its two engines, or fully laden behind a bomber with four. All concerned chose the latter.

The discovery was made at a relatively late hour. From 15 July glider pilots who had passed into the regiment began conversion courses to the Horsa at the Heavy Glider Conversion Unit formed at Brize Norton in Oxfordshire. No. 6 Maintenance Unit, RAF, assembled fifty-six Horsas on the airfield. Staff Sergeant Wally Shearer found conversion,

. . . a bit daunting at first – it seemed so big after the Hotspur. But most of us got the hang of it quickly. We flew 'light' at first, no load at all, then moved up to various weights, using sandbags as ballast, though this was stopped in the first week of my course. We were briefed on load limitations two or three days later.

Sergeant George Seal wrote home in late August,

. . . sitting out on the grass in glorious sunshine, so far from anything warlike, waiting a turn to fly. I feel a fraud. It's so enjoyable – can't say I feel as if I'm contributing to 'the war effort'!

Soon Horsas were being assembled on the 38 Wing airfields on or round Salisbury Plain, Hurn, Netheravon, and Thruxton. The target of thirty on each airfield was achieved in September; the output from the factories was now reaching operational units.

The 2nd Battalion began to form in August. Major Chatterton was selected to command, but within a matter of weeks this was changed. During a night flight, Lieutenant-Colonel Rock's tow rope broke and, seeking to land on Shrewton airfield in darkness, the Hotspur he was flying hit a telegraph pole. The sudden check in speed impelled the ballast forward from the hold into the flight compartment. He was mortally injured. This was a very considerable loss. Chatterton became commanding officer of the 1st Battalion and the senior officer of the regiment. Major Iain Murray was appointed to raise the 2nd.

These arrangements were just completed when Major-General Browning was informed of plans to land Anglo-American forces in French North Africa. On his advice a British parachute brigade was allocated to the Commander-in-Chief, General Dwight D. Eisenhower, in addition to the American battalion then in training with 1st Airborne Division. False notions in the War Office concerning the prerogatives of General Eisenhower and his army commander then excluded General Browning and his staff from all further part in the planning of the landings. The division was simply required to reinforce and equip the 1st Parachute Brigade to take the field.

'We were feeling rather flat', Major-General Browning was later to remark, 'when I was ordered to mount a glider operation into Norway.'

# CHAPTER SIX

# Operation Freshman

From February 1941 British airborne forces had been involved periodically in small-scale operations under the instructions of Headquarters, Combined Operations. Two had been of the 'butcher and bolt' category, but were stood down shortly before execution. One had struck at the Tragino aqueduct in southern Italy, another had successfully captured a German radar from its station at Bruneval in northern France. None employed gliders, even in a supporting role.

The first hint of Operation Freshman was whispered to 1st Airborne Division at the end of September 1942. An airborne raid into Norway was under consideration by the Chief of Combined Operations to demolish the production of 'heavy water' in a major hydro-electric plant, an essential part of German plans to manufacture atomic weapons. Major-General Browning ordered his Commander, Royal Engineers, Lieutenant-Colonel M.C.A. Henniker, to assess the task.

While representing several reservations as to the practicability of the operation, he advised that the demolition could be accomplished by a detachment of field engineers but that the numbers should be doubled to optimize the chances of success. In discussion with Major-General Browning and Group Captain Norman, the three decided that, of the two options for delivery – parachute or glider – they should use gliders.

This minute was sent to the Chiefs of Staff on 18 October 1942:

*MOST SECRET. OPERATION FRESHMAN*

The attached notes by the Chief of Combined Operations on Operation FRESHMAN are circulated for consideration by the Chiefs of Staff at their Meeting on Monday, 19th October.

2. At this stage the C.C.O. asks for approval in principle for the Operation and for the action required –

Three Halifax aircraft, and crews, to be allotted forthwith to No. 38 Wing for experiments in long distance towing, fitting the Rebecca apparatus, and ultimately for towing the gliders taking part in this operation.

This was approved; similarly, the selection of glider pilots, and volunteers from 9th Field and 261st Field Park Airborne Companies, Royal Engineers. Though all were fit, they needed to acquire the skills to move among mountains in winter: a march of five to six hours across snow to the Norsk Hydro plant in the county of Telemark lay ahead of them; following the raid, their escape route lay across central Norway into Sweden. Thirty were required, two sections each of an officer and fourteen. Thirty-six were picked to dispose a reserve against injury or illness during training. They were to travel in two Horsas, drawn from a pool of three tugs and three gliders.

Photographs, sketches, and local information provided by a Norwegian agent were closely studied in divisional headquarters.

A detachment from an Austrian battalion guarded the plant at Vemork: ten on the dam above the plant, six at the headworks of the pipeline, six at the power station to which it led. About thirty others were known to be at Vaer and Rjukan nearby. A number of engineers worked on the tunnel between dam and plant.

The plan was to fly from Skitten airfield, a satellite of RAF Wick, to a landing zone adjacent to Mosvatn lake, a distance of 360 miles. In the final approach, the 'Rebecca' radar device fitted in the Halifaxes would evoke a response from the 'Eureka' complement at the landing site. The latter had been carried in previously by a Norwegian Army team. In company with a local resistance group, these men would then light flares to mark the landing zone and the Horsas would disconnect from the tugs and descend. Rolls of butter muslin were loaded into the Horsas to conceal them on the ground.

Guided by Norwegians to the power station, individual engineer sub-sections were detailed to demolish items identified in the power house and the electrolysis plant. Two of the glider pilots were to smash the telephone in the office buildings, the other two meanwhile securing Norwegian civilian workers in one of the rooms. The job done, the airborne party were to move off in twos and threes towards Sweden.

Lieutenant-Colonel Henniker's anxieties were not eased by events from mid-November. For reasons unknown, Bomber Command did not supply aircrew; the Halifaxes were finally manned from trials teams with the Ministry of Aircraft Production, not all of whose members were familiar with them. Weather conditions did not permit the completion of their familiarization. Engine problems and poor weather prevented movement northward on 13 and 14 November. Two Halifaxes and an Albermarle towing the reserve glider finally reached Skitten on the 17th. Group Captain T.B. Cooper, the coordinating officer, decided that the persistent unserviceability made it essential to bring up the third Halifax, which he collected personally, returning to Skitten on the 18th.

As a deception measure, and to discover the extent to which the target area could be observed visually at night, the two Halifaxes undertook leaflet-dropping sorties to Oslo on the night of the 18th. One carrying Lieutenant-Colonel Henniker and Sergeant Doig (a glider pilot) as passengers was obliged to return prematurely with a partially seized engine. The other, with Group Captain Norman aboard, passed over Lake Mosvatn. Looking down, he could see no detail of the ground; in the moonlight mountains and valleys looked 'like the back of a tiger – stripes of dark and light'. Still, the moon was only just entering the most favourable phase: in the absence of cloud, the valley would be moonlit between 18 and 26 November. The operation was to be launched between these dates.

Group Captain Norman later reported,

*19th November* First weather report unfavourable but later in the morning it was decided that conditions might be possible, and in view of the extreme improbability of getting better weather conditions and the importance of the operation it was decided to try to carry it out. . . .

> Take off was fixed for 17.30 hours but the first aircraft was delayed for half an hour attempting, without success, to get the intercom gear [the telephone between tug and glider] serviceable. . . . Crew 'A' with the addition of Group Captain Cooper took off at approximately 17.55 hours and Crew 'B' . . . half an hour later, also having had an intercom failure.

The two Horsas rose in succession behind their tugs: Staff Sergeant M.F. Strathdee and Sergeant P. Doig behind Halifax A, Pilot Officer Davies and Sergeant Frazer, both of the Royal Australian Air Force, behind Halifax B. These four men had been flying gliders since the days of sailplaning at Ringway. Many demands had been made on their skills but none matched the challenge of that evening as they climbed in combination through drizzling rain into the night.

The Horsas were heavily laden. To reduce drag, their undercarriages were released on take-off, as planned, exposing the skids for landing. The loss of telephonic communication to the tug captains was a serious matter. Light signals were available but were unable to convey more than a limited number of simple messages. In an emergency, they could communicate by radio but that would alert German monitors to their presence. The Halifax B combination had the additional problem that the starboard wing-tip light, relied upon by the glider pilots for station keeping, was defunct. Unknown to both glider crews, the Rebecca apparatus in the Halifaxes became unserviceable in flight.

Climbing and turning to penetrate breaks in the overcast sky, Squadron Leader A.M.B. Wilkinson, captain of Halifax A, brought tug and glider above the cloud at 5,000 ft. Reaching 13,000 ft, the course led directly to southern Norway. About 22.30, they turned towards the target.

Reliant on map reading, they looked for lake patterns but saw none that resembled Mosvatn and its neighbours. Searching, they turned east, running on dead reckoning from an identified point. No lakes appeared. The same means was tried on a course south east and after some doubt another set of lakes was recognized, providing another starting point. But it did not bring them to Mosvatn.

Clouds were gathering. Squadron Leader Wilkinson became concerned that his remaining fuel might be insufficient to carry the combination back to Scotland. He set course for the nearest airfield at Peterhead. Halifax and Horsa began to climb to clear rising cloud banks. In doing so, he reported subsequently, the tug,

> . . . collected some ice. Although the engines were put to take off revs and full throttle, it was then impossible to maintain height or even speed, and the aircraft sank into the tops of the clouds where more ice was formed. It was now absolutely essential to get down to below the freezing level and there was no possible alternative but to attempt to do so through the clouds. All lights were put full on and the glider followed steadily down to approximately 7,000 feet. At this height conditions became extremely bumpy with cloud much thicker and at 23.11 hours, after two or three very violent surges, the tow rope broke or the glider cast off.

Detachment was almost certainly due to a break. Staff Sergeant Strathdee and Sergeant Doig had been flying for more than five hours at this point – flying manually; the Horsa had no automatic pilot. With immense skill they had maintained station with the tug and they had no reason to think it would be sensible to detach themselves in the middle of a dense cloud.

In any case, the Halifax flew on, sending a brief muddled signal to Skitten indicating that a glider was in the sea. In fact, the Horsa was still over Norway, about 90 miles south west of its target, losing height among mountains but over small valleys which contained a number of open spaces for landing. But either while the glider was still in cloud, or shortly after descending through it into the deepening shadows of the passing moon, it crashed among mountain tops above Lysefjord, to the east of Stavanger. The pilots, Lieutenant D.A. Methven GM and five of his Royal Engineer section were killed outright, ten survived, though five of these were seriously injured. They were all discovered by the Germans. The injured men were murdered by Gestapo and Sicherdienst agents in Stavanger hospital. The remainder were taken to Grini gaol, near Oslo, to be murdered by a German firing squad on 18 January 1943.

Halifax B combination certainly reached Norway, crossing the coast at Egersund, south of Stavanger. At 23.41 a signal apparently from her captain, Flight-Lieutenant Parkinson, asked for identification of his position by radio direction finding, and the response placed him below Egersund. All that is known after that is that he crashed into mountains south of Helleland when the entire crew was killed. The Horsa he had been towing crashed shortly beforehand to the northeast of this site. Fourteen survived this accident to be taken prisoner. All were murdered at Slettebo on 20 November 1942 and buried at Brusand.

These crimes were the consequence of Hitler's categorization of all special or raiding forces as spies.

Operation Freshman thus ended in tragedy. Probably, if the Rebecca equipment had worked, the gliders would have got down in the right place. At all events, the glider pilots had demonstrated beyond dispute that they were capable of operating over considerable distances. Given improvements to their equipment – for example, the tow rope and its intercommunication cable – they would be ready for strategic as well as tactical intervention on the battlefield.

# CHAPTER SEVEN

# Husky – Theory into Practice

By the end of 1942 the Army had come to accept airborne forces in the sense that they were no longer regarded solely as a set of cut-throats, or cranks obsessed with the idea of swooping into the ground battle from the air. In the curious way of established military forces, respectability was acquired in part by the badging and titling of the new corps, and the grant of unique items of dress.

Major-General Browning had decided shortly after taking up his command that airborne soldiers should wear berets because they could be tucked away readily during parachute or glider exercises. Black berets were worn by the Royal Tanks, green by the Commandos. He took various other colours made up for him by the Royal Army Ordnance Corps to General Alan Brooke, a noted birdwatcher with a keen eye for colour, to ask him which he favoured. A corporal put on each beret in turn to assist judgement.

'Which one do you like?' the CIGS asked the corporal.

'The maroon one, sir.'

'So do I.'

The maroon beret was adopted, though subsequently misnamed 'red'. Maroon and Cambridge blue had been suggested to Major-General Browning as airborne colours by his wife, the novelist Daphne du Maurier. These were used in the formation signs, depicting the warrior Bellerophon astride Pegasus the winged horse. In time, a Glider Pilot Regiment shoulder title was introduced with a base in Cambridge blue.

The brevet introduced on 11 April 1942 for Air Observation Post and glider pilots alike on qualification displayed blue wings on either side of the crown topped by a lion. Major-General Browning, who had qualified as a light aircraft pilot before the war, passed an intensive course to become also a glider pilot.

Yet, acceptable as a regular as distinct from an irregular body within the Army, and reckoned by the CIGS to be 'as much a part of the Army as are armoured forces', the Royal Air Force continued to question the value of airborne forces in relation to the air resources demanded for them. Air Marshal Sir Arthur Harris, Air Officer Commanding-in-Chief Bomber Command, had particularly strong views on this subject.

He believed that his forces alone, given the necessary strength, would ultimately defeat Germany. Asked to comment in August and September 1942 on his ability to supply additional aircraft from time to time as transports or tugs for airborne assaults, he gave an uncompromising answer:

10. The creation of an airborne division at a time when the Air Forces needed for its transport do not exist has already seriously interfered with the expansion of Bomber Command and is one of a . . . multitude of ill-considered causes which have reduced the Command to its present meagre proportions. Already an establishment of 172 Whitleys and

10 Halifaxes in Army Co-Operation Command has been authorised and hundreds of glider pilots have been trained in E.F.T.S.'s to the exclusion of Air Force pilots. A vast amount of industrial effort has been and is being put into the building of hundreds of gliders and a large building programme of hangars requiring about 30,000 tons of steel has been put in hand in order to house them. The production of the Lancaster, which is our best bomber, the only one really adequate for its work, and the only bomber likely to be operationally useful in 18 months' time, is being interfered with by the conversion of a considerable number of them [with glider towing points] to transport duties. Finally, I am informed that a small $8^1/_2$ ton tank, utterly useless on the battlefield, is being produced by the Army solely because it is the largest size that can be fitted into a glider and that large gliders to transport it are also being produced. If this is true it is deplorable.

11. The crux of the matter is this – is Bomber Command to continue its offensive action against Germany or is it to be turned into a training and transport Command for carrying about a few thousand airborne troops to some undetermined destination for some vague purpose? . . .

This invigorated the air staff. The Harris letter was used as a basis to propose that 1st Airborne Division should be reduced in size – principally in its air landing forces. The issue returned to Mr Churchill on 23 October 1942 in his capacity as Minister of Defence. General Alan Brooke set out for him the characteristics of airborne forces:

Great strategic mobility
Ability to bypass ground obstacles
Surprise and moral effect

The details of the paper provided for the first time a comprehensive case for their operational potential in both major and minor roles. It was the product of an Air Directorate recently organized within the War Office and staffed by officers who had served in the early airborne units. The conclusion was that the United Kingdom should maintain four parachute brigades – two as independent formations – and a strong air landing brigade of four battalions.

For a third time, Mr Churchill was obliged to arbitrate on the future form of airborne forces. On this occasion he was persuaded that it was more important to expand bomber operations than the capacity for airborne assault. The advice that 'the United States are raising considerable airborne forces' probably weighted the scales in favour of the Royal Air Force case; he had no doubt that the successful liberation of Europe would depend upon partnership with the Americans. On 16 November he directed that a draft should be prepared for his signature instructing the Army to reduce the air landing element of 1st Airborne Division by 50 per cent.

This was a small matter for the Prime Minister among others of greater importance on his desk. He may thus be forgiven for underrating an important means of delivering British airborne forces from dependency on converted bombers – a factor of which the air staff surprisingly made no mention in their submission – the American C–47. There was every reason to expect that these would be supplied to the Royal Air Force in due course. Meanwhile, the Army Department in Washington had shown that it would share its air transport resources as contingencies arose;

United States Army Air Corps' C–47s would lift the British 1st Parachute Brigade during the forthcoming occupation of French North Africa.

As it was, in mid-November 1942, in constraining Army demands on RAF training and bombing resources, Mr Churchill also ordered the cutting back of Horsa production but left open a door for re-entry. 'The whole position should be re-examined in about six months' time – say 1st June.'

Strangely, the Chief of the Air Staff had some doubts about cutting glider manufacture. If orders following the completion of 1,200 Horsas were cancelled, three to six months would be required to reopen the line. Production rates were thus sustained.

Meanwhile, events began to suggest immediate reconsideration of the number and strength of airborne formations for future operations. General Montgomery's advance across the Libyan desert, the CIGS remarked, would have been accelerated if he had disposed an airborne division. Precisely because the First Army in French North Africa was unable to advance in strength across Algeria and Tunisia at speed, the Germans were able to reinforce the latter by air and sea.

> . . . Had we been sufficiently prepared to use the Airborne Division comprising ten battalions of infantry, with a full scale of supporting arms, Tunis and Bizerta might well have been captured in the early days. . . .

The commanders-in-chief, Middle East, wished to raise a parachute brigade in that theatre. At Casablanca in January 1943 the strategy adopted for the remainder of that year envisaged an offensive against the Axis forces in the Mediterranean, to be launched from North Africa following its final clearance, and re-entry to north-west Europe if an opportunity arose. To meet these tasks, the CIGS gave notice on 24 February to his fellow chiefs of staff, he would require two airborne divisions. One, 1st Airborne, should be sent from the United Kingdom to North Africa as soon as possible. A second should be formed from elements gathering in the United Kingdom, to be made ready for the cross-Channel operation, whenever that should be.

However much the air staff may have wished to challenge this proposal in its entirety, agreement between the Prime Minister and President Roosevelt had been specific in the fundamentals of the operational plan. American and British airborne forces would be involved in the next phase, the occupation of Sicily. The 1st Parachute Brigade was already in North Africa, distinguishing itself in ground fighting. The 4th Brigade was forming in Palestine. The divisional headquarters and troops, 2nd Parachute Brigade, and 1st Air Landing Brigade of two battalions would be concentrated in Algeria as soon as possible. As regards the gliders,

> Neither the Horsa nor the Hamilcar can be flown to North Africa. . . . The American Waco glider, on the other hand, is designed for breaking down for shipment, and can be tugged by smaller aircraft than would be required for the Horsa. . . . an initial equipment of 200 Wacos would lift the anti-aircraft and anti-tank units of an airborne division.

A further conclusion foresaw the delivery of the division into operations in one lift employing five hundred aircraft and two hundred Wacos. These calculations related to Operation 'Husky', the capture of Sicily.

In so far as 'Husky' was concerned, the Royal Air Force saw no difficulty in providing the means to mount it, and no wonder: the United States had agreed to contribute the major share of the five hundred aircraft required, and the Waco gliders then being crated for shipment from American factories. There was common agreement that sufficient glider pilots would be available and that, in this operation at least, each glider should be flown by two pilots.

However, the CAS was not ready to provide air training for the second – what was to be called the 6th – Airborne Division in the United Kingdom, which appeared to have an inflated establishment.

General Brooke had kept the 1st Air Landing Brigade intact, contrary to the Prime Minister's instruction in November 1942, on the basis that half its fighting strength – two battalions – would be required for the air landing brigade in 6th Airborne Division. The Air Ministry did not understand this.

On 4 March 1943 Air Chief Marshal Sir Charles Portal reproached his Army colleague:

. . . 8. Although the airlanding element in the target force for the United Kingdom [6th Airborne Division] is stated to be one Brigade of two battalions, it is clear from paragraph 6 of CIGS's paper and the estimate of glider requirements . . . that a full brigade of four battalions is contemplated. . . .

When the chiefs met next day, General Sir Alan Brooke was able to demonstrate that this was erroneous, a small point of advantage but one which, in the view of the Army Air Directorate, 'improved the climate of our discussions. They had accused us of trickery and had to say they were wrong'.

They capitalized on this by showing that, contrary to Air Marshal Harris's contention, his command would not be diverting forces to fly a few thousand airborne troops about to prepare for undetermined operations. For one thing, the aircraft removed from him were overwhelmingly medium bombers no longer suited to operations. Then, while it was true that numbers of Royal Air Force officers and men were supporting the Army's airborne forces – and for that matter Air Observation Posts – they were a tithe of the soldiers passed to the Royal Air Force for aircrew duties. And there were clear operational commitments: immediately, for Husky, in the medium term for Roundup – the codename for the invasion of north-west Europe.

The key requirement was glider pilots. As the final paper remarked:

The number of gliders required to lift the whole of the air landing troops [the brigade and divisional troops] of a full airborne division has been reduced from 760 to 630. On the other hand it has been decided that a second pilot for each glider is an operational necessity.

Assuming that the 1st Division in the Mediterranean and the 6th in the United Kingdom would each undertake three successive operations, and that American gliders and pilots would be available to contribute to this requirement, they would need a total of 1,800 British glider pilots. Mr Churchill's ruling allowed for the training of a thousand, to be completed by October 1943. The Army accepted that to add a further eight hundred to this number by that date would severely strain RAF resources. But, and this point was omitted from the paper, the British chiefs did not believe that Roundup would take place before 1944, contrary to the wishes of the United

States government and chiefs to land in France in 1943. It was therefore accepted that the target for 1,800 glider pilots should be set for completion by July 1944, an arrangement which would require no more than an additional fifty medium bombers or transports – C–47s – with air and maintenance crews.

On this basis, an agreement was struck on 28 April 1943 with one caveat by the Chief of the Air Staff: they should wait upon the results of Husky to see whether a major airborne operation against the Germans was practicable.

.    .    .    .    .    .    .    .

The meeting of the Prime Minister and the President of the United States at Casablanca concluded on 24 January 1943. The airborne assault, which opened Husky, began on 9 July, some five and a half months later. It might be thought that this gave plenty of time for preparation. This did not prove to be the case, particularly for the glider pilots.

During February and March, planning and movement arrangements were carried forward in London and Washington for the concentration of the additional forces, ships, aircraft, equipment, weapons, ammunition and stores for Husky. They could not be placed in position during the late winter months; the German and Italian forces in Tunisia were not finally defeated until 9 May 1943. Due to insistence on changes in the strategic concept by General Montgomery, work on the final plan for the landings in Sicily did not begin until that same week. However, 1st Airborne Division was already concentrating in Algeria from 26 April.

The decision to commit the division to the Mediterranean hastened certain changes in the structure of airborne forces. The Air Directorate was expanded in the War Office. Major-General Browning relinquished command of the division to assume responsibility for the organization, training, and development of British parachute and glider forces, including those in the Middle East – 4th Parachute Brigade – and in India. Major-General Hopkinson was promoted from 1st Air Landing Brigade to command 1st Airborne Division. The 6th Airborne Division began to form up on Salisbury Plain in the accommodation vacated by the 1st. The agreements reached in the chiefs of staff committee resulted in the replacement of the Whitley in 38 Wing by Albermarles and Halifaxes. All seemed to be moving forward smoothly to provide a major airborne assault capability for forthcoming operations. On Salisbury Plain it was seen somewhat differently.

The increased intake of glider pilots from the flying schools simply added to the numbers needing to maintain, let alone extend, their flying skills. Due to bad weather and servicing problems, Whitley flying rates had been unable to provide sufficient sorties to meet the demand for tugs. The problem was confounded when Albermarles and Halifaxes entered 38 Wing, requiring the progressive conversion of the Whitley aircrew. But the regiment had coped with such circumstances before. Given time, Colonel Chatterton and his senior officers believed, they would find ways and means of raising the level of flying training.

Early in April it became apparent that a major task was in prospect, though neither dates for a move nor a destination were notified.

In April the entire division paraded before His Majesty King George V, marching past finally across the tufty grass of the 'Divisional Dropping and Landing Zone' between Bulford and Netheravon. Embarkation leave followed.

Colonel Chatterton had been ordered to embark his headquarters and two companies (the title of 'squadron' came later) for an operational theatre. At sea, their destination was announced: North Africa! This was the favourite among the betting men. They landed at Oran on 26 April and were transported by truck to a camp containing a few water taps and some deep trench latrines, prepared for but as yet unoccupied by prisoners of war. Issued with two-man bivouacs – American 'pup tents' – they were ordered to make themselves comfortable pending the arrival of their baggage and vehicles 'in the next week or so'.

This did not suit Colonel Chatterton. He visited the advanced elements of divisional headquarters at Mascara, failed to find anyone interested in glider training, but received a message as he was leaving to meet the divisional commander in Algiers. In an office at Allied Force Headquarters, General Hopkinson gave him the impression that he had persuaded General Montgomery, British Land Force Commander for Husky, to employ 1st Airborne Division. It was a false claim. General Montgomery had from the outset embraced the idea of an airborne assault.

More importantly, a series of high secrets were disclosed to Chatterton during this meeting on 1 May: the target was Sicily; the operation was to open on the night of 9/10 July; gliders were to be used extensively. In the latter connection, a number of potential objectives and landing zones were shown to him on air photographs. What did he think of them?

His response did not please General Hopkinson. He judged the scheme to be impracticable: his pilots lacked recent flying training and most had never made a night landing; they had never seen a Waco glider; the obstructions on the landing zones indicated to him would smash any glider – these and other difficulties raced round his mind. But short of refusing an order, they had to be overcome.

At Allied Force Headquarters he met American officers of the Military Air Command. From them he learned that a consignment of Wacos had just arrived at Oran airfield, the first of the two hundred allocated for British use. Returning to his unit, he sent a strong party to find the Wacos and, if possible, to to get them ready for flying. His primary aim was to use the following nine weeks to restore flying proficiency and extend this to night operations.

At Oran, one of the party observed:

Planes were landing throwing up red dust, hundreds of trucks seemed to be driving about – more dust – and no one seemed to be in charge of anything except their own little activity. We hung about for a bit while some of the officers tried to find where the Wacos were. After about two hours, we discovered that they were quite close by on the edge of a mass of stores, including a lot of tyres.

One of the American ground technicians servicing C–47s, a corporal, was sent over to help us – not that he knew much about gliders but he was one of those guys who could turn his hand to anything requiring a spanner. He brought a crowbar to open the first crate and, glory be, there was a handbook inside showing all the parts and how to put them together, and a set of tools for every glider! You'd never have got that with a British issue.

Starting slowly, proceeding at a pace as they became more familiar with the assembly process, the glider pilot detachment built the aircraft they were going to fly. Working through most of the daylight hours, living off American rations, they lived comfortably in a village of empty crates lit at night by paraffin pressure lamps.

Meanwhile, Colonel Chatterton obtained leave to move his base closer to the sites due to be occupied by the American 51st Troop Carrier Wing, the air transport formation which would be lifting the division in the forthcoming operation. He made contact with its newly appointed commander, Brigadier-General Ray A. Dunn, and discovered that his C–47s were scattered, hauling passengers and freight across French North Africa. But the general needed no urging to begin training with his ally, and was impressed to learn that British glider pilots were assembling Wacos at Oran. By way of response, he sent one, shortly two more, C–47s to ferry the Wacos to the strips constructed for him on the Mascara plain and two French airfields in the vicinity, Froha and Relizane.

Colonel Chatterton recalled that he,

decided to try a moonlight landing, so I took up a Waco . . . It was entirely different from a Hotspur or Horsa, the British gliders, for whereas these were made of wood, the Waco was made of steel and fabric. Its glide was flat and the whole scheme of flight was different. It was dual-controlled, with a large cockpit capable of carrying thirteen men or one jeep. The nose lifted up so that the load could be run out of the glider, and it could land on a fixed undercarriage or on skids. It was a pleasant aircraft to fly and handled very easily.

On take off, perhaps the most disconcerting thing was the huge dust cloud that was blown up from the airstrip by the tug . . . something one got used to after a practice or two.

I took the glider up and released at about 2,000 feet. It was quite a thrilling feeling, and I found that I could see the ground quite clearly. We gradually descended and the moon was so bright it was very similar to landing by day. Gently turning into the airfield I brought her down as easily as if it had been lit up by the sun.

This gave him confidence; they were to land in moonlight in Sicily, though this destination and timing were, just then, known to himself alone in the regiment.

First, however, all pilots had to fly the Waco by day. The advantages noted by Colonel Chatterton notwithstanding, the glider had substantial limitations. Stability was questionable when flying at speeds in excess of 150 mph indicated air speed. The glider floor was flimsy; jeep or gun wheels broke through it on hard landings. The tail section was weak. One tore away from the remainder of the glider while ferrying the Air Landing Brigade to the launching area in Tunisia on 27 June. None of the aircrew or passengers, a detachment from 2nd Battalion, The South Staffordshire Regiment, survived the miscarriage. And the payload offered, 3,700 lb, was less than the British airborne planners had been advised. This latter constraint was removed when Major-General Browning and Air Commodore Sir Nigel Norman revived an early proposal, made at the outset of the Mediterranean deployment, that Horsas should be flown out to North Africa.

For some time the Air Ministry continued to object that the flight involved too many risks: attack by German aircraft over the Bay of Biscay, weather hazards and fatigue during a ten-hour flight, and lack of diversion facilities. But they were won round by the argument that the division's assault would be inhibited by a lack of Horsas, and by the reflection that the deployment would demonstrate to the enemy and the American ally alike that the Royal Air Force was not daunted by range and attendant hazards.

Training was advanced for this high challenge when Norman was killed in an air accident on 20

May. He was en route to North Africa to establish an advanced element of 38 Wing. His loss was considerable as a man, a commander and partner to Browning – in North Africa to Hopkinson – and in the depth of knowledge he had acquired. His influence with the Americans at that time was irreplaceable.

The sixty glider pilots who had arrived at Oran on 26 April had been joined in June by a further fifty who had each received some twelve hours flying training by 38 Group in England over six weeks. This had been valuable but excluded night flying. A pool of second pilots was made available by Brigadier-General Dunn to 1st Airborne Division to raise the numbers required for the air landing operation into Sicily. The Horsas began to join the Wacos from 4 June.

Twelve Halifax tugs were involved in ferrying. They were organized as A Flight, 295 Squadron, under Squadron Leader Wilkinson, the surviving captain of Operation Freshman. As in that event, he was the only pilot fully conversant with the aircraft. Others qualified during a work up within Great Britain. Additional aircraft and crews were brought in to replace those lost by enemy action or accident.

Pilots apart, several important modifications had to be made, notably the fitting of additional fuel tanks in the Halifax bomb bays. The Horsa undercarriages were to be jettisoned on take-off but each was to carry a spare set to be fitted in North Africa. Three glider pilots formed the crew for each sortie. After an abortive launch on 31 May, four combinations departed on 3 June. Thus began RAF Operation Beggar, Army Operation Turkey Buzzard. Ahead lay three journeys: Portreath in Cornwall to Salé – Rabat – in Morocco, 1,400 miles; Salé to Froha – Mascara – 350 miles; Froha to Kairouan in Tunisia, 600 miles.

There were mishaps and mortalities. Few accidents were more extraordinary than the discovery by one crew that an undercarriage section, prematurely released on take-off, had bounced back from the runway to imbed itself in the Horsa's starboard wing. Sergeant Percy Attwood was only just able to regain control and, with assistance, maintain it through cloud turbulence. Major Alistair Cooper's tow rope broke over the Atlantic. Rescued from the sea by a warship, the three crew members returned to ferrying, when two were again forced to ditch following an attack by Focke-Wulf Condors, and again survived. Several combinations simply disappeared, almost certainly as a result of air attack. At one point or another en route Halifaxes were lost due to engine malfunctions. At Salé, servicing and maintenance was carried out by the aircrew.

Gradually, the Halifaxes of 295 Squadron joined the Albermarles of 296, which had arrived as an entity somewhat earlier, principally as a parachuting aircraft. In June, Group Captain Cooper, RAF coordinator during Freshman, took command of the 38 Wing advanced detachment. He sought to open a joint control post with 51 Wing. The Americans welcomed his forces but were disinclined to offer partnership. For a brief period in May, Air Commodore Sir Nigel Norman might have struck such an arrangement on the basis of his contacts in the Mediterranean Air Command. By the beginning of June, Brigadier-General Dunn and his staff were extremely busy converting British glider pilots to the Waco, in training the C–47 aircrew and British soldiers in parachuting, and in meeting a number of general air transport tasks passed to 51 Wing on a day-to-day basis. They had also drawn close to 1st Airborne Division, whose commander and staff had embraced them in the absence of a 38 Wing planning and training team. Thus, although there was a readiness to accept the matured ideas of Group Captain Cooper and his officers on occasion, Brigadier-General Dunn wanted the Royal Air Force component to cooperate on the basis of the American way of doing things.

By the beginning of July considerable progress had been made in making the air transport forces ready for Husky. As a means of validating later judgements, it should be noted that the 116 British glider crews completed over 1,200 hours flying between 21 May and 3 July, about one-third at night. And while this was far from the target of eight hours a month for the individual, and much night training had been confined to spins lasting fifteen minutes, it was a considerable advance on their situation earlier in the year. Lieutenant John Mockeridge spoke for most of his comrades when he later recalled that he had not flown at all between 3 March, on leaving the Operational Training Unit at Brize Norton, and commencing conversion to the Waco on 23 May at Relizane in Algeria.

There were penalties for this desuetude; inevitably some loss in skills, some in confidence. Accidents were numerous in the early phase, trivial and momentous, some fatal. But extraordinary mishaps, such as the sight of Sergeant Hampshire looping on take-off for the final exercise in Algeria – the consequence of an incorrectly rigged tow rope – did not daunt them. Understandably, however, apprehensions about the reliability of the Waco became widespread after the tail separation in flight to Tunisia, manifest in a minor incidence of premature releases from tugs when pilots fancied malfunctions or excessive air speed. Formal administrative or disciplinary action was invoked in one or two cases: Colonel Chatterton had the power to RTU – return to unit of origin outside airborne forces – any member of his command. But squadron leadership largely overcame this problem, and comradeship. Quite a number of glider pilots felt anxieties periodically about the nature of their flying but the greatest worry, as the time for the operation approached, was that some last minute problem, such as engine failure in a tug, would leave their particular glider on the airstrip.

Early in July 1943, then, 1st Airborne Division was concentrated in the area of Sousse, M'saken, and Kairouan in Tunisia, its units encamped among olive groves. The summer heat was now intense. Quantities of water melons were purchased daily from carts parked on perimeter roads. German or Italian agents may well have been among the Arabs selling these and other fruits – an ammunition dump was destroyed by sabotage in this period – but the briefing arrangements, though crude, maintained security. Each unit had a barbed wire enclosure containing a hut or an improvised shelter concealing the maps and air photographs of the objectives and routes to them. Stage by stage, information and orders were passed down the chain of command.

Two airborne formations were engaged in Husky: the United States 82nd Airborne Division and the British 1st; the former with General George S. Patton's Seventh Army, the latter with General Montgomery's Eighth.

The Americans planned initially to launch a parachute regiment – that is, in British terms, a brigade – into the area behind Gela on the south-eastern shore of Sicily. This was Operation 'Husky 1'. It was to take place on the night 9/10 July, the 10th being D-Day, when the seaborne assault would begin.

On this same night, the British 1st Air Landing Brigade was to land close to the port of Syracuse on the eastern shore, the first of three airborne operations prepared by the 1st Airborne Division. Brigadier P.W.H. Hicks, the brigade commander, had instructions to capture a bridge, the Ponte Grande, spanning a double canal one mile south of the city, to extend his force to capture the harbour, and to destroy a coastal defence battery covering the beaches to be used in the British seaborne assault. He had sufficient gliders to lift part of his own and divisional headquarters, his two battalions, 1st Battalion, The Border Regiment and 2nd Battalion, The South Staffordshire, the greater part of 9th Field Company, Royal Engineers, and 181st Field Ambulance. This was Operation 'Ladbroke'.

The air plan carried the air transport stream due east from their Tunisian bases to Malta and then north-north-west past Cape Passero, the south-eastern tip of Sicily, from which the British would proceed northwards to Cape Murro di Porco immediately below Syracuse. Launched in daylight, the combinations would arrive over the release points in darkness relieved by a quarter moon.

Group Captain Cooper had never cared for this scheme. He objected that,

. . . the release was over water, and involved judging distances from the shore, that the glider pilots were to make a straight glide in and would have no surplus height, that no marks were going to be put out on the ground because the Americans said they would cause confusion, and the Army considered they would attract the enemy, and that the release run was made down moon.

But his advice was not heeded. As a means of assisting navigation, 38 Wing produced black and white night or 'moonlight' maps – shore-line profiles – for all pilots. Horsas towed by Halifaxes were to retain their undercarriages, and indeed some were wired on to prevent accidental release. Exceptionally, the undercarriage of the single Horsa to be towed by an Albermarle was to be shed because the additional drag might drain the latter's fuel reserve.

The North African Troop Carrier Command had developed an excellent system of marshalling tugs and gliders to permit rapid launching. Less satisfactory was the intercommunication arrangement between tug and Waco; the cable end in the latter had to be disconnected before the tow rope was disconnected, otherwise the telephone apparatus would be pulled through the windscreen.

As the day of 9 July grew oppressively hot, the glider pilots left the olive groves and were carried in trucks to their appointed airstrip, one of six marked by the letters A to F. Wacos and Horsas were already loaded with freight. In the late afternoon a meal was brought round to the dispersal sites before they began to prepare for the arrival of their passengers at 18.00. The sun was then descending, the day cooling, and a wind rising. Weather reports from Malta forecast an offshore wind of 30 to 35 mph when 1st Air Landing Brigade began its assault.

Colonel Chatterton and Brigadier-General Dunn discussed the implications of these details for the run-in. They agreed that gliders should cast off, as planned, 3,000 yd from the shore, but raised the release heights to 4,000 ft for the Horsas, and 1,400 to 1,800 for the Wacos.

At 18.40 hours, Colonel Chatterton was sitting in the first Waco:

. . . the propellers of the [C–47] Dakotas started up with a whirl, dust flew off the runway and whipped into the air, and the tug slowly moved into position. Gripping the controls, I gave the thumbs-up signal, the rope taughtened, and I heard over the intercom. the faint sound of the Dakota pilot's voice, but the crackling and interference was so bad that from beginning to end of the trip we were never able to hear each other clearly. We moved slowly forward, then faster and faster across the dusty strip until the Dakota disappeared in the dust and I was forced to hold the glider in position by the tow rope's angle. Then, still gathering speed, we were out of the dust and in the clear, and there, below, was the silver Dakota tug, and below her again the sea, smothered in foam. It was extremely rough, the glider jumping up and down and from side to side, and I held on like grim death, concentrating on holding position above the Dakota. But soon I was able to relax as I became accustomed to the movements of the aircraft and its behaviour.

After a while I handed over to [Captain] Peter Harding [his adjutant], but he was very sick and in no state to fly, so I took back the stick and without relief piloted the glider for the next 400 miles, a tow of four hours. . . .

. . . I wondered if German fighters were likely to intercept, and I remember experiencing a sense of astonishment when they did not come, and, as the darkness descended, a feeling of elation that we had got away with it, for we would have been sitting ducks if a force of fighters had come across us. And what a target we would have made!

The storm did not abate, and as the sun went down, glowing red on the horizon, the foam still sweeping through the gloom, the sea changed from cold blue to dark green, and then to a menacing black.

One hundred and forty-four combinations eventually took off: 110 C–47s towing Wacos, 26 Albermarles towing Wacos, 1 Albermarle towing a Horsa, and 7 Halifaxes towing Horsas. Height and time separated the different types of tug. The C–47s and Wacos were first away because they were the slowest, travelling in echelons of four at 120 mph. They were also the lowest, maintaining 300 ft above the sea until they approached Sicily. The RAF tugs flew in a single stream, one combination behind another, the Albermarles at 125 mph at 350 ft, the Halifaxes at 140 mph at 500 ft.

Seven combinations failed to reach the operational area, chiefly due to technical problems in tug or glider. An eighth, Flight-Lieutenant D.A. Grant's Halifax, took off among the last of the stream at 20.05 and his starboard inner engine began to fail as he took to the air. He informed his Horsa captain, Staff Sergeant D. Galpin, that he was returning to airstrip E, but as they positioned to land the fuel regulator recovered itself. As a safety measure he climbed to 2,000 ft for the run to Malta, during which,

. . . my starboard outer radiator temperature gauge went unserviceable, so did the D.R. compass and the automatic pilot . . . my navigator managed to take several drifts on the way to Malta and after we turned towards Sicily. He calculated that there would be a wind of 30 m.p.h. against the glider pilot after releasing. We decided to climb to 5,000 feet instead of 4,000 feet and to release the glider over land two miles nearer the target. As we were running along the coast of Sicily my navigator told me the wind was dropping considerably. We then decided to keep to our height of 5,000 feet and to release him in the pre-arranged position.

The Horsas were carrying two companies of the South Staffords, with headquarters elements, anti-tank guns, mortars, engineer and medical detachments, a force tailored primarily to capturing the Ponte Grande across the parallel canals.

Staff Sergeant Galpin had listened with interest and occasional apprehension to Flight-

Lieutenant Grant's problems, but apart from a brief and potentially dangerous increase in air speed close to Malta, the flight gave him no difficulties. Once Sicily was in sight, the Halifax navigator indicated points on the coast as they appeared. Point 'D' was the release point and the glider pilots, Galpin and Sergeant N. Brown, cast off as they reached it.

Theory and practice ran together for them. They knew their position. They had a course to steer which would bring them on to the Ponte Grande landing zone. But they were now alone in a dark night with little illumination from the quarter moon. Galpin reported later:

> . . . at first I could not make out exactly where we were. However I was able to make out the shape of the coast line and after flying for a few minutes realised I had flown over the objective and was over Syracuse itself. On turning back I soon saw our objective, standing out exactly as depicted on the night map. I had too much height at 2,000 feet and the ground defences got on to us by searchlight and flak so I had to head out to sea to lose height then came in towards the bridge flying fairly low and fast. Just as we crossed the coast a searchlight beam showed the bridge and landing zone for a few seconds and I immediately pulled the nose up, applied full flap and landed. Although a ditch broke our nose wheel and caused damage to the floor of the cockpit, it did . . . enable us to stop.

Lieutenant L. Withers and No. 15 Platoon of the South Staffords immediately alighted and captured the Ponte Grande. It was 23.00, scarcely three hours after take-off.

Taken in isolation, this event would suggest a triumphant entry by the air landing forces. But numerous gliders had been released that night. Due to the misbehaviour of Flight-Lieutenant Grant's Halifax, Staff Sergeant Galpin was among the last to cast off his tow rope. What of these others?

Staff Sergeant [later, Major] H.N. Andrews was flying a Waco behind a C–47 and described his experiences as they approached Sicily:

> . . . At last a shape of land; it looked nothing like the moonlight map – it was much darker out there and much more difficult to locate any distinctive feature. There were distant shellbursts over Syracuse and searchlights. . . . I asked Morris [Flight Officer M. Kyle, an American warrant officer flying as second pilot] if the tugs could get closer to the land and gain a bit of height. He carried on another strange conversation over the phone and it did seem as if we were going higher. In the process, however, we overshot the release point and I hung on grimly, requesting Morris to enquire if we could go round again. Once past Syracuse the tugs turned round gently in a big circle and for a short time we were heading back out to sea and then on a reciprocal of our original course. . . .
>
> . . . not forgetting to disconnect the phone, we threw the cable out of the window, and I pulled off. I went into a slow climbing turn to the left to gain as much altitude as possible so I could then get back to the most efficient gliding speed by touch and feel on the controls; the wind speed was unknown to me and there was a long way to go. As I slowly trimmed back on the overhead wheel I gently felt my control column go a bit slack, the speed settled back and Morris kept saying 'Get the speed back'. . . . These few seconds after a release seemed as long as the whole of the rest of the flight put together. There was a silence and the passengers said

nothing. I concentrated again on the blue searchlight; it seemed we were sinking too fast and I had my first doubts – could I make it? . . . I swallowed hard, wetted my lips, and in my calmest possible voice said, 'I don't think we are going to make it; you'd better get your equipment off and blow up your lifejackets.' . . . Colonel Henniker barked back in his best orderly room voice, 'Don't be a damned fool, we've got to get to land.' . . . Perhaps there was a chance. Obviously the blue searchlight was manned by troops and it did seem to stick out a bit further than the dark shape that must be the coastline. It was our only hope and that's when I decided to land. . . . Those last few seconds before we touched the ground seemed a long time to wait. A strange calm, almost a peace, came upon me . . . and as always the ground came up very quickly just before a landing. I just had time to say, 'We're going to make it,' and there was a light bump. No appreciable run along the ground; the left wheel seemed to stick a bit and we swung to the left and stopped.

Landing successfully, on the edge of a minor precipice, crew and passengers were certainly not on a selected LZ. They were shortly under enemy fire but, led by Colonel O. Jones, deputy brigade commander, the majority were soon attacking every enemy position they came across.

Colonel Chatteron was released either too far from the shore or too low. He ditched with Brigadier Hicks and members of his headquarters. Intermittently under fire from weapons ashore, they decided to swim to an apparently deserted point on the beach, Chatterton cursing his luck at being, as he imagined, the only pilot to land his glider in the sea. But many others were in worse position. Seven Wacos towed by Albermarles and one Horsa were in the water with sixty-one of the Wacos towed by C–47s. In fact, only forty-nine Wacos and five Horsas had landed in Sicily. Four gliders had crashed into major obstructions killing the pilots and passengers by the force of impact or the explosion of ammunition aboard. Thirteen other landings had involved some degree of injury.

From these, and the survivors of sea landings, some 900 of 2,075 who had emplaned began to gather in groups to carry out their tasks. Their capacity was diminished, however, because they had few support weapons – mortars and anti-tank guns – or communications. Their ammunition was also limited to whatsoever they could carry on foot.

Captain A.F. Boucher-Giles had landed his Waco in a field close to LZ 2. He carried an anti-tank gun and crew of the 1st Border, among whom 'the only serious injury was to Sergeant Hodge. . . . The gun had worked loose in its moorings during the bumpy crossing and when we landed had slipped forward and dealt him a frightful blow in the back'.

Leaving one man with the sergeant, Boucher-Giles set off to find others, and fell in with echelons of divisional and brigade headquarters and some field engineers. The whole finally arrived at the Ponte Grande. Lieutenant Withers was delighted to be reinforced, he had been fighting off intermittent counter-attacks with small arms and light mortar fire since his arrival, and, while he had removed the Italian demolition charges under the bridge, was anxious to have them destroyed. The engineers obliged. Command of the defences, now eighty-seven strong, passed to Lieutenant-Colonel G. Walch. Boucher-Giles took command of a detachment of twenty, principally glider pilots.

An Italian force attempted to recover the bridge during the morning but was repulsed. Thereafter, mortars and a field gun harrassed the British defence pending the arrival of an infantry battalion whose concentration and movement were delayed by the guerrilla tactics of other fragments of 1st Air Landing Brigade. Eventually it reached those surrounding the bridge. Attacks by this strong and well armed body wore down Lieutenant-Colonel Walch's positions and progressively exhausted the ammunition of the men within them during the afternoon. When the Italians finally pressed in, a few of the British managed to escape but most were captured.

Yet the bridge did not remain long in enemy hands. Royal Scots Fusiliers and Northamptons were marching towards it from the beaches and, within half an hour, captured the position and released the prisoners.

On 13 July the survivors of the air landing force embarked at Syracuse to return to their camps in Tunisia. They carried with them the thanks and good wishes of the sea assault force and General Montgomery.

> . . . In spite of all difficulties and setbacks, the main objective had been captured and held. For those responsible for this particular action he was filled with admiration. Others, who, by their own initiative, fought isolated actions on various parts of the battlefield, had played no small part in this most successful landing action. Had it not been for the Air Landing Brigade, the port of Syracuse would not have fallen until very much later, because the enemy would inevitably have formed a strong defensive line on the canal south of the town.

These remarks were not a gesture to raise morale; they were made in the knowledge of the enemy's own reaction – German and Italian – gleaned by the intelligence staff from plain language intercepts and prisoners of war. The arrival of the gliders had alarmed and considerably confused the system in the hours prior to the landings from the sea. The coastal battery had been put out of action by the forces under Colonel Jones and others. The Ponte Grande was not demolished but kept intact for passage northwards of the seaborne units.

Undoubtedly, the cost was high. To 490 casualties among 1st Air Landing Brigade, including 252 drowned, there were added 101 glider pilots. Of these, less than half survived the operation.

As Brigadier Hicks' brigade made contact with units of General Dempsey's 13 Corps on the road to Syracuse, the remainder of 1st Airborne Division was standing by for successive operations. The 2nd Parachute Brigade had loaded its aircraft, including eighteen gliders containing jeeps and anti-tank guns, for landings on 10 July in the Augusta area north of Syracuse. This was cancelled on 11 July as 13 Corps' advanced guards seized the objectives. However, a second formation of 82nd Airborne was landed near Gela that night.

A third British option then remained: the capture of the bridge across the River Simeto giving access to the Catania Plain – Operation 'Fustian'. This was the task of 1st Parachute Brigade.

Nineteen gliders containing loads similar to those provided for the 2nd Brigade, and, indeed, including several of the gliders previously allocated to the brigade, were allotted a landing zone separated from the parachute dropping zones. Seventeen – ten Horsas and seven Wacos – took off behind RAF aircraft, following the C–47s into the air from 21.43 on the night of 13/14 July. Winds were reported as light, 12 to 15 mph.

In the final approach, anti-aircraft fire from two sources seriously disrupted the operation. Allied warships fired on the C–47s, which passed over instead of outside them, causing minor injuries and disruption. Over land, they encountered enemy flak. Eleven gliders were shot down.

Two RAF tugs were lost, one containing Squadron Leader Wilkinson. Others were hit and their occupants wounded. The Dakota streams broke up to escape the fire.

Pathfinders of 21 Independent Company dropped successfully early in the operation to light marker flares for the gliders but the Catania Plain was covered with illuminations of one sort or another as the Horsas and Wacos began their descent. At first, all Staff Sergeant H.G. Protheroe could see was 'fire and smoke'.

> . . . The tug pilot said, 'Here we are' or words to that effect. I replied I had no idea where we were. The tug pilot came back and said he could make another run in and this he did. On the second approach I could see the reflection of the moon in the river, and later the bend in it, and a silhouette of the superstructure of the bridge.
>
> Now I was ready to pull off. . . . As we approached the road south of the bridge I put on full flap so that we would land as near to the road as possible and avoid running into the River Gornalmaga on the other side of the landing zone. Sergeant D.F. Kerr said, 'Don't forget the electric pylons.' I said, 'We're OK, we are almost over the road, the pylons were behind us.' No sooner had I said that than there was a hell of a crash and sparks flying in all directions. (Later, I could see we had struck what looked like telephone wires and a post.) The next thing I was aware of was being propelled along the ground in what was left of the cockpit, with my head making contact with the ground. I could tell we were going at a fair speed.

The crews of four Horsas under Captain Barrie joined the parachutists at the Primosole bridge during the night, and next morning Lieutenant Thomas and his second pilot brought in the jeep and 6 lb anti-tank gun from their glider wrecked in a ravine 7 miles distant. Staff Sergeant Protheroe and Sergeant Kerr had preceded them with their own gun and jeep. The glider pilots manned these weapons – finally, three in number – with the Royal Artillery throughout 14 July.

The 4th Armoured Brigade, was expected during the morning of 14 July but did not appear until 19.45 that evening. By that time the parachute elements on the northern bank of the river had been driven back to the south. The bridge was not lost, however; parachutists and glider pilots continued to cover it with fire. Infantry and armour of 13 Corps began the task of clearing the road to the north on the morning of 15 July, when the last unit of 1st Parachute Brigade withdrew. By 30 July all had returned to North Africa.

Concerned to discover exactly what had happened in their joint operations, 38 Wing and 1st Airborne Division conducted a close enquiry among ground and air forces as soon as they had resettled into their bases. Fortunately, the main elements of their findings survive, though they tend to be neglected in favour of anecdotes and partial judgements.

In the first few weeks after the operations, the British felt that their difficulties were due overwhelmingly to two failings among the American aircrew: their navigation was of a poor standard, and they panicked as soon as they came under anti-aircraft fire.

The first was a fair judgement. The pilots were proficient, many highly experienced in flying Dakotas on internal civil air routes in the United States before the war, but they followed familiar routes in this profession; their navigating skills were thus not taxed. Each Royal Air Force aircraft had a navigator. Many of the C–47s had none and relied for directional adjustments on the navigators with their formation leaders. If any of these miscalculated their positions, those following were similarly astray. This was the reason why many Dakota captains released their gliders when they were at a distance greater than 3,000 yd from the shore. But not all were lost. The figures below show that somewhat more than a third assessed their positions correctly:

|  | 38 Wing aircraft | US aircraft | Total |
|---|---|---|---|
| Glider pilot released immediately after take-off | 2 Waco | 0 | 2 Waco |
| Glider did not cross N African coast | 4 Waco | 1 Waco | 5 Waco |
| Tug returned to base with glider | 0 | 4 C–47 and Waco | 4 C–47 and Waco |
| Glider landed in sea | 7 Waco 1 Horsa | 61 Waco | 68 Waco 1 Horsa |
| Gliders landed in Sicily | 11 Waco 5 Horsa | 38 Waco | 49 Waco 5 Horsa |
| Unaccounted for | 2 Waco 2 Horsa | 6 Waco | 8 Waco 2 Horsa |
| Totals: | 26 Waco 8 Horsa | 110 Waco | 136 Waco 8 Horsa |

The following figures add illumination:

|  | Landed in Sicily | Ditched | Total |
|---|---|---|---|
| Gliders released within 3,000 yd of coast | 41 Waco 5 Horsa | 4 Waco | 45 Waco 5 Horsa |
| Gliders released more than 3,000 yd from coast | 9 Waco | 64 Waco | 73 Waco |

The United States official record suggests that much of the landing failure on Ladbroke was due to the inexperience of the British glider pilots. It is a fact that the Glider Pilot Regiment investigation discovered that a minority of its pilots failed to pick up the correct course when released; several turned on to the opposite of the course to be followed. But these were exceptional cases. Half at least of their number had greater experience than the American glider pilots including those who instructed on the Waco. Almost all the latter did not complete basic training until March 1943.

The second charge, alleging an absence of resolve by American pilots, is at odds with the facts.

On Ladbroke, flak was not intense. Many C–47 captains readily agreed to circle and run in a second time at the request of glider pilots. On Fustian, fire from the surface was considerable. Some undoubtedly came from the Royal Navy, partly because poor navigation carried the aircraft into the inshore zone. Following that, enemy fire was persistent and accurate, wounding aircrew and passengers, particularly among the parachuting aircraft.

The C–47 aircrew were completely inexperienced in operations. Unlike the British converted bombers, their aircraft had neither the design nor modifications to mitigate damage. Though some broke away completely, including those captains who considered it wrong to discharge their loads into such fire, the majority persevered as the following indicates:

| | *38 Wing aircraft* | *US aircraft* | *Total* |
|---|---|---|---|
| Number took off | 11 | 105 | 116 |
| Aircraft returning without dropping | 2 | 24 | 26 |
| Aircraft returning with some parachutists | 1 | 17 | 8 |
| Number of aircraft shot down | 1 | 10 | 11 |
| Number of aircraft which dropped on DZ/LZ | 4 | 26 | 30 |
| Number dropping within $\frac{1}{2}$ mile of DZ/LZ | 5 | 34 | 39 |
| Number dropping over $\frac{1}{2}$ mile from DZ/LZ | 4 | 44 | 48 |

These details manifest a high proportion of misadventures, but one important item among them must not be overlooked. Staff Sergeant Galpin and Sergeant Brown, in combination with Flight-Lieutenant Grant and his crew, reached the correct release point despite malfunctions in the Halifax. When cast off, the two glider pilots then carried through the gliding plan to land their passengers at precisely the right point. This was not a fluke. It was due to a combination of skill and spirit. The accomplishment showed that an air-landing assault was a feasible operation of war.

# CHAPTER EIGHT

# Operation Overlord

From the moment that American partnership made it possible to contemplate re-entry to France, Mr Churchill was haunted by fears of an Allied bloodbath on the invasion beaches. The experience of Gallipoli weighed upon him. Hence his wish to strike through the 'soft underbelly of Europe', a process begun with the occupation of Sicily, followed at once by exploitation to the Italian mainland. The 1st Airborne Division was moved by sea to Taranto to clear the south-eastern province.

The United States government and high command accepted the value of opening a front in southern Europe directly engaging German forces but they did not regard it as a substitute for the more direct and more accessible route to Germany through northern France. By the time President and Prime Minister met in Quebec during the third week of August 1943, the latter had come to recognize that his preference had become untenable. Accordingly, plans for Operation Roundup, renamed 'Overlord', took precedence. The Combined American and British Chiefs of Staff reported that,

> (a) This operation will be the primary United States–British ground and air effort against the Axis in Europe. (Target date, May 1, 1944.) After securing adequate Channel ports, exploitation will be directed towards securing Channel areas that will facilitate both ground and air operations against the enemy. Following the establishment of strong Allied forces in France, operations designed to strike at the heart of Germany and to destroy her military forces will be undertaken. . . .

The settlement of strategy affected the organization and preparation of airborne forces almost immediately. In the Mediterranean, 1st Airborne Division was withdrawn from ground operations in Italy in November 1943 to be transported home by sea. To meet the needs of the Mediterranean Commander-in-Chief, the division shed the 2nd Parachute Brigade to operate under his command as an independent group, including a squadron of the Glider Pilot Regiment. Thereafter, two British formations, the 1st and 6th Airborne Divisions, would be available in Britain singly or collectively for Overlord and whatsoever operations followed from it. To this end among others, Major-General Browning's authority was enhanced to embrace all British airborne forces, and his staff augmented to provide a corps headquarters. At the same time, the United States began to concentrate two airborne divisions in Britain, the 82nd, withdrawn from the Mediterranean, and the 101st directly from the United States.

Reports on Ladbroke and Fustian by Generals Alexander and Montgomery, despite some qualifications from air commanders in the Mediterranean, persuaded Air Chief Marshal Sir Charles Portal that airborne operations were viable and offered a strategic as well as a tactical potential for the campaign in north-west Europe. The British Chiefs of Staff accepted on 27

September the lessons drawn from 1st Airborne Division's intervention in Sicily. One asserted that future airborne operations should be planned, mounted and launched under command of the air commander-in-chief in the theatre concerned, duly advised by the appropriate Army senior commander, a principle welcomed by the Royal Air Force. The Chief of the Air Staff agreed to expand 38 Wing to 180 aircraft to meet day-to-day training requirements, and indicated that he would convert it to a group under an air vice-marshal commensurate with its greater strength and authority in formulating operational policy.

The decision to bring 1st Airborne Division back to Britain facilitated the expansion of 38 Wing to group level. By inter-Allied agreement, the American XII Troop Carrier Command assumed the task of lifting 2nd Parachute Brigade in airborne operations, and thus the Royal Air Force Albermarles and Halifaxes were recovered to their bases in southern England. From their departure in the autumn of 1943, Major Robin Coulthard and the Brigade's 1 Independent Glider Squadron operated entirely with C–47 tugs for the remainder of the war.

The good news that they would be at home for Christmas spread swiftly among all ranks of 1st Airborne Division. All assumed that they would be returning to their barracks and camps on Salisbury Plain, and some were vexed when they discovered that these were occupied by 6th Airborne, a formation of which they were then scarcely aware. The 1st would be located principally in the east and north Midlands. Their glider pilots were among those most put out by the discovery that there was no place for them on Salisbury Plain. The greater the distance from the 38 Wing airfields, it was reasoned, the greater the difficulty of maintaining flying skills. Their commanding officer, Lieutenant-Colonel Chatterton, had anticipated the problem.

Following his return to Tunisia in late July 1943, Chatterton was called to London to attend a series of meetings relating to the concentration of airborne divisions in Britain; for although he was simply the senior of two unit commanders, he had become by experience and personality the commander *de facto* of the regiment.

Many matters were still uncertain during the late summer and autumn of 1943, the most pressing being the capacity of the Royal Air Force to increase the numbers of men and aircraft engaged in elementary flying and conversion training of pilots, and the ability of the Ministry of Aircraft Production to meet the demands of the two British divisions for Horsas, to which was now added, post-Husky, an order by the United States for 1,500. It was chiefly on this account that the planning staffs proposed the return of 1st Airborne Division to the United Kingdom to reduce the expense of maintaining such a large detachment at a distance.

Chatterton decided that the moment had come to press an idea maturing over some months in his mind. Glider pilot squadrons should be located, he believed, whether at home or abroad, with the air transport squadrons, sharing their domestic and working accommodation, subordinate in great measure to the respective air force station commanders. This would have two advantages. Blue and khaki aircrew would get to know one another and become familiar with the operating potential and limitations of their partners. No less important, joint training would be organized on the station, adjustments for flying hours lost due to unserviceability or bad weather could be made on the spot, and travelling to and from airfields by Army pilots obviated. To oversee this arrangement, he proposed that a glider pilot headquarters should be located at Headquarters, 38 Wing.

Browning advised him that cohabitation with the tug squadrons was a matter wholly for the Royal Air Force, but he promised to support the proposal. As a part of the uprating of his own headquarters to the status of a corps, he had proposed the establishment of a 'Headquarters, Commander, Glider Pilots'. Both men were surprised to find that the air staff made no objection to sharing their airfields with Army glider pilots. 38 Wing welcomed it. Other problems were not so easily resolved.

Well before the Quebec conference, planning assumptions had been issued for Operation Overlord. One of these foresaw a requirement to launch three airborne operations in divisional strength in succession. It was at once evident that 38 Wing would have to be doubled to cope with the numbers of parachute and glider forces to be exercised, hence the total of 180 aircraft in nine squadrons notified by the Chief of the Air Staff to his inter-service colleagues in September 1943. At the same time, for a matter of months, the wing's capacity to offer training hours would be constrained by the conversion of additional aircrew to the incremental Halifaxes, the newly disposed Stirlings, discarded by Air Chief Marshal Sir Arthur Harris from Bomber Command, and reserve crews for the Albermarles.

In so far as glider supply was concerned, 1,800 Horsas and 120 Hamilcars would be available by June 1944, exceeding the original order accepted by the Ministry of Aircraft Production. This went some way to provide a balance to meet the American request. Efforts would be made to raise output by a further five hundred Horsas and fifty Hamilcars for the latter. Requests to provide thirty gliders for the gathering Indian airborne division could not, however, be satisfied in the foreseeable future. Negotiations began to supply them with Wacos from the United States.

Feasibility studies assumed that 430 gliders would be employed in each of the three prospective operations: 400 Horsas, and 30 Hamilcars for heavy equipment. On the basis of two-man crews, 860 glider pilots would thus be required on each occasion. The 2nd Parachute Brigade's requirement was assessed at 80. To meet the overall demand for 940 pilots, the accumulation of the 380 returning from North Africa, and those in the United Kingdom assessed as 530 by 1 March 1944, provided a total of 910.

Standing over the needs of the Mediterranean theatre, there would be a surplus of fifty pilots for the first operation, but losses in each of the three had to be taken into account. It was reckoned that casualties would average 20 per cent, say, 170 on each occasion. The surviving 80 per cent were expected to be recovered to the United Kingdom bases and be available for the next task within a month. If the schools continued their output, they might just be able to mount the three operations given a month between each but, if casualties exceeded 20 per cent, there would be a deficit.

It was clear to the Army's Director of Air, Major-General K.N. Crawford, that any suggestion that they should double the output of initial flying training was pointless. The Royal Air Force basic course employed one EFTS, two Glider Training Schools, and a Heavy Glider Conversion Unit to qualify a trainee over twenty-four weeks. That was the limit of their resources at a time when they were doubling the strength of 38 Wing for the benefit of the two divisions.

Investigations had shown the way to a solution within their means. It was accepted that the second pilot of a glider did not require the same level of qualification as the first pilot. As the assistant, he had to be able to fly the glider and land it in an emergency, but the events of Husky suggested that the first pilot would survive in a majority of sorties. A second pilot could be trained in twelve weeks, half the time required for a first pilot. The assessment conveniently doubled the output of the schools to fifty a month, excluding the fluctuating number of those who failed, and may prompt the suspicion that it was an expedient to production at the expense of safety. At all events, the policy was soon to be tested in battle.

The Second Pilot scheme was adopted in mid-August 1943 – officially, on the 19th – jointly by the Army and RAF. Last minute reflections perhaps added a caveat: Second Pilots should not be committed to operations without at least a work up over a month in their squadrons. All First Pilots would hold at least the rank of staff sergeant. Second Pilots would be promoted to sergeant on qualification and wear a distinctive brevet containing the letter 'G' at the centre of the wings in place of the lion and crown.

As the winter of 1943 began, the various resolutions were effected. 38 Group was formed and Air Vice-Marshal L.N. Hollinghurst appointed to command it. He quickly proved to be an enterprising and cooperative friend to airborne forces, hastening the scheme of co-location and setting an example in welcoming the Glider Pilot Regiment as members of the Royal Air Force messes, an agreement which had scarcely been honoured prior to his arrival. The 1st Battalion of the Glider Pilot Regiment, returning from the Mediterranean and redesignated '2 Wing', was deployed among his own squadrons, while the 2nd Battalion, now '1 Wing', joined the airfields of 46 Group. The latter was raised by Air Commodore A.L. Fiddament in January 1944 and equipped with C–47s; for within six months of making a promise to do so, the Americans had supplied sufficient of these aircraft to equip five squadrons. There were more to come.

Browning, promoted to lieutenant-general, controlled comprehensively the Army's airborne base. He was subordinated in his capacity as a corps commander directly to 21 Army Group under General Montgomery. Within this reorganization, Chatterton, promoted to colonel, formed Headquarters, Commander Glider Pilots, embracing the two wings and depot. His staff opened a small operational planning cell and became the executive agency for training, standard operating procedures, manning, and equipment development.

At the beginning of 1944, Britain was filled with the ground and air forces of many nations besides those of its own men. These included the 82nd Airborne Division in the north Midlands, alongside 1st Airborne, and the 101st, neighbours of the British 6th in the Wessex counties. The veteran Polish Parachute Brigade, under Browning's command, exercised with both the Americans and British.

Throughout the remainder of the winter, the days of these soldiers were filled with periodic air and a great deal of ground training by day and night, maintaining the practice of six days work and one of leisure in each week. The pubs were full on holidays. It is not surprising that there were fights at turning-out time among this mass of fit and mettlesome men, among the British, among the Americans, and between each other; it is surprising that the bouts were few relative to numbers. Sore heads were more often due to drinking beer to excess. Training restored health swiftly and painfully on the following day.

The glider pilots lived a somewhat different life. They followed the working pattern of their comrades in the divisions but somewhat less rigidly. Flying was their principal interest. More opportunities became available with the expansion of 38 Group but many sorties were confined to take-off, climb to 6,000 ft, release and landing, a process lasting about fifteen minutes. Though far from despised, the process simply whetted the appetite for more. Thus every pilot was on the look out for an opportunity to gain extra flying, even on a leisure day. Gossip in the officers' or sergeants' mess might disclose that the captain of an aircraft was preparing a supernumerary sortie. He would rapidly be asked if he wanted to tow a glider in the process. Even a few additional minutes in the air to extend flying skills, instrument use, and the art of navigation was highly valued.

One small but prized concession had come to the glider pilots as a result of their location with the air transport squadrons. The Royal Air Force had agreed that, subject to passing a test satisfactorily, the First Pilot would take responsibility for checking the serviceability of his glider before take-off, previously reserved to tug captains. This was another subject for study and practice.

At least half their days were spent in drill, weapon handling, fieldcraft, and ground tactical training. As one glider pilot put it:

> The fact that the great majority of us were senior NCOs cut no ice in our military training. In your flight and section, in battle practice, you were allocated a job as a Bren gunner or a scout on a particular exercise. Then, you took a share in all the domestic duties, including guards – often as not simply doing what was a private soldier's job. In fact, the people who had the easiest life in the squadron were the very few junior ranks who had set jobs to do and were largely left to themselves.

The officers and warrant officers bore the burden of preparing training at various levels, supervising or taking part in it, keeping up their flying skills, and taking a share of administrative duties. Not for them the outlook of the early Royal Flying Corps officers who did not appear on the airfield unless they were flying. Regimental Sergeant-Major Briody, who qualified as a Second Pilot in 'fits and starts' when he could get away, remarked:

> It was not easy for the officers, particularly the young officers to make their mark as leaders. They were doing the same job in flying as the NCO pilots, anyway the First Pilots. And in the training as soldiers they were dealing all the time with senior NCOs, intelligent and generally educated men who needed instructing in a different way to junior ranks. My position was different. I was the sergeant-major and my place in the unit was more like that in a battalion. One thing was to make our mark on the stations by being smart, alert, and hot on saluting. You know, because we set a good standard, the Royal Air Force picked up as well, even the aircrew!

Part soldiers, part airmen, Colonel Chatterton used to worry that the other members of the two airborne divisions felt his units were 'a cut above themselves'. They did not. But those who were wholly soldiers sensed that the glider pilots were men of another order, not quite like their brothers in the same brigade, or their first cousins in other arms of the division; second cousins, perhaps, members of the same family withal – very much members of the same family; the red beret united them.

There were, as a matter of fact, none outside the Glider Pilot Regiment who understood what was involved in their principal function, though the tug aircrew who had taken part in Husky probably glimpsed it. It did not lie in the phase of taking off successfully a loaded glider in a high wind, though that involved considerable skill, or in following the tug on a course, though that could be hazardous in heavy weather. It lay in those minutes after casting off at night, over alien territory, poorly illuminated if lit at all, when the pilots assumed the huge burden of finding their way down to a precise patch of ground, a few hundred square yards surrounded by obstacles any one of which might shatter the ply and canvas fuselage in a fatal collision.

Some pilots readily admitted that those minutes in the darkness, as they found themselves descending irrecoverably, were the most challenging of their lives. If the target area was occluded by shadow, they were tempted to abandon all plans and concentrate solely on finding any clear ground on which to land safely. Every fragment of self-discipline and self-confidence had to be mustered by the First Pilot to deliver his contribution to the battle and preserve the passengers sitting behind him. In such circumstances, the steadiness and cooperation of his Second Pilot were of considerable value.

Colonel Chatterton knew all this from his own experience. In the winter of 1943/4 he endured moments of despair when he considered the task of landing a mass of gliders in France amid extensive defence works garrisoned strongly by German troops. The pilots returned from the Mediterranean had not flown since Husky; in Italy they had operated as infantry. The majority of those in England lacked experience, and the amount of refresher training available to them had been limited. Night flying had been negligible.

In the spring of 1944, these anxieties diminished. The policies agreed between August and October 1943 had borne fruit in the greater provision of tugs and the benefits derived from living with the tug squadrons. By that time, too, the nature of the tasks the regiment would be undertaking was apparent.

General Eisenhower and General Montgomery, now respectively Supreme Allied Commander of the invasion host and Commander-in-Chief *ad interim* of the Land Forces, had adjusted and confirmed the plans for Overlord. These directed the landing of an American and a British army simultaneously on the coast of Normandy between the Cotentin peninsula in the west and the River Orne in the east.

The British Second Army beaches lay in the eastern half of the sector. Its commander, Lieutenant-General Sir Miles Dempsey, had selected three infantry divisions and commando forces to capture the coastal defences by assault from the sea on D-Day, and an airborne division to secure the open eastern flank across the River Orne. Two infantry divisions, an armoured division and two armoured brigades, would rapidly follow into the beach-head. D-Day was to be selected from best options of moonlight, tides, and weather on 5, 6, or 7 June 1944.

At the beginning of the year, Mr Churchill had prodded the Chiefs of Staff to ensure that all four of the airborne divisions would be available for simultaneous use by General Eisenhower if he so wished. They were able to show that, despite their best efforts, current stocks and new production of transport aircraft were insufficient to lift more than two and a half at the same time, though the possibility existed of delivering a second lift on D-Day less the transports lost or damaged on the first. As observed, there were sufficient gliders to carry all the British air landing forces and limited freight for the parachute units.

With General Montgomery's agreement, the American army commander, Lieutenant-General Omar N. Bradley, decided to employ the greater part of two airborne divisions, the 82nd and 101st, on the western flank to hasten clearance of the Cotentin peninsula and the opening of the great port at Cherbourg to the allies. This restricted the number of aircraft available to the selected

British division, the 6th, in the first lift. Its commander, Major-General R.N. Gale, decided to mount the 3rd Parachute Brigade, 6th Air Landing Brigade, divisional headquarters and an element of his divisional troops initially, to be followed by the 5th Parachute Brigade as soon as the air transports had returned to their bases and made ready to fly again. The residue would land from the sea.

Briefly, the task of 6th Airborne Division was to secure the high ground east of the River Orne and the Caen canal, parallel waterways, to prevent its use by German forces attempting to strike into the eastern flank of the Second Army, and to destroy the coastal battery at Merville which threatened ships and men landing in that area.

The timing of the airborne landings, American and British, was discussed at length. The Air Commander-in-Chief, Air Chief Marshal Sir Trafford Leigh-Mallory, responsible for the air plan overall, argued persistently against night landings, at any rate by the gliders. He was overruled by General Eisenhower. The airborne assault was to begin shortly after midnight on D-Day, the seaborne landings in daylight from 06.30–07.45, a bracket made necessary by the tidal differences between the American and British sectors.

The 6th Airborne Division plan was completed by 18 March 1944. On 17 April, however, new air photographs of the landing and dropping zones disclosed unpleasant information: wooden poles, 10 ft high, had been raised to obstruct all open ground likely to be used by airborne troops in the anticipated invasion. Close examination showed that they would not seriously impede the parachutists but General Gale was unwilling to land a host of gliders among them. He changed the order of entry, replacing 6th Air Landing Brigade by 5th Parachute Brigade. The former would fly to France early in the evening of D-Day.

Even so, the characteristics and carrying capacity of gliders made them indispensable to the first lift. First, two bridges were to be captured, the canal and river crossings between Bénouville and Ranville. These were needed to link the divisional area with its neighbour, 3rd Infantry Division, as it crossed the beaches, and to provide a means of passage for Lord Lovat's Special Service Brigade to join Major-General Gale's command. Both bridges had been prepared for demolition, probably at very short notice. Surprise, speed, and concentration of the capturing force were essential to success. The best, perhaps the only, means of securing these was by simultaneous glider landings on the targets, the method employed for the capture of the Ponte Grande in Sicily. The task was given to Major John Howard, commanding a reinforced company of the 2nd Battalion, The Oxfordshire and Buckinghamshire Light Infantry – known as the 52nd – and a detachment of field engineers, transported in six Horsas. Flight-Lieutenant Grant, captain of the Halifax which had dropped Staff Sergeant Galpin over Sicily, was appointed to train the tug aircrew.

Second, the Merville Battery was to be captured by the combination of a glider *coup de main* and an assault by parachutists of the 9th Battalion, the Parachute Regiment. Three Horsas were allocated to this task. Four Horsas were allocated to bring in supporting detachments and heavy weapons for the battalion.

Third, the transportation of the division's anti-tank guns, armoured reconnaissance and other essential vehicles, depended upon delivery by glider. A first group of seventeen Horsas, bearing these and the loads for the 9th Battalion, would have to take their chances among the pole obstructions. But 249 Airborne Company, Royal Engineers, and a company of the 13th Battalion, the Parachute Regiment, were detailed to clear a landing zone in time to receive a second and larger group, 94 Horsas and 4 Hamilcars, at 03.45 on D-Day.

From March to May, exercises advanced to massed landings by night on flare paths, passing on to landings in moonlight. The Horsas were joined by the Hamilcars, comparative giants but highly manoeuvrable. Irrespective of types, the tugs released them at thirty second intervals. The numbers of gliders thronging the approaches to a landing zone raised the danger of collisions in the air. Various ideas were circulated to establish a form of traffic control, perhaps by a code of precedence. Chatterton suggested the projection of a notional funnel to order the final descent but it was resisted by his pilots. They had enough difficulties to contend with at that point. Working out the parameters of an imaginary funnel would exacerbate them.

Despite the increase in flying opportunities in the spring of 1944, there were complaints among the glider pilots when it was discovered that tug aircraft were engaged in lengthy operations. Hours spent on operations were hours denied to glider towing. The 38 Wing crews had long sharpened their expertise by leaflet dropping over enemy territory. Now 38 Group was delivering Special Air Service detachments and agents deep into France. Because they lived among the aircrew involved in this work, the glider pilots who resented what they saw as a diversion of their resources were soon brought to see that the RAF crews were gaining experience on these sorties in night navigation and flak evasion which would serve tug and glider combinations well on D-Day, notably in determining the location point for glider release.

In this connection, the Horsas had been successively uprated in instruments and design. For example, gyro compasses had been fitted. The nose of the Mark 2 was hinged, like the Waco, to permit a vehicle or gun to be run forward directly out of the fuselage. If the nose was jammed by damage or obstruction, a number of both Marks 1 and 2 dubbed 'Red' models were fitted with an explosive surcingle embracing the rear end of the fuselage which would blow it off, though this sometimes blew up the freight as well! There were greater apprehensions that the charge might be detonated by enemy fire in the air. As an alternative, spanners were issued to disconnect the eight bolts securing the rear section of the glider, a method dubbed 'White'. Some passengers actively sought to be allotted to White Horsas. As an aid to braking, twin arrestor parachutes were fitted optionally under the tail.

On 25 May all units of 6th Airborne Division other than the glider pilots entered sealed camps on or close to their despatch airfields. In specially prepared accommodation the secret of their targets was revealed during the ten days remaining before D-Day. Outside, row upon row of Stirlings, Halifaxes, Albermarles, and Dakotas, Horsas and Hamilcars, 364 aircraft, 98 gliders, filled the close dispersal sites on airfields in Gloucestershire, Oxfordshire, and Dorset. All had three white bands painted on the rear of the fuselage to identify them as friends to other Allied aircraft and warships, a precaution suggested by the experience of Ladbroke and Fustian. The entire air transport armada was committed to 'Neptune', the delivery of the Allied forces into France. Royal Air Force stations were not sealed until 2 June, and the glider pilots followed that arrangement. During their briefing, they received a message for good luck from General Sir Alan Brooke. The CIGS had recently become the first colonel-commandant of the regiment.

As June opened there was growing anxiety about the weather. Cloud and wind had succeeded the clear skies and light airs of May. Neptune was postponed for twenty-four hours. The immense burden of decision lay upon General Eisenhower as the Channel waters grew rough and the optimum phase of moon and tide began to slip away. He discharged it well. From 04.00 on 5 June the orders were issued to begin the invasion by airborne assault that night, D-1 day.

Now at last they were released. Loaded, in some cases overloaded, the transports of 6th Airborne Division rose into the evening sky darkened by clouds. The launching airfields fell behind, Down Ampney and Blakehill Farm, Fairford, Broadwell, and Brize Norton, Harwell, Keevil, and Tarrant Rushton. The westerly breeze buffeted the gliders – some of the strained tow ropes broke in flight – but as the transport streams approached the French coast shortly after midnight the clouds thinned temporarily, admitting shafts of moonlight. Closing at 6,000 ft, the pilots saw the flicker of bombs exploding on targets ahead, and soon the smoke and flashes of flak among the formations. Tugs and gliders were hit at random, some fatally. Passing safely through this fire, Staff Sergeant S.G. Bone and his tug were abruptly restrained as the parachute arrestors streamed from the Horsa's tail, an accident in which the combination lost 4,000 ft as the pilots fought to recover control above the Channel waters.

Below them in the darkness, the pathfinder landings had been unsuccessful: all the Eureka beacons, complementing the aircraft Rebecca systems, were damaged on landing; some pathfinders set up on the wrong DZ, others in crops which obscured their light signals; some were dropped far from their assembly points.

All this was incidental to the six Horsas of C Squadron swooping towards the bridges across the Caen canal and River Orne. This was Operation 'Deadstick'. Three were directed upon the canal, three to the river bridge. All were crewed by First Pilots. Staff Sergeants J. Wallwork and J. Ainsworth, O. Boland and P. Hobbs, G. Barkway and P. Boyle landed on LZ 'X' at sixteen minutes after midnight, though not without loss: Barkway lost an arm among six other casualties in his glider, one fatal. But the bridge was taken after a sharp fire fight and with some loss by two of Major Howard's platoons over some fifteen minutes. A third platoon was then despatched to clear Bénouville village.

The river bridge site required a steep angle of approach by the Horsas piloted by Staff Sergeants A. Lawrence and H. Shorter, S. Pearson and L. Guthrie, R. Howard and F. Baacke. The first of these landed wide by mischance on the Dives river bank to the east. The second and third landed about half a mile to the north of the Orne river bridge to which the two platoons of the 52nd within them hastened, finding to their surprise that the bridge was undefended and the demolition charges absent – they were in the German billet close by. Captain Neilson and his Royal Engineers drew the demolitions from the canal bridge. Digging in, infantry, engineers, and glider pilots disposed successfully of several parties of Germans attempting to use the bridges, and an investigating tank. They were glad when 7th Battalion, the Parachute Regiment, appeared by way of reinforcement, the more so when the Germans launched counter-atacks, but the five Horsa crews had again demonstrated the tactical rewards of accurate navigation and determined handling of their gliders.

Meanwhile, their comrades to the east were beginning their descents for Operation 'Tonga' through rolling cloud with few features to aid their landings. This comprehended the glider assault on the Merville battery and the first delivery of heavy weapons, vehicles and other freight.

Between midnight and 02.30 in the early morning of D-Day, parachuting and tug aircraft directed to the easternmost landing sites fell into confusion due to the loss of navigating aids, lack of contact with the ground, and flak. Released low, the glider pilots, led by their commanding officer, Lieutenant-Colonel Iain Murray, had little time to make judgements when they broke through the cloud base. Of seventeen Horsas of A, C, E and F Squadrons, one crashed, a total

On target: the Horsas which landed at and permitted the capture of the Orne canal bridge, night 5/6 June 1944 (*AAC, Museum of Army Flying*)

loss, three were severely damaged by pole and other obstructions, five landed safely but at a distance. Captain B. Murdoch's tow rope had broken over Winchester and he had force landed nearby. Eight, however, landed on or near the divisional landing zones. Like many of the 3rd Brigade's parachutists scattered in delivery, glider pilots, passengers, vehicles and guns began doggedly to seek their parent bodies, many becoming involved with other small groups in clashes with German patrols. Glider pilot officers and NCOs also turned their hand to crewing anti-tank guns in clashes with German armour.

Scattering considerably affected the 9th Battalion, the Parachute Regiment. Lieutenant Colonel T.B.H. Otway, its commanding officer, had orders to destroy the Merville battery before the sea-landing began, a responsibility which weighed upon him and his unit. Just before 03.00, more than

Elements of 6th Air Landing Brigade waiting for orders to emplane, afternoon, 6 June 1944 (*Trustees of the Imperial War Museum, London, H 39176*)

Gliders – Horsas and Hamilcars –- and Halifax IX tugs await launching at RAF, Tarrant Rushton, Dorset, 5 June 1944. Note the identification bands painted round wings and fuselages (*MOD*)

an hour and a half after their parachute drop, only 150 of some 500 officers and men had arrived at the battalion rendezvous. No less importantly, the heavy weapons, field engineers and their equipment, and naval bombardment teams carried among the seventeen gliders, had not arrived. The colonel decided that he must move, nonetheless, to the battery.

His advanced party, landed earlier, had done excellent work, reconnoitring the perimeter wire, opening gaps in it, lifting mines and booby traps, and locating the nearest enemy posts. On arrival, the skeleton of one company formed breaching parties, the amalgam of two others under Major Alan Parry comprised the assault force.

At 04.30, as the break in was about to begin, two gliders emerged from the darkness, one high, one low. Otway assumed correctly that these belonged to his *coup de main* group containing the infantry and engineer assault party complementing the attack by his main force.

The tow rope of the third glider had broken shortly after take-off. Safely landed in England, it appeared later. Of the two on target, one contained Staff Sergeant Bone and Sergeant L.G. Dean, whose arrestor parachutes had vexingly inflated over the Channel – they had been jettisoned, but release action also carried away the starboard undercarriage – the other, Staff Sergeant D. Kerr with Sergeant H. Walker. Both combinations had broken cloud and then, confident in their navigation, and gallantly ignoring bursts of flak, spent some time in circling the area looking for the pathfinder's marks. Horsa and Albermarle navigation lights were switched on intermittently as signals of desperation when there was no response from the ground. Bone thought he recognized the lineaments of the battery in the light of 20 mm tracer engaging him and released his tow rope, saw then that he had made an error and inadvertently flew over the battery to land in a field several miles away. Kerr thought he saw ground flares, released to a spiral descent, was hit by flak – four passengers were wounded – suddenly saw the casemates below, was hit again and, streaming his parachutes, managed to put down in an orchard, shearing off his wings. The platoon he carried escaped through the broken fuselage followed by the pilots as the glider caught fire. If nothing else, this brought a reinforcement to the 9th Battalion.

Even as Kerr landed, Colonel Otway launched his attack. The assault was led with great gallantry by Major Parry and Lieutenant Alan Jefferson, Company Sergeant-Major Ross and Colour Sergeant Long. Losing men killed and wounded in the rush to the gun positions, they nonetheless destroyed them all.

Meantime, at Ranville, A Company of Lieutenant-Colonel Peter Luard's 13th Battalion, the Parachute Regiment, had been labouring in cooperation with the engineers of 295 Company. Their task was to collect the obstruction poles blown down by explosives and to lay them as a floor on the axis of LZ 'N'. Stripped of their equipment but carrying their personal weapons in that hostile environment, the teams completed their work at 03.15, thirty minutes ahead of the main glider landings.

These involved ninety-eight combinations: Albermarles and Halifaxes towing ninety-four Horsas, and four Hamilcars. The latter contained 17 pounder anti-tank guns, then the most powerful in British service, and their towing and support vehicles, the former 6 pounder anti-tank guns, vehicles and equipment for the divisional and parachute brigade headquarters. It was the final phase of Tonga, led by Major S.C. Griffith, with gliders from his own A Squadron, B (Major T.I.J. Toler), and D Squadron (Major J.F. Lyne).

Although it landed successfully, the stream was not complete. Five gliders including a Hamilcar had landed in England, and one in the Channel, with broken tow ropes. Turbulence in cloud obliged seven to cast off over Normandy but short of their release points. Twenty-five were hit by flak without loss to men or gliders, though a number of pilots were killed or wounded on landing. Major-General Gale's Horsa, piloted by Major Griffith, was brought to a halt by a solid bank of earth which thrust the nosewheel through the cockpit floor. Leaving pilots and fellow passengers to unbolt the tail for the unloading of his jeep, the general set off on foot to his headquarters site.

With Tonga completed, Operation 'Mallard' within Neptune began. The greater part of 6th Air Landing Brigade, including two of its three battalions, 1st Battalion, the Royal Ulster Rifles and the remainder of the 52nd, with a further element of divisional troops, was to be put down by 21.00 on D-Day in the divisional area.

Major Napier Crookenden, the brigade major, had been waiting throughout the night of 5/6 June at Major-General Browning's headquarters in England for the outcome of the airborne assault. In his comprehensive account of the event, *Dropzone Normandy*, he recalls that they were awaiting news in mid-morning when a report arrived from a Spitfire pilot. He had seen,

. . . some markings in a field near a large farmhouse in le Bas de Ranville. The pilot's sketch of the markings baffled everyone at first, then [I] had a thought, took the paper from the operations officer, turned it upside down – and there clearly was the essential battle message code for 'All objectives taken'. Within minutes the decision was taken to dispatch the second lift and all airfields in 38, 46 and 11 Groups were informed.

. . . By [17.30] the men were sitting in the evening sunshine by their gliders which were drawn up in rows each side of the runway with tow ropes laid out so that each tug and glider operation could start their take off runs with the minimum of delay. Half an hour later they emplaned and at [18.40] the first combination took off. . . . The weather was fine, visibility was 10 to 15 miles for the whole flight and the escorting fighters from 11 Group wheeled and zoomed above and below the long stream of aircraft and gliders. Unhappily, there were absentees. At Brize Norton a Horsa glider carrying five signalmen, a jeep, a trailer and a No. 22 radio set, weaved excessively from side to side on take off and crashed into a corner of one of the hangars, killing everyone on board. Two tug aircraft turned out to be unserviceable and failed to start, four tow ropes broke over England and two over the Channel; both Horsas involved in the last of these incidents ditched close to Allied shipping, but in one of them six men of [A Company, 12th Battalion, The Devonshire Regiment] were drowned.

Over the Channel conditions became a little bumpy and some high scattered cloud appeared. . . . By [20.45] the French coast was in sight and the aircrew and glider pilots could clearly see the Orne estuary. Spread out to the right lay the invasion fleet – a splendid spectacle. Gun flashes from the bombarding ships were visible and over the land hung masses of smoke and haze. . . . A little light flak arched up from the coast and the outskirts of Caen, and one Dakota tug aircraft heeled away and down with an engine on fire. . . .

. . . Each glider pilot released from the tug at about 800 feet . . . made a steep diving turn through 180 degrees and steadied on his final approach to the landing zone over Ranville and its characteristic church. Full flap was applied, the men inside tightened their seat straps, put their arms round each other's shoulders and lifted their legs off the floor, ready for landing. In a few seconds each glider was down, bumped along for 100 yards or so and stopped. Some had their wings knocked off by the anti-landing poles and one or two collided, but it was a remarkably successful landing. . . .

This stream of 248 tugs and gliders alarmed the local German forces and was a further indication to the local enemy command of Allied capability to introduce additional airborne forces beyond the bridge-head. Indeed, the glider pilots were progressively gathered under Lieutenant-Colonel Murray to return to England in case 1st Airborne Division should be employed in expansion of the territory seized. But there were to be many plans, and several months were to pass, before 1st Airborne was to enter the battle from the air.

# CHAPTER NINE

# Ready for Anything

On one day in November 1943, Brigadier C.H.V. Pritchard was Commander of 2nd Parachute Brigade within 1st Airborne Division, on the next he was commander of the only Allied airborne force in the Mediterranean, adviser on airborne operations to the Supreme Allied Commander in Algiers, and to General The Hon. Sir Harold Alexander, Commander-in-Chief of the Allied armies in Italy. The division was on its way home and his formation, now 2nd Independent Parachute Brigade Group, had been detached to provide a strategic reserve in the theatre. Pritchard was told to report to General Alexander at Caserta, just north of Naples.

The two men met in the magnificent *palazzo* occupied by the headquarters of 15 Army Group, and at once discussed the state of the brigade's readiness for operations. It had to be said that the parachutists had not dropped since their final exercise for Husky in June. The glider pilots left behind by the 1st Battalion had not flown since early July. They had been sent to the American airborne base at Oujda in Morocco to assist in ferrying Wacos.

'So what is your actual state of readiness for airborne operations?' the general asked.

'We are somewhat in need of training, sir,' said Pritchard. 'But we're ready for anything.'

They agreed that airborne training was the first priority for the brigade group, and the commander-in-chief promised to secure aircraft from the United States Air Force. Pritchard drove back to his base at Gioia del Colle and called a conference of his commanding officers. Before they could meet, however, fresh orders were received: 2nd Independent Parachute Brigade Group was needed by 8th Army to enter the line in the Adriatic sector, a commitment expected to last a few weeks. By railway and road they moved forward on 1 December 1943, crossed the Sangro, and joined the 2nd New Zealand Division in the foothills of the Apennines. Thus began a term in contact with the enemy which lasted until 27 May 1944. In almost six months the brigade was out of action for an accumulation of only eight days.

Meanwhile, 1st Independent Glider Squadron under Major G.A.R. Coulthard became more independent than most. Transported in C–47s to Oujda, about 100 miles south west of Oran, officers and men discovered a large airfield of the American XII Troop Carrier Command, a base and ferry centre which contained also the United States Airborne Forces Training Centre. It had been established originally to serve the 82nd Airborne Division and was maintained for Operation 'Anvil', the invasion of southern France, though security arrangements precluded any circulation of this intention at the time.

They were certainly independent at Oujda, 1,000 miles from brigade headquarters in Italy. The town was located just inside the Moroccan border, the climate perfect in the winter season. Fruit, flowers, crops, livestock and wine were abundant. Coulthard and his squadron were made most welcome by Colonel E. Ready, the base commander.

Their first task was to refresh their flying skills, using the Wacos on the base. There was no shortage of tugs. The local American commander was anxious to bring everyone to operating status and used the British unit to ferry Wacos arriving in crates at Casablanca to Oujda. Flying hours rose in the glider pilots' log-books. Days passed rapidly as ferrying progressed. During an evening party with a South African transit detachment on the base, one of the hosts asked, 'How long are you staying?'

'Forever, I hope,' said his British guest, 'but I suppose it's too good to last.'

He was right. As soon as the Wacos were concentrated, the Training Centre was ready to move forward. Their destination was Comiso on the edge of a mountain range in south-western Sicily.

The airfield at Comiso had been occupied until July 1943 by a German fighter wing, when it was allotted as a forward base for the 51st and 52nd Troop Carrier Wings. Though its runway had been rapidly repaired following the Husky landings, its buildings were still holed and scarred by Allied aerial bombardment. But, here, too, the climate was good. Services had been restored and power was assured by American generators. Major Coulthard's squadron settled into a barrack block, repaired the roof, doors, and windows, and established itself comfortably. All arrived by 12 December apart from a small party with heavy vehicles which followed by road and sea, a journey lasting some twenty days but put to good use as they had discovered a NAAFI store en route and an order for two months' rations of spirits, beer, tobacco, and other rarities had been supplied.

Towards the end of January 1944, Major Coulthard was called to base headquarters. An instruction had arrived that three Horsas were to be collected from one of the airstrips round Kairouan in Tunisia, and to ferry them to Bari, a port on the southern Adriatic Sea. No other information was provided. A party of glider pilots was flown to the site in North Africa, now derelict, from which they had mounted Ladbroke and Fustian. Captain Cornelius Turner, Major Coulthard's second-in-command, described later what they found:

. . . at dusk on the desolate, abandoned air strip. There the gliders were, looking utterly lonely and dejected, the last remnants, but for the wrecks and the rusty tin cans, of the masses of men and machines that had packed these air strips, roads and olive groves. . . . These Horsas had been at the mercy of wind, rain and the Arabs for six months, but there was no question of a proper inspection, nor indeed anyone who was qualified to carry one out. In the morning the pilots got in, tentatively checked the creaking controls, patted the woodwork trustingly and flew them 250 miles across the Mediterranean to Sicily. . . .

Before proceeding to Bari, Major Coulthard thought it expedient to apply loading tests, though they no longer possessed Horsa loading charts. Ballasting to 7,000 lb was accomplished by,

. . . arranging the load so that a body swinging from the tail could just raise the front wheels clear of the ground. Our well attested experience was that this simple method is always successful. The flight to Bari, with the tow-ships barely clearing the high hills, was an unpleasant experience for all concerned. . . .

It also supported their judgement when the object of the Horsa collection was revealed. Force 133, located in Bari, was the base organization for clandestine operations in Yugoslavia. Orders had been received from London to convey a Russian military mission to join Marshal Tito and his partisan forces. The chosen method of delivery was by glider.

Horsas, however, were not to be used, Captain Turner and his team of glider pilots asserted once the dimensions of the flight were disclosed. The two engines of the C–47 were remarkably powerful but they lacked the ability to tow Horsas over the Dinaric Alps. But the Waco was available; the C–47 would have no difficulty in towing this glider laden even to 4,500 lb. Tests from Bari airfield reassured all concerned, all, indeed, for the whole mission took part in flight tests at the insistence of their chief, Lieutenant-General Korneyev. Fitzroy Maclean tells us that the group included 'Major-General Gorshkov, a noted expert on partisan warfare . . . A quantity of colonels and majors including at least one obvious representative of the NKVD [secret police]'.

Preceded by bombers on a diversionary raid, escorted by American and British fighters, the three Wacos took off at 11.00 on 19 February 1944, crewed by Captain Turner with Staff Sergeant Newman, Staff Sergeant McCulloch with Staff Sergeant Hill, and Staff Sergeant Morrison with Staff Sergeant McMillen. The C–47 tugs of 64th Group were led by the commanding officer, Lieutenant-Colonel Ed Duden. Operation 'Bunghole' began.

The distance was 250 miles to a landing zone in the valley of an uplands river, the Una. The skies were clear but the air cold, and colder still when, passing over Split on the coast, the snowy ground ascended sharply. At 13.40 the combinations saw the ground beacons of burning straw. Tow ropes were cast off and,

> . . . within a few yards of each other the gliders touched down, or rather flopped with a sickening jolt into the snow about three feet deep . . . After being embraced by incredibly filthy and bearded natives we were all hurried to a hut in the forest which verged on the valley . . . .

Having concluded this unique task successfully, the detachment from 1 Squadron were obliged to join Brigadier Maclean's British mission – and share the partisan life – for some weeks, until the snow abated sufficiently to admit a Royal Air Force Dakota to carry them out.

They returned in March. In that month Brigadier Pritchard succeeded in laying the foundations of a base for airborne operations, holding equipment including parachutes, training recruits to replace his battle casualties, and functioning as a contact point with detachments. Although he was unable to draw his brigade out of the line immediately, he wisely decided to send his pathfinders, 1st Independent Parachute Platoon, under Captain Peter Baker, to Comiso, and with them 300 Air Landing Anti-Tank Battery, Royal Artillery, employed temporarily as infantry because there was no possibility of armoured warfare in the Italian mountains. The pathfinders were thus able to work up their task of providing visual and radar beacons to C–47s and gliders. The gunners provided battle loads for pilot training and themselves refreshed their skills in loading and unloading guns and towing jeeps, and passenger drills on landing.

In April, Pritchard learned that he might expect to mount an airborne operation in June as part of a reinforced corps landing in southern France – Anvil – to complement Overlord, but this was quickly stood over. It later became apparent that lack of assault shipping obliged the postponement. Finally, mid-August was chosen and a new title allotted, 'Dragoon'.

Much had happened in France by the beginning of August. The British Second Army joined by the Canadian First were breaking out from Caen towards the Seine. On their right, two American armies, the First and the Third were striking south towards the Loire and east towards Chartres and Orleans. These thrusts had obliged the Germans to draw on their forces in central and southern France. The aim of Dragoon was to deliver an uppercut to the remainder, opening a line of communication from the French Mediterranean ports to General Eisenhower's main forces. At the same time, General Alexander was to attempt the destruction of the German forces in Italy.

The Allied Seventh Army of American and French divisions had been formed and trained under Lieutenant-General A.M. Patch to secure a lodgement in France along the coast from Marseilles to the Italian border, prior to exploiting northwards along the Rhône valley. With limited assault craft, the coastal defences were to be broken open between Frejus and Saint Raphael by three United States divisions forming the VI Corps under Lieutenant-General L.K. Truscott. This opening operation was to be facilitated by airborne assaults on the enemy garrisons behind the coast line.

A task force was formed of divers American airborne units and 2nd Independent Parachute Brigade Group under a United States commander, Major-General Robert T. Frederick. But the Mediterranean XII Troop Carrier Command was unable to find sufficient aircraft to lift the nine thousand parachutists and the glider forces. IX TCC in England was thus instructed to send a further wing temporarily to the Mediterranean together with a number of elements experienced in mounting an airborne operation. 'By April', a British staff officer at the Supreme Headquarters remarked, 'we had stitched the whole thing together.' He was evidently an optimist. Several important omissions in the arrangements were yet to emerge.

2nd Parachute Brigade came out of the line at the end of May into a tented camp south of Salerno. They needed a rest. They also need training; battle hardened, their experience lay in the confined struggles of the winter defence line. Open warfare lay ahead. More pressingly, they needed to remind themselves how to mount and carry through an airborne assault. But the pathfinders were ready, and, above all, the glider pilots.

Apprised of the Dragoon plan in April, Major Coulthard was confident that his squadron could deliver whatever was required of them in Wacos, but he hastened to remind Brigadier Pritchard that they could not lift an anti-tank or light field gun in combination with its towing jeep. To do that, they needed Horsas. The staff at Caserta was asked to investigate the possibility of renewing the Horsa ferry service from Britain. The planners in Algiers then had to admit to the error, following Operation Bunghole, of assuming that the Independent Squadron was equipped with Horsas. Further enquiries were made in haste.

An extraordinary discovery followed. There were fourteen more Horsas in Tunisia, twelve on the old E airstrip, kept in condition by a small detachment of Royal Air Force technicians. Two more were at Blida airfield, a site chosen for the concentration of the British gliders after Husky but abandoned after 1st Airborne Division was called at short notice to ground operations in Italy. These were collected with their RAF grooms. A further twenty were to be sent from Britain in packing cases carried in a fast sea transport. Did anyone in the high command recall at that time the solemn assumptions of 1942 that Horsas could neither be ferried to the Mediterranean nor withstand transportation by sea?

Actually, only nineteen were sent from the Royal Air Force maintenance unit concerned but, with the three sent to Bari for Bunghole and recovered, thirty-six were to hand. It would have been difficult to crew more. The squadron reconverted itself to the Horsa before moving to Salerno to join the remainder of the brigade.

On 12 July the whole force moved north to a tented camp between its base at Ostia Lido and Rome. The Independent Squadron established itself with 51st Troop Carrier Wing at Tarquina airfield, one of five sites from which the air transport force would launch the airborne force.

Three lifts were envisaged, a limitation imposed by the numbers of C–47s available. Preceded by the British and American pathfinders, the first lift would drop all the British and the majority of the United States parachutists from 04.23 on D-Day, 15 August, to capture and block the road centre between La Motte and Le Muy. At 08.14 the second lift would deliver thirty-six Horsas and forty Wacos into the same area shortly after the landing of the first seaborne assault force at 07.00. Finally, at 18.10 that evening, as the seaborne landings continued, the United States Gliderborne Regimental Team would land to enlarge the airborne ground perimeter.

On the night of 14/15 August the task force made ready. The first aircraft departed and dropped the pathfinders about thirty minutes ahead of time. The parachutists followed along the common route for the air stream, cutting the tip of Elba and Corsica before the next landfall between St Tropez and Nice. A dense cloud then came into view, drifting across the sea west of Corsica, enveloping the coast.

The parachutists were dropped ashore through this cloud. When the head of the glider stream reached Corsica its base was only a few hundred feet above the sea. The Wacos in the first echelon began to circle the island hoping that a rising sun would break the cloud mass, but the Horsas, heavier and thus more demanding on their tugs' fuel, turned back for Rome.

By 08.00 visibility was improving. Those on the Corsican circuit, turning back on to course, were soon able to see the Côte d'Azure from 2,000 ft and the wake of ships landing troops. The Wacos, including 64 Air-landing Light Battery, Royal Artillery, with their 75 mm guns, were released at 09.10. They unloaded 'in bright sunshine. We were in warm air scented by shrubs. White houses were scattered round about among low stone walls. I remember seeing a field full of grapes on the vine. . . .'

Major Coulthard was among those flying back to Rome. Via his tow rope telephone cable, he asked his tug captain if any instructions had been received about relaunching the stream, but radio security precluded such exchanges. Many of the Horsa pilots apprehended banishment to some distant corner of the base so as to keep the marshalling and take-off area clear for the third lift. If that happened they would not themselves remount and return to the operational area before nightfall.

They reckoned without the presence of Major W.H. Ewart-James, sent from England by Colonel Chatterton to observe the launching of the gliders for Dragoon. Waiting in the Wing operations room for news of progress, he learned that the Horsas were returning and at once proposed to organize their reception and remarshalling. The consequence was that the Horsas and tugs were accorded pride of place in the marshalling scheme to be relaunched at 14.30. The most difficult task was the servicing of the gliders; there were none in reserve. One, indeed, had not returned to Rome, though it was believed that this had landed in Corsica.

At 14.30 they took off once more. Visibility was excellent all the way to France and the Horsas began landing about 17.30, not without difficulties; a number of the fields on and around the landing zone were obstructed by poles and, unexpectedly, a group of the enemy had re-entered the area shortly beforehand. Sergeant Jenner was killed by cannon fire just before landing. Major Coulthard overshot into a wood and was one of three seriously injured. But the anti-tank battery and minor loads for brigade headquarters and units were unloaded safely. In the final minutes of the air-landing, those on the ground were in danger of collisions, for the air was suddenly filled with the Wacos of the American glider regiment. Next day, a tally showed that few of the gliders would be fit for recovery.

In the following week, after the seaborne had joined the airborne forces, the Allied components went their separate ways. The Seventh Army began its pursuit of the Germans up the Rhône valley. The British were to return to Italy to make ready for another airborne operation, embarking in sea transports on 26 August, 'just as we were settling down to enjoy the Riviera', Captain Mockeridge remarked. But Rome called, and more insistently, the Supreme Allied Commander, General Sir Henry Maitland Wilson.

The brigade had scarcely concentrated in Rome before it was moved by road to makeshift camps, hot and dusty round San Pancrazio in the heel of Italy, a 'wretched site' in the opinion of one officer, 'suitable for a penal battalion'. The glider pilots joined 64th Troop Carrier Group on the three airfields at Manduria nearby. They were in this remote area because it was the nearest point of take off for Greece.

> Before leaving Italy at the end of August 1944, [Mr Churchill wrote in his recollections of the Second World War], I had asked the Chief of the Imperial General Staff to work out the details of a British expedition to Greece in case the Germans there collapsed. We gave it the codename 'Manna'.

The British and United States governments did not want to expend forces on yet another invasion to eject the Germans from the northern shores of the Mediterranean but they were equally determined that, as operational pressures from Russia and north-west Europe necessitated the recall of enemy garrisons to the most threatening fronts, there should be no power vacuum in Greece. Of the two national guerrilla movements, the strongest, EAM ELAS, was controlled by communist cadres. There was a danger that the latter would organize a *coup d'état* as soon as the Germans began to evacuate Athens. Mr Churchill's plan was to insert limited British forces to keep the Germans moving and to ensure stable conditions for the resumption of power by the Greek government-in-exile as a prelude to democratic elections. Commando forces were to be positioned off the west coast aiming, if possible, to prevent a blockage of the Corinth canal. An armoured brigade group was embarked to land in Piraeus. But Athens was the key. The 2nd Parachute Brigade Group was to be ready for launching at forty-eight hours notice to enter the city and secure its airfield.

Briefing arrangements hung fire in the San Pancrazio camps for the remainder of September. The time was not wasted for the glider pilots: a team under Captain John Mockeridge had ferried forward the remnant of Wacos from Tarquina but they needed a good deal of servicing by the Royal Air Force maintenance party. At Manduria, the new squadron commander Major J.L. McMillen arranged a loading and flying trial for a light bulldozer unfamiliar to the squadron. But all this was done by the first week in October, and still the Germans showed no signs of leaving Athens.

They were waiting for the evacuation of the Peloponnese and the island garrisons. Once these had cleared Athens, the German commander was ready to withdraw his main forces, concentrated to discourage guerrilla interference. Suddenly agents reported that the Germans were moving north, protected by a screen covering the city. These dispositions required a new landing site, Megara airstrip 40 miles from Athens, for which there were no proper maps or photographs at San Pancrazio. The objective was nonetheless secured by a detachment of 4th Battalion, the Parachute Regiment, and 2nd Parachute Engineer Squadron under Lieutenant-Colonel H.B. Coxen on D-1, 12 October. But a strong wind inhibited entry. A number of the parachutists were dragged among rocks and mortally injured. Airborne operations were postponed.

On the 14th it was still gusting to 30 mph but political requirements were no less persistent. Captain Turner was ordered at very short notice to lead six Wacos loaded principally with engineer stores and the bulldozer to Megara. The airstrip and shore had been secured but was under occasional artillery fire from a German rearguard. In the last thirty minutes of flight, Staff Sergeant T. Gillies was struck by 'the deep cutting of the Corinth canal, blocked by a small steamship scuttled half way down'. Passing the city of Corinth, the gliders were towed southwards in a half circle to bring them into the north wind. Watched by a crowd of admiring Greeks, they touched down without accident. Next day, they were joined by the remainder of the squadron, bringing vehicles, radio sets and reserve ammunition.

The brigade was soon drawn north but Captain Turner, acting as squadron commander, and Captain Mockeridge made all arrangements to service and fly the Wacos back to Tarquina, a task completed in the first half of December. It was a fine effort and not in the least diminished by the fact that sixty crews under Major Lyne had successfully ferried twenty-seven Horsas across France to Ciampino airfield at Naples on 9 and 10 October. The Independent Squadron knew nothing of this because they had no contacts at Ciampino. The base commander assumed that someone would eventually give him instructions for their disposal. Such is the pantomime of war.

# CHAPTER TEN
# An Airborne Carpet

The German positions round the Normandy bridge-head were progressively broken from the end of July 1944. The American First and Third Armies – 12 Army Group – soon to be joined by Patch's Seventh Army from the south of France, began to stream out, their columns radiating within a great arc from the coast of Brittany in the west to Paris and Nancy to the east. In the coastal sector the First Canadian and British Second Armies – 21 Army Group – thrust towards the lower reaches of the Seine, the Somme, and the Belgian frontier. Ground objectives apart, the aim was to prevent the Germans from establishing a new defence line by maintaining the momentum of advance, breaking resistance wherever it was offered.

In July, with the break out impending, General Marshall again advised early use of airborne troops to facilitate the general advance. He was assured that they would be employed at the first opportunity. General Eisenhower's chief concern in this matter was to ensure that he had an organization in place to launch them without delay. In July he carried forward an idea under consideration for several weeks, the formation of an airborne army, commanded by a senior American air corps general.

There were objections to this structure, particularly by his Air Commander-in-Chief, Sir Trafford Leigh-Mallory, who foresaw the loss of his own authority to influence airborne intervention and to make use of the transport aircraft between operations. They did not persuade General Eisenhower to change his mind. On 17 July Lieutenant-General Lewis H. Brereton was appointed to command what was to become known as the First Allied Airborne Army. It consisted of:

A headquarters staffed by American and British Army and Air Force officers, at Sunninghill, near Ascot.

*I British Airborne Corps*
1st Airborne Division
6th Airborne Division
1st Polish Parachute Brigade
1st Special Air Service Brigade
52nd Lowland Division (trained and equipped as a light mountain formation)

*XVIII United States Airborne Corps*
17th Airborne Division
82nd Airborne Division
101st Airborne Division

Airfield Construction Engineers

IX Troop Carrier Command

38 and 46 Group, Royal Air Force (for specific operations)

It was not designed as an army to take the field, but as a preparatory and mounting 'agency' – Eisenhower's term – to train, plan, marshal the necessary aircraft, and lift the soldiers into battle. Up and running, Lieutenant-General Brereton and his command were ready for business from 12 and 21 Army Groups. Unhappily, there was no custom except for occasional parachute or glider forays carrying French and British Special Air Service contingents behind enemy lines. A series of airborne options was therefore projected by General Eisenhower's staff. Several were carried to a mounting stage, but none were launched.

From mid-August, General Bradley, commanding 12 Army Group, was positively opposed to airborne intervention on his front, though he wanted the transport aircraft to 'bring gas to George Patton's [Third] Army'. Patton's armoured divisions, racing forward, reached the Meuse on 31 August. The American First Army was between the Oise and the Meuse, aiming for Mons and Namur in Belgium but slowing as their petrol supply was reduced to benefit Patton. Motor fuel was short everywhere because Cherbourg had not been fully cleared and storms had severely damaged the Mulberry harbours on the Normandy beaches. As commanders pressed their troops forward eagerly to the Rhine and Moselle on the frontiers of Germany, the supply lines lengthened. A port on the Channel coast was needed urgently. The number of aircraft employed in carrying motor fuel to France reached a peak at the beginning of September.

The British and Canadian armies crossed the Belgian frontier to enter Brussels on 3 September. When Antwerp was reached on the following day it was believed that this great port would soon be in use, shortening the supply line by 300 miles. Hopes rose that the war in Europe might be won in 1944.

During August a combination of factors including the supply difficulties and pace of advance led to differences of view within the high command. Montgomery wished to concentrate forty divisions in one or the other of the Army groups to advance in mass to the Rhine and cross into Germany. Bradley did not care for the idea; he suspected that command of such a number would pass to Montgomery. He and Patton proposed to continue to the Rhine between Wiesbaden and Karlsruhe, with a subsidiary thrust along the Main valley.

No doubt personalities – and politics – played a part in these ideas. Politics certainly influenced General Eisenhower's decision in the first week of September to give equal support to the thrusts of both Army groups. The Americans would not have accepted the major land command returning to a British general. The British would have resented the marginalization of Montgomery, renowned for his success in battle and recently promoted to field marshal.

With Bradley's rejection of airborne assistance, First Allied Airborne Army's resources were passed exclusively to 21 Army Group. Field Marshal Montgomery decided that he would project a division to capture the Rhine crossings from Arnhem to Wesel, Operation 'Comet'. Troops were briefed to take off on 10 September at 06.00, but were stood down at 02.00. The advance of the British XXX Corps had been checked short of the Dutch frontier. This was the fifteenth consecutive operation to be cancelled for 1st Airborne among the divisions in the Airborne Army.

That afternoon, 10 September, Major-General Browning's headquarters issued fresh instructions. It was still the field marshal's aim 'to cross the Rhine as quickly as possible'. I Airborne Corps was to throw 'an airborne carpet' across the waterways from Eindhoven to Arnhem, notably the Maas (Meuse), Waal, and Rhine, together with associated canals.

> The carpet is very long so it will necessarily be narrow [Montgomery remarked to Browning on 9 September]. The essence of the business is to capture those bridges intact. And this will mean dropping as many men on the bridges as possible from the word 'go'.
>
> How long do you think we shall have to hold the bridge at Arnhem? [Browning asked].
>
> Two days [the field marshal replied]. They should be up to you in two days.

Three divisions were allocated for the operation: the 101st and 82nd United States Airborne Divisions, and the British 1st together with 1st Polish Parachute Brigade. In that order, they were to drop from south to north, taking Eindhoven and seven major and minor bridges along the route north. The Maas bridge at Grave, the Waal bridge at Nijmegen, and the Rhine bridges at Arnhem were the greatest of these. Immediately beyond the Rhine, 1st Airborne had the task of holding a bridge-head within which XXX Corps could deploy to break any investing German forces. If possible, the 52nd Lowland Division would fly in to reinforce the area, using Deelen airfield or airstrips prepared by the United States Airborne Aviation Engineers.

The spreading of the 'carpet' and the opening of the route across the waterways was given the codename 'Market'; the passage to and beyond Arnhem by XXX Corps was called 'Garden'. D-Day was to be 17 September.

Eight months had passed since 1st Airborne Division had returned from the Mediterranean for leave and reinforcement. At full strength it began to train in February for a part in Overlord and was much disappointed when operations in Normandy were concluded without its intervention. But, maintained at short notice, the division received the greater share of resources for airborne exercises into late August. Throughout this period it had benefited from the training plan of a very experienced commander, Major-General E.E. Down, the inceptory commander of 1st Battalion, the Parachute Regiment, and the 2nd Parachute Brigade. But he was sent to prepare the Indian Airborne Division for operations in the Far East and was succeeded by Major-General R.E. Urquhart, proven as an infantry brigade commander, but lacking any knowledge of an airborne assault. A brave and modest man, he was unable to speak with authority at a crucial phase of operational planning.

The Glider Pilot Regiment had also needed reinforcements when 2 Wing came home from the Mediterranean but, as agreed between the two services, it received a steady flow of Second Pilots each month from the truncated flying training scheme, and regular opportunities for the more experienced Second Pilots to uprate their status to First Pilot. In June, all squadrons contributed in greater or lesser degree to Neptune so that the breadth of operational experience was considerably increased. The regiment incorporated the lessons learned in subsequent continuation training. The formation of 46 Group raised the number of flying hours available to individual pilots; the desired average of eight hours a month was achieved in July and August within 38 and 46 Groups.

Colonel Chatterton and his staff were involved in the fifteen plans made between the conclusion of Neptune and the abandonment of Comet. Some of these matured to the point of briefing squadrons. Inevitably, as in all units concerned within I Airborne Corps, expectancy waned. This mood prevailed in the planning for Market.

General Brereton's opinions dominated the development of the air plan which in turn influenced the final ground plan. He was not confident in the ability of the IX Troop Carrier Command aircrew to navigate at night, in contradistinction to those of 38 and 46 Groups, and thus insisted that the operation should be launched in daylight. This was a sound decision. However, as there were insufficient aircraft to lift all three divisions and the corps headquarters simultaneously, the question of sortie rates arose.

Against the advice of Air Marshal Hollinghurst, Brereton ruled that there should only be one lift per day, a decision which necessitated delivery over three days. He cited crew fatigue and the uncertainty of weather conditions in mid-September as his reasons. But although Holland was further from England than Normandy, it would have been possible to mount two sorties on the first day on the basis of a return journey of six and a half hours duration with two hours on the ground for turn round between each. At the very least, a significant number of second sorties could have been made on D-Day using reserve aircrew. The weather factor argued for itself. If the weather was good on D-Day, they should take advantage of it to deliver as many units as possible. There was no guarantee of fair weather conditions on immediately following days. The general officers commanding the corps and divisions should have made the point that the forces landed on the first lift were insufficient to ensure the immediate capture of essential targets such as the bridges and their retention against counter-attacks.

In the 1st Airborne Division area, the dropping and landing zones were distant from the prime target, Arnhem bridge, some by as much as 8 miles. The polder – drained fens – south of the river but immediately adjacent to the bridge structure was suitable as a dropping zone and probably as a landing zone for Horsas, though extrication of vehicles and guns might have been difficult. Air Chief Marshal Sir Trafford Leigh-Mallory objected that, all else apart, the site was covered by flak, though it was soon discovered that the whole area was within the same Deelen flak zone. Major-General Urquhart did not feel that he was sufficiently experienced to argue that if they did not land by the bridge the operation was questionable. The polder was therefore rejected for the first day as unsuitable on the grounds of its surface alone but, curiously, considered acceptable as a dropping zone for the Polish brigade on the third.

The final plan for the three days ran as follows:

| | |
|---|---|
| D-Day | A pathfinder drop at H minus 20 minutes |
| H-hour | Parachute drop of 1st Parachute Brigade |
| H-hour | Glider delivery of part of 1st Air Landing Brigade, divisional headquarters and troops |
| D plus 1 | Parachute drop of 4th Parachute Brigade<br>Glider delivery of remainder of 1st Air Landing Brigade and divisional troops<br>Supply drops |

D plus 2    Parachute drop and glider delivery of 1st Polish Parachute Brigade and
            878th Aviation Engineer Battalion
            Supply drops

On the night of Saturday 16 September 1944, two hundred Lancasters of RAF Bomber Command and twenty-three Mosquitoes attacked German airfields within range of the Airborne Corps objectives. Fifty-nine RAF bombers attacked flak sites in Holland, while others combined with American aircraft in diversionary raids. Air strikes continued after daylight on Sunday, the 17th.

The glider pilots completed their briefing on the Saturday afternoon. By that time, all those involved in Market were concentrated on their launching airfields. Early morning mist threatened a postponement. At 09.00 the decision was taken to fly.

The pathfinders departed at 09.25. All crews and passengers were by then emplaned. Engines were started. Aircraft began to position on the runway thresholds. Glider tow lines grew taut. The first chalk numbers of I Airborne Corps were on their way. 'Like a great swarm of bees ascending and droning' parachute aircraft and glider combinations rose from the airfields of Hampshire, Berkshire, Wiltshire, Gloucestershire, Lincolnshire, Northamptonshire and Cambridgeshire.

Three hundred and fifty-eight British crews were among the five hundred gliders taking off that morning, thirty-eight carrying the advanced elements of corps headquarters to be established in the 82nd Division sector near Nijmegen. The remainder, 307 Horsas and 13 Hamilcars, were loaded with vehicles and equipment of 1st Airborne Division.

As on Neptune, some combinations fell away from the outset. One glider was damaged by a passing vehicle in the marshalling area. A tug had engine trouble and was obliged to return after two false starts. Their loads were transferred to the second lift. Twenty-four gliders became separated for one reason or another as they rose through clouds, one of which crashed, killing pilots and passengers. Twenty-two returned to join the second lift. Four gliders ditched over the sea, two with broken tow ropes, two because their tugs had engine faults; all those aboard were rescued by the recovery craft in the North Sea. Nine gliders were lost over Holland.

Navigation arrangements were excellent, though once the dense cloud was left behind on the English coast direction was largely a matter of follow-my-leader. The British combinations were flying in loose pairs at ten second intervals. As the several streams, British and American, coincided the passage of more than a thousand aircraft on each of the two approach routes generated turbulence which made flying difficult for the gliders. This was undoubtedly a cause of tow ropes breaking in flight.

Allied fighters ensured that there was no air attack upon the transports but from the moment of crossing the Dutch coast at 2,500 ft all were vulnerable to random flak. The Rhine came into view, the red roofs of Arnhem and the outlying towns and villages, the railway running west north west and the ground chosen for the four landing zones 'L', 'S', 'X' and 'Z' on either side of it. The pilots' recollections of the prospect were broadly similar. On recognition, 'I picked it up straight away, everything looked like the briefing model'; '. . . no problem, it was all laid out in front of us'. Visibility was good: '. . . we were under the cloud at 2,500 feet [release height], I reckon we could see everything in the area'; 'we weren't worried about the cloud, more about tracer from the ground close to one of the combinations ahead'. Several of those who had taken part in Husky and

Neptune commented on a daylight approach: 'Landing in full daylight was the easiest thing in the world. Course, descent – everything was simple'; 'I thanked God that we weren't going through that nightmare of finding our way down into the darkness . . . .'

For those hit by flak it was another matter. One glider pilot,

> . . . had barely got my map out in front of me and was bending over, tracing our course, when I heard a sudden very rapid and curious swish-swish sound which was quite loud. I couldn't make out, for a fraction of a second, what was causing it, but when I looked out of my window I saw a lot of little red sparks shooting upwards from beneath the cockpit and past my port window. Next second there was a tremendous bang right in the cockpit and a thin wisp of greyish smoke. I automatically grasped the control column and as I did so I could smell high explosive; then poor Ralph [Second Pilot] rolled sideways in his seat as far as his straps would let him. I shouted for someone to come forward and see what could be done for Ralph, and the platoon sergeant poked a startled head into the cockpit, but before he could do so Ralph was dead, so I told him to leave him in his seat and to shut the door.
>
> By this time I was considerably frightened because I realised that if I was incapacitated, nobody else knew how to get the glider on to the ground in one piece, and I was terribly sad about poor Ralph, who was a grand boy and a personal friend. I remember ringing up Jeff, the tug pilot, and asking him if he could possibly weave about a bit as we had been hit by flak and Ralph was dead. Jeff apologised and said he was very sorry that he had not enough boost to jink around – in fact I think he was rather worried to think that he would not get us to the LZ. . . .
>
> . . . As we arrived at the LZ Jeff rang up and wished us good luck and said to pull off when we were ready, and this we did. Fortunately there was air in the flaps and I went straight down almost vertically. I think we must have been shot at from somewhere on the ground as, after landing, I discovered that we had two other casualties in the back, though neither was fatal.
>
> . . . As I moved off to my own rendezvous, I was very deeply touched by a young private of the Borders who came up to me, stood smartly to attention and said: 'Sir, I just want to thank you.'

Another First Pilot discovered that his RAF tug captain, flying a C–47 of 575 Squadron, had been killed. The aircraft was being flown by a navigator who had no training as a pilot but agreed to continue with the operation. When the Horsa ailerons were destroyed by flak he returned the combination to Belgium and then flew back to England to land the Dakota safely.

Working on a margin of time, the pathfinders had laid all the aids. Winds were light and variable. The only fault in landing was a high approach speed. Some overshot – one pilot was killed crashing into a tree – many landed at the far end of the LZ, but others braked successfully in the air to land 'perfectly', 'we had a brilliant landing' as remarked by members of 7th Battalion, The King's Own Scottish Borderers, the KOSB, landing with their comrades of the Border Regiment and part of the South Staffords. On one landing zone the ground was rutted. Horsa undercarriages were forced up through the floor of their fuselages, slewing the gliders into collisions. Those carrying the divisional reconnaissance squadron sustained the worst damage.

Gliders on Landing Zones Z and X, Arnhem, 17 September 1944 (*Trustees of the Imperial War Museum, London, CL 1172*)

Two of the Hamilcars overturned, killing the pilots and severely damaging their loads of 17 pounder anti-tank guns and towing vehicles. But taken as a whole, the first lift landed successfully. Arriving from 13.00 onwards on a warm, sunny afternoon, 1st Air Landing Brigade set about its task of defending the landing sites for those following over the next two days.

Resistance was initially scant. The local Dutch people came out to welcome their liberators and to pass the information that there were no Germans in the immediate area.

They were reporting what they knew. What they did not know was that the Commander-in-Chief of Army Group B, Field Marshal Walter Model, was about to lunch in his headquarters at Hartenstein on the western outskirts of Arnhem and was thus an observer of the airborne landings. Forgetting the food and wine on the table, he gave immediate instructions for the deployment of the forces in and close to the city before hastening off with staff and radios to a distant site. Elsewhere, the Allied landing plan was taken from the body of a dead American and passed to General Kurt Student, Commander of the First Parachute Army at Vught, just north of Eindhoven. Although this title was misleading – the majority of his troops were not airborne units

Horsas interlocked on Landing Zone X at Arnhem. Regimental HQ of the Airborne Light Regiment, RA, unloading, 17 September 1944 (*Trustees of the Imperial War Museum, London, BU 1164*)

but scratch divisions which included men graded as unfit for active service – his numbers were sufficient to maintain a continuous defence and had, indeed, delayed the advance of XXX Corps. Student's staff relayed the details of the airborne plan to all headquarters in the area including II SS Panzer Corps at Doetinchem, 15 miles east of Arnhem.

The Dutch underground had recently reported the presence of this formation to London, but it was also known that the two divisions in the corps, 9th and 10th SS Panzer Divisions, had lost heavily in the break-out from Normandy and were recuperating on the borders of Holland and Germany. Brigadier E.T. Williams, Field Marshal Montgomery's senior intelligence staff officer, was later to admit that he underrated their capabilities, but he was not alone in this error. That evening, the 9th organized as *Kampfgruppe* Harzer – Lieutenant-Colonel Harzer was the senior officer of the divisional remnant – began to move into Arnhem from the east and to circle its northern outskirts. Major-General Heinz Harmel, commanding the 10th, was meanwhile winning a race to secure the mighty Nijmegen bridge across the Waal.

On Monday 18 September heavy rain clouds in England delayed the departure of the second

Hamilcar on tow by Halifax IX (*Charles E. Brown*)

lift until 11.00. The glider combinations were swelled by those returning the previous day to 296, including fifteen Hamilcars and four Wacos. Of these, 241 were unloaded successfully on or around the landing zones after touching down in a north-westerly 10 knot wind. By that afternoon, therefore, and discounting those who had landed with I Airborne Corps headquarters at Nijmegen, more than a thousand British glider pilots, the greater part of the two wings, had entered the battle zone.

Although the regiment was proud of its ability to contribute to the ground fighting after landing, it had become the firm policy of the War Office that glider pilots should be used only in defensive duties and recovered as soon as practicable to assure a pool of pilots for following operations. But as ever in an airborne assault, recovery could not be effected until there was a secure withdrawal route to the rear areas.

As the result of the experiences in Neptune, Colonel Chatterton had thus,

. . . detailed the pilots on landing to form into squadrons under command of their respective headquarters. No. 1 Wing would be under Headquarters, 1st Airborne Division and No. 2 Wing under 1st Air Landing Brigade whom they were respectively carrying. . . .

There was one exception to this. Chatterton was concerned that the small number of pilots flying to the corps headquarters would be insufficient to defend it. Major T.I.J. Toler, commanding B Squadron, was instructed,

> . . . to take twenty crews or one flight who land on the first lift straight to Nijmegen to assist in the defence of Corps HQ. This is all very well but it is through twelve miles of enemy territory. I don't think this is on [Major Toler noted in his diary on 16 September] and say so in no uncertain terms. Major Royle agrees and we decide to remain with the unit until Division HQ is established and then see how the land lies and whether it is possible to get to Corps – how little we knew what was to turn out. . . .

The events of Operation Market have long since been established and described. In recounting the part played by the members of the Glider Pilot Regiment it is essential to view it as they saw it at the time. In a long running battle, the information available to junior officers and men is often limited, mostly confined to what is happening in their company, squadron, or battery. At Arnhem the glider pilots who gathered under one or the other of the wing commanding officers, Lieutenant-Colonel J.W. Place with the Air Landing Brigade and Lieutenant-Colonel Murray at divisional headquarters, fought as entities and, being at headquarters, tended to receive a flow of information from the wireless net to the extent that it was functioning. The officers and NCOs who were with other units by design or the chance of war became involved in the process of fragmentation as casualties and enemy penetration necessitated the amalgamation of remnants. Lacking wireless sets, these frequently received no regular information about the run of the battle. News was passed up and down streets, for example, among the men holding houses or factories but few knew its source. Local chains of command were established but as often broken by the renewal of enemy assaults.

Major Toler spent the remainder of the 17th and the morning of the 18th with the half battalion of the South Staffords – the remainder were to arrive on the 18th – covering part of the landing zones. His squadron was slowly assembling; some had landed 6 miles from the rendezvous. Between taking a turn at digging defences and the night watch, he organized salvage among the damaged gliders. A light, tracked, Bren carrier found in a Hamilcar was put into squadron service.

After breakfast on the 18th, the Staffords commanding officer, Lieutenant-Colonel McCardie, told Major Toler that General Urquhart had been captured (actually, he was isolated by enemy fire in Arnhem, from which he escaped) and that Brigadier Hicks, the brigade commander, was acting as divisional commander. It was also reported correctly that the railway bridge had been destroyed but the 2nd Battalion, The Parachute Regiment, had secured the north end of Arnhem road bridge. The Staffords were ordered to move forward to support the parachutists in that area.

The morning was sunny, and warm in more than one sense. As Major Toler accompanied the battalion forward, he saw German aircraft strafing the landing zones, and shortly afterwards the column came under sniper fire. German and British dead bodies lay about on pavements and roads as they approached Arnhem. Yet the Dutch people were moving about freely, offering fruit drinks to the soldiers. Major Toler was glad to find a missing flight. He also picked up an unusual party, a Royal Air Force radar section whose glider had force landed south of the Rhine. They had crossed by the civil ferry. But firing intensified as they moved forward; the civil populace took refuge in air raid shelters.

Lieutenant-Colonel McCardie ordered Major Toler to take his party to divisional headquarters. Withdrawing, the glider pilots met other Staffords – the second lift had brought them in that afternoon. But they were not on a safe road; bursts of tracer came down it. Major Toler drew to one side to await daylight.

Staff Sergeant L. Gibbons landed with the second lift and joined the remainder of his flight at the rendezvous. He jotted down diary notes later as night fell:

> . . . we are somewhere on the road to Arnhem; our leading columns have run into trouble and there is a bit of a battle going on a few yards ahead. We are guarding the flanks. Enemy fighter is now overhead; has just strafed the column a few hundred yards down.
>    . . . our leading columns have run into trouble . . .

Field Marshal Model had been engaged since Sunday afternoon in sending reinforcements to II SS Panzer Corps, including self-propelled guns and *PzKw IV* tanks. More of these and 'King Tiger' tanks were to follow from an armoured vehicle park just across the German border. Hitler had ordered the *Luftwaffe* to make extraordinary efforts to attack the British airborne troops and the transports arriving daily to reinforce and sustain them.

By the time 4th Parachute Brigade arrived under Brigadier J.W. Hackett on the Monday afternoon, a considerable German force was in occupation of their objective, the high ground north of Arnhem, supported by strong artillery and mortar fire, backed by a handful of Harzer's tanks. The DZs and LZs were under mortar and small arms fire. In the city the enemy continued to wear down 1st Parachute Brigade. The Air Landing Brigade was at once trying to hold the western sector, hold 4th Brigade's landing sites, and relieve with others 2 Para's positions on the bridge. The aircraft dropping supplies on 18 September received persistent shrapnel and cannon fire from flak detachments which had escaped British bombing by frequent redeployment among houses and woods.

The German striking groups also kept moving, but for a different reason. By concentrating at selected sites they were able to bring overwhelming strength to destroy the British defences in, say, a row of houses, a block of flats, or along a railway embankment, concentrating now at one point, now another. These successes drove in the perimeter. Some 380 glider pilots were involved on the periphery and the support areas immediately in the rear.

They helped to man 6 pounder anti-tank guns as in Sicily and Normandy: '. . . two of us with the bombardier – "Rocky", I never discovered his other name – covered the highway for the remainder of the day. We were told to pull back, so when it was dark we pulled the gun out by hand; a mortar had smashed the jeep.' Elsewhere, when the last rounds had been fired, 'we hid the gun in a garage – I thought some Dutchman's going to be surprised when this is over'. Many were in composite groups: '. . . we joined six from the 3rd Battalion [of the Parachute Regiment] and two from 1 [Battalion]. We stayed in that position all through Wednesday [20 September] and the Thursday afternoon when the Jerries brought up a flame thrower and set fire to the house.'

There were many rumours. 'Lieutenant Smith got a message that the Second Army [XXX Corps] had reached the south side of the river and was attacking across the pontoon bridge with the Poles.' The Poles had arrived on the 21st, diverted from the main Arnhem bridge, but were fighting their own battle to survive south of the river. The pontoon bridge was destroyed and the ferry sunk. 'It was raining on the Saturday [23 September] and there was a lot of shelling that morning. But some REs in position on the other side of the road said we would be relieved that night by the Second Army. But nothing appeared that night and we had to move back as the line was drawn in.'

The glider pilots, being officers and senior NCOs, frequently took command of leaderless groups, none more gallantly than Lieutenant M.D.K. Dauncey, defending the guns of the Air Landing Light Regiment:

. . . On three occasions the enemy overran the sector necessitating a counter-attack. Lieutenant Dauncey, on his own initiative, organised and led each sortie with such determination that the positions were regained with heavy loss to the enemy. Wounded on three occasions [he] refused to be evacuated from the area. On September 24th a more determined attack was made by the enemy using tanks and SP [armoured, self-propelled] guns. Lieutenant Dauncey, whilst leading his men in a further counter-attack was wounded again – losing the sight of one eye. In spite of pain, and handicap of defective vision, he continued . . . recapturing the lost ground. On September 25th . . . [an] enemy SP gun penetrated the positions. Lieutenant Dauncey . . . assaulted the enemy vehicle single handed with Gammon [high explosive] bombs.

Successful in this sortie, Dauncey was wounded for a fourth time and captured. Sergeant R.F. Tilley, working at a casualty collecting post, took charge of the evacuation of wounded, forayed for ammunition to supply those defending the area, and ultimately took command.

Field Marshal Montgomery had expected that 1st Airborne Division would have to hold at Arnhem for two days. General Browning believed that they would hold it for four, even though he judged that they were stretching the carpet 'a bridge too far'. On Sunday 24 September they had been holding for a week.

The delay has been attributed to numerous causes but the prime cause was the failure to deliver two lifts on the first day, and to land on or near to the bridges. It is true that XXX Corps should have been launched earlier and fought through the night to link up with the 101st Division, and that greater attention should have been given to the presence of II SS Panzer Corps, but these omissions simply underline the deficiency of the air plan.

At last, on the second Monday, Major Toler noted,

. . . we hear from Colonel Murray that orders for withdrawal across the river have been given. It is to start at 20.45, up until then Colonel Murray has had the Pegasus divisional Flag ready for when the Second Army arrived. . . . Colonel Murray is wonderful; he very tactfully suggests that if we are getting out tonight we don't want the rest of the Army to think we are tramps and offers to lend me his razor and a minute bit of lather which he has conserved over many shaves. I manage to get the worst off and it is amazing how much better I felt both mentally and physically. . . .

2 Para at the bridge and various others among of the defences had been captured and men made prisoner but no position in or outside the perimeter had surrendered while it had the means

to challenge possession. The survivors drew off quietly that night under cover of the Second Army guns. Some were killed or wounded on the river bank waiting for the assault boats brought over to collect them, some drowned after boats were hit. Lieutenant-Colonel Murray commanded what remained of 4th Parachute Brigade after Brigadier Hackett was wounded, together with others in the vicinity. Glider pilots acted as guides on the evacuation route used by this force to the north bank of the Rhine.

About one quarter of 1st Airborne Division was recovered eight days after Market began. The Glider Pilot Regiment had lost 23 officers and 124 NCOs killed. A further 31 officers and 124 NCOs had been wounded, some of whom were in company with the 313 unwounded pilots captured, in all, 615.

With their British and American comrades, they had clawed a huge corridor in the enemy defences; and if this had fallen short at the last waterway it was not for want of trying. A few days later, as Major-General Urquhart reflected on the events of Operation Market, he wrote to Colonel Chatterton,

On behalf of the 1st Airborne Division I should like to thank you, Lieutenant-Colonels Murray and Place, and all the Glider Pilots who took part in our operations near Arnhem.

The glider-borne elements of the Division made possible the best landing that has ever been achieved to date. The skill of the pilots was quite first class, and all ranks appreciated the benefit of the good start given by the pilots to the operation.

Very early in the 9 days of the battle it became more and more apparent that we had to call upon the Glider Pilots to the full. They played all kinds of parts, but everything they were asked to do they did whole-heartedly.

I am afraid your losses were rather heavy, but I think that those who became casualties and did not return with the Division will have the satisfaction of knowing that their efforts contributed to the results achieved. . . .

CHAPTER ELEVEN

# Getting it Right

None of the British or American armies crossed the Rhine in 1944, though the Americans attacked expensively into the German marches in November. In the east the Russians were held on the Oder. Thus the war was not brought to an end in Europe in that year.

The optimists in the west were misled by the rapid clearance of France and the liberation of Brussels between the end of July and the first week of September. For a time it had seemed that nothing would stop the onrush of the armies. General Eisenhower was among those who underestimated Hitler's power to command obedience and the capacity of his military apparatus to respond. In December, a German offensive employing thirty-four divisions opened in the Ardennes, striking towards Antwerp.

Though this great sortie failed, it obliged the Allies to draw heavily on their reserves. The 6th Airborne Division, for example, was brought from England to reinforce the line. It also prompted a fresh look by the western Allies at their strategy for 1945.

Eisenhower believed that 'one more great campaign, aggressively conducted on a broad front' would bring victory to his forces. There were British doubts as to the advisability of the broad front concept. Some senior members of his staff advised that the offensive should wait until the spring when better weather would enhance the prospects for the reinforced armies and air forces. But he knew that eighty-five divisions and the material to support them would be in his hand by February. The Germans had been thrown into disarray by their defeat in the Ardennes and he had no intention of offering them time to recover. His only concession as regards frontage was to ensure that his American commanders would concentrate on thrusts of opportunity rather than broadly at a venture.

On this reckoning the offensive was renewed in February. The principal drive into Germany would be made by 21 Army Group, including the United States Ninth Army: 'from the lower Rhine north of the Ruhr to be followed up by a great thrust to join up with the Russians'. Bradley's Army Group would launch a complementary attack north east to Kassel. General J.L. Devers' 6 Army Group would make a subsidiary attack into southern Germany. These instructions were issued in January 1945.

The first stage in all sectors was to clear the west bank of the Rhine to secure crossing places. The 1st Canadian Army with XXX Corps began this operation on 8 February, a move inhibited by a thaw and flood waters. On their right the Ninth Army was checked by the opening of the Roer dams which further raised the river levels along the northern front. But the Americans prepared with exemplary care to overcome this obstacle and crossed it by surprise on 23 February. British and Americans north, centre and south thrust irresistibly along the western bank of the Rhine. On 7 March the United States 9th Armoured Division seized the only crossing still standing on this great river, the railway bridge at Remagen, 10 miles south of Bonn. The bridge-head was temporarily contained by the enemy, but it was plain that the German line was frail, the reserves behind it scant. While the Americans sought to exploit their successes, Field Marshal Montgomery continued with his plan to cross and break away to the east from the broad expanse of the lower Rhine. This included a major airborne assault.

The British capacity to contribute to fresh airborne operations had been considerably reduced by the losses at Arnhem. This was due not so much to the reduction of 1st Airborne Division to cadre strength but to the loss of glider pilots. The Army planning staffs assumed that two or more major launches lay ahead in the final campaign in north-west Europe with a month between each. Beyond these, perhaps overlapping in time, offensive plans in the Far East comprehended airborne operations. Immediately, the numbers of pilots were inadequate for a single divisional operation in Germany. Then, while it was understood that pilots would be selected from imperial and Indian Army units in the sub-continent, instructors and cadres would be required from Britain to bring them to readiness. If this requirement was met, the deficit in pilots at home would be even greater. By coincidence, War Office and Air Ministry policies were moving to resolve the issue.

During July 1944 the Air Ministry had raised at a joint meeting with the War Office the idea of seconding Royal Air Force pilots to the Glider Pilot Regiment for duty as First Pilots. The Director-General of Training (Air) had pointed out that 1,500 officers and airmen were employed solely for the benefit of the Army in the EFTS and the Glider Training Schools while there was a rising surplus of RAF aircrew. At the same time, as a matter of general manpower policy, 10,000 RAF tradesmen were being compulsorily transferred to the Army to meet its deficiencies in many arms. He proposed that both services would benefit by RAF secondment and the closure of the Army glider pilots' training organization.

As the meeting progressed, however, the balance of argument moved against the idea: differences in flying pay between Army and RAF were cited, the unsatisfactory nature of a hybrid force, the difficulties of persuading RAF pilots to accept secondment. Besides, the loss of Army glider pilots on Neptune had been lower than expected, and the Army expected to find the numbers required to enter flying training of 135 a month, the number needed to ensure 50–60 qualifying. Some of the 10,000 airmen being transferred would probably volunteer for the Glider Pilot Regiment. It was decided to let arrangements stand for two months when they would meet again to review the matter.

Passing this information to the Vice-Chief of the Air Staff on 31 July, Air Vice-Marshal Douglas Colyer, who had chaired the meeting as Assistant Chief for Personnel, mentioned a consideration omitted from the discussion:

> . . . There are also several difficulties in regard to the proposal that RAF pilots should be used for this work, the main ones being that this would eventually lead to the majority of the glider pilots being airmen and thus a gradual wasting away of the glider pilot regiment of which the Army are justly proud and of which, incidentally, the CIGS is Colonel-in-Chief [actually, Colonel-Commandant].

On 31 August 1944 the Royal Air Force met by themselves preparatory to the inter-service review. They discussed short- and long-term policy, for none then knew how long the war in the two hemispheres would continue. In the short term, the meeting,

. . . considered an immediate requirement for 110 Royal Air Force crews for operations planned for the Indian theatre during the early part of 1945. . . . If approved, the Army expected to provide 1,000 glider pilots (the maximum figure they could achieve) and the balance was to be made up by 220 Royal Air Force pilots (110 crews) with some additional help from the Americans. . . . the training of 110 RAF crews at short notice could only be undertaken at the expense of Army Glider pilot training.

In the long term,

. . . The view of the meeting was that the primary role of a glider pilot was to fly a glider and that his participation in the land battle was unnecessary. It was therefore felt that the higher efficiency of RAF glider pilots combined with the great advantage of having an RAF glider pilot/tug-pilot team outweighed the known objection of the War Office to the disbandment of the Glider Pilot Regiment.

The minutes of this meeting manifest the reappearance of an old prejudice, a rooted opinion: if the vehicle is a flying machine, the Royal Air Force alone must drive it. The resuscitation was probably encouraged by an impression rising in the service that it was being run down for the benefit of the Army. Resentment was inevitably strongest among regular officers, in particular, senior officers. It found expression even in 38 Group just after Air Vice-Marshal Hollinghurst relinquished command. A party of glider pilots ferrying Horsas to the Mediterranean in October under Major Lyne were excluded from aircrew briefing and neglected administratively, a severe if fortunately exceptional departure from the goodwill long since established between the regiment and Royal Air Force at station level.

On 29 September the Air Ministry proposed formally that, 'the intake of Army personnel for glider training should cease at the earliest date convenient to the Army Council. . . . [Royal Air Force] pilots would be employed in this capacity for not less than 12 months or more than 18 months'. No challenge was offered to the use of Army pilots in the longer term; the expectation that RAF glider pilots would predominate within the regiment eventually and thus bring about its demise was understandably not mentioned. For the time being it was true to say: 'these proposals are put forward by the [Air] Council because of the urgent need for economy in trained manpower both now and during the Japanese war phase and . . . they are without prejudice to any question of post-war policy for the provision of glider pilots'.

This letter reached the War Office five days after the survivors of 1st Airborne Division were recovered across the Rhine into Allied territory. The War Office was primed as to the losses in the Glider Pilot Regiment and the immediate consequences. Colonel Chatterton informed Major-General Crawford, Director of Air, that it was essential to accept Royal Air Force manning within his organization, and that, by bearing individuals, as distinct from RAF sub-units, on his establishment he would be able to maintain the regimental character of his units.

Responding on 30 October the War Office reminded the Air Ministry that it required glider pilots to be able to operate equally as soldiers. That said,

. . . it is therefore considered that the RAF pilots should be attached to the Glider Pilot Regiment to fill vacancies in the establishment of the Army glider pilot units. . . .

Arrangements have already been made, in connection with the scheme for the immediate training of RAF pilots to meet urgent operational requirements, for a temporary cessation of the intake of Army personnel for glider training. It is understood that arrangements are also in hand for those [Army volunteers] who have reached a certain stage in training to receive further instruction [in operational squadrons] so as to be enable them to attain the standard necessary for them to take part in operations. The remainder, comprising those who have either not yet started or completed the course in Elementary Flying Training School, will for the time being continue with their military training, but I am to say that the Army Council consider it essential that these personnel should, at the earliest time possible, be brought forward to complete their flying training.

By this means the Army conveyed the view that they were not prepared to relinquish primacy of role in the Glider Pilot Regiment.

As plans developed for an airborne assault across the Rhine, the Royal Air Force discovered that its requirement for aircrew was greater than reckoned at the end of 1944. In any case the demand for glider pilots in South East Asia was less urgent than previously advised. The Air Ministry proposed to contribute 534 crews to a total of 1,030 by April or May 1945, the remainder to be provided by the Army. While this would limit the capability to a single British airborne division, it would be possible, if a critical need arose at short notice, to mount a second divisional assault, by lowering the overall standard required of glider pilots. As an immediate measure, with the reduction of demand for basic flying training, one of the glider conversion units should be converted to refresher training. With some reservations, the War Office accepted this policy.

They accepted because they were confident that their own senior commanders were determined to avoid in future the prime errors of Operation Market. Landings would be made on or adjacent to principal objectives. There must be sufficient aircraft to carry in one lift the forces required to accomplish their tasks. With this the commanders of 38 Group (Air Vice-Marshal J.R. Scarlett-Streatfield) and 46 Group (Air Commodore Laurence Darvell) concurred.

Detailed planning for the airborne operation across the Rhine, codename 'Varsity', began early in February 1945. The force selected to perform it was the XVIII Airborne Corps under Major-General Matthew B. Ridgway who had commanded the 82nd Airborne Division in Normandy. His deputy was Major-General Gale, formerly commander of the 6th. It comprised two divisions: the 6th and the 17th, British and American respectively.

The 6th returned to the United Kingdom in January from the Ardennes battle, took ten days leave (they had been in the line over Christmas) and entered a brisk training programme on return to their camps on Salisbury Plain, culminating in several exercises involving massed descents. The 17th, unfledged in airborne operations, had become well acquainted with the battlefield on the German frontier, from which they did not emerge until February, when they were concentrated in primitive camps in France.

Corps and divisional general officers together with the British and American brigade commanders attended a planning exercise in England to consider the operational situations which might arise following the landings and the measures they would take to deal with them.

Major-General E.L. Bols now commanded 6th Airborne Division, Major-General W.M. Miley the 17th. Their task collectively was

. . . to disrupt the hostile defence of the Rhine in the Wesel sector by the seizure of key terrain, by airborne attack, in order to deepen rapidly the bridgehead to be seized by an assault crossing of the Rhine by British ground forces, and facilitate the further offensive operations of Second Army.

This statement was not a model of plain language but the details emerged subsequently as to their precise objectives in the overall plan.

First, Field Marshal Montgomery rightly regarded the Rhine crossing as a preliminary, though potentially hazardous, step to breaking into the heart of the Ruhr and advancing thereafter to meet the Russian armies approaching from the east. The river was to be crossed on the night of 23/24 March by divisions of the British Second Army on the left and the United States Ninth on the right between Rees and Rheinberg. They would be landing on the flat and open ground of the Rhine plain, waterlogged through much of the winter but now drying. It was essential to expand into this with all speed, clearing the east bank to secure bridging sites and securing the communications centre of Wesel for the subsequent break out. They could not secure strategic surprise; the Germans were well aware that a crossing was impending. But there was scope for tactical surprise in time and location of the landing from amphibious craft. One area offered the enemy the ground for a grand redoubt, from which artillery, mortar, and anti-tank fire might be directed for some time, the high ground of the Diersfordter Wald north of Wesel. Moreover, it fronted the Issel, no mean stream; it was then 50 yd in width and too deep for a tank to wade, a potential check line to those advancing from the Rhine to clear the plain. It was known that the German 84th Division was sited in this area, backed by the Karst Anti-Air Landing Division.

The 15th (Scottish) Division had orders to make the crossing opposite the Diersfordter Wald early on 24 March. The 1st Commando Brigade was to infiltrate across the river to Wesel during the same night. XVIII Airborne Corps would pass over the former in daylight, seize the Diersfordter Wald, the town of Hamminkeln, and selected bridges over the Issel. At the earliest moment, elements of 6 Guards Tank Brigade would come forward to support the airborne corps by D plus 1 day, 25 March, the remainder of the brigade following as ferry options permitted. Although the artillery of Second Army would cease firing in this sector while the landings were in progress, strong support would be available to the corps immediately thereafter.

The air plan comprehended a launching from East Anglian airfields for 6th Airborne Division and former German airfields round Paris and Amiens for the 17th. The two streams were to converge over Wavre, immediately south east of Brussels, and drop their loads simultaneously. Because the parachute troops descended more quickly than the gliders, it was decided that they would drop first. Lieutenant-General Brereton left the choice of dropping zones and landing zones to divisional and brigade commanders in consultation with 38 Group and Colonel Chatterton. The latter argued successfully for a policy of tactical landing; that is, landing on or beside tactical objectives.

At the beginning of March, General Gale discussed the zones selected during a visit to Regimental Headquarters, concluding, 'I hope we've taken in all the lessons of the past, George. I want to get it right this time'.

On the 17th, 6th Airborne Division moved to East Anglia where their temporary accommodation was sealed for briefing. This placed them close to the launching airfields. The glider pilots, organized in seven squadrons under Lieutenant-Colonel Iain Murray with 1 Wing headquarters, were in position on the airfields with the tug aircraft of 38 and 46 Groups, Stirlings, Halifaxes, and C–47s.

It was Lieutenant-Colonel Murray's fourth operation. On this occasion, however, his wing was manned as much by Royal Air Force officers and NCOs as his own regiment. The RAF had spent many hours learning the soldier's trades of weapon handling and fieldcraft, the use of maps to a scale of 1-inch to the mile, and hard physical exercise. The officers had attended tactical courses, the most successful of which was run by the Oxford University Senior Training Corps staff over ten weeks. In combination with foot and arms drill, some had developed 'as budding Napoleons, keener than the Army types', one flight sergeant complained. A flight-lieutenant discovered that his former easygoing colleague, a squadron-leader, had become a 'ferocious' commander of his glider pilot squadron.

Even so, neither the Glider Pilot Regiment nor the Royal Air Force observed the full discipline of sealed camps. A number of aircrew slipped out during the evenings of waiting to see relatives or friends, though none breached security by word or deed because they remained unbriefed until a relatively late hour, 22 March. This was due to the late arrival of 46 Group from other transport commitments, and an absence of aids, in particular vertical and oblique air photographs showing the whole landing zone. Those available were close shots of approaches, welcome but providing less than an adequate picture. Several stations also lacked the scale models of the ground which appear to have been appropriated by others under briefing. Air and ground maps supplied essential information but failed to supply a direct visual image of the target area.

The area of operations was not unknown to some members of the division; it had been studied for a potential operation towards the end of 1944, but the majority of the officers and men in 6th Airborne were looking at ground disclosed in their briefing sessions from 18 March for the first time. With few exceptions, commanding officers' orders were given to their units *en masse*. On the instructions of Supreme Headquarters, the two Royal Air Force group commanders had raised the number of tugs to 440 by pressing into operations aircraft and aircrew in the training schools, by raiding maintenance units, and severely reducing the number of reserve crews.

Flight-Lieutenant D.J. Richards recalled that,

We were woken at 2.30 or 3 [on 24 March] for breakfast, final briefing and loading checks and we were out by the marshalled gliders well before 5 a.m.. Take-off was in semi-darkness about 6 a.m. on a cold and completely windless morning, and the 16,000-lbs of loaded Horsa took a long run – indeed contrary to the normal practice the Dakota became airborne first and we had to struggle to avoid her slipstream and an involuntary and premature positioning in the low tow position, which was normally only adopted over 500 feet. . . .

Captain Boucher-Giles remembered,

. . . a thrill of excitement as we swept over Brighton in the van of what must have been a most impressive spectacle and looked down at the crowds who had assembled to stare at us. The weather was perfect for flying and we did the whole of the journey in the low tow position (the best petrol saver for the tug) so that the pilots could see the black form of the bomber like a gigantic crow in the perspex window just above the level of our heads. There was no rough air, and as we were in front [of the stream] we fouled no one else's slipstream. . . . It was only after we had flown quite low over the roofs of Brussels and had left the field of Waterloo behind us that we began to join up with other tug and glider formations. . . .

'P' hour, a term recently adopted to denote the departure of the first parachutist from his aircraft, was at 10.00 on that morning of 24 March 1945. Ninety minutes before that the aircraft of the two divisions converged as planned over Belgium. The following had taken off successfully:

*from England with 6th Airborne Division*

| | | |
|---|---|---|
| 243 C–47s of the US 52nd Wing | – | carrying all the parachutists |
| 319 Stirlings and Halifaxes of 38 Group | – | towing 271 Horsas 48 Hamilcars |
| 120 C–47s of 46 Group | | towing 120 Horsas |
| *Total* | – | 1,123 aircraft and gliders |

*from France with 7th Airborne Division*

| | | |
|---|---|---|
| 303 C–47s} US 52 72 C–46s} and 53 | – | carrying parachutists |
| 610 C–47s} Wings | – | towing 916 Wacos (592 in double tow) |
| *Total* | – | 953 aircraft and gliders |

6th Airborne Division was approaching to clear the northern half of the Diersfordter Wald, to capture Hamminkeln and the two road bridges across the Issel. Now travelling in parallel in the air, the 17th was to clear the southern half and the Issel crossings in its sector. Ground radar and visual markers indicated the separation line between the streams which was perfectly observed in navigation. A greater problem was the adjustment of flow in relation to cruising speeds. The British Dakota tugs were travelling at 115 mph, the Stirlings and Halifaxes at 145 mph. In the American stream, the seventy C–46 Curtis Commandos, larger and more powerful than the C–47s, were obliged to circle to maintain their place. Given these circumstances, it is not surprising that the head of the column reached the dropping and landing zones slightly outside the schedule, some eight or nine minutes ahead of time. Artillery and fighter ground strikes on these sites were thus stopped before they had completed their final programmes.

Those in the leading waves could see the Rhine clearly despite a smoke haze, and were encouraged to observe considerable friendly activity on the east bank. The 51st (Highland)

Horsas which landed on enemy positions north of Wesel, 24 March 1945 (*Museum of Army Flying*)

Division had crossed at 21.00 on the night of 23 March at Rees on the left, the 15th (Scottish) at 02.00 with the American 24th on their right. The Commandos had slipped across to enter Wesel. All had been supported by prolonged artillery fire, and air attacks.

The parachutists jumped, the glider pilots made ready to cast off. Of 439 combinations successfully launched in England, 404 had arrived over the assault area. Four had fallen out rapidly due to unserviceability or broken tow ropes. Similar difficulties carried away ten more close to the coast. Over the sea, two gliders ditched but passengers and crews were rescued by RAF launches. Engine failures, broken tow ropes, and other causes including the break-up of one Horsa, subtracted a further nineteen.

Below them lay their six LZs: 'A', 'B', 'O', 'P', 'R', and 'U'. Winds were light: under 10 mph from the south-south-east. Visibility was poor; the remnant of the smoke fired earlier to obscure daylight crossings of the Rhine, smoke from the artillery fire of both sides, burning buildings, and enemy flak, combined to screen the view from 2,500 ft. Fire from the latter began to hit tugs and gliders as they parted.

It was later to be suggested that the early arrival of the aircraft stream had prevented the final destruction of enemy flak sites. This stemmed from the quaint idea prevalent among the supporting forces that shellfire and air strikes could destroy every weapon in the array. The fact was that gun and aircraft systems were incapable of hitting small targets with perfect accuracy. Hence, while widespread damage had been done to the 84th Infantry Division on and around the Diersfordter Wald, they still had fighting power.

Smoke haze, fire and, probably, the inadequate provision of air photographs for the briefing,

Railway station at Hamminkeln used by Major P. Jackson as his squadron headquarters, afternoon of 24 March 1945, Operation Varsity (*Trustees of the Imperial War Museum, London, BU 2404*)

contributed to landing errors. 'I was due to land on [LZ] U but ended up in the middle of R', and '. . . although I caught a glimpse of my LZ [R], I found when I got down we were with the Americans on N'; these were typical comments of those who went astray. Some crash-landed inside and outside the zones having been damaged by fire on the descent. One, out of control, struck the commanding officer of the 8th Battalion, the Parachute Regiment, as he was directing an attack, but happily this robust officer suffered only concussion and severe bruising.

These were no more than the mischances of joining battle. Over two-thirds of the crews reached their correct landing zones, three-quarters were within 500 yd of it. Numerous landings were precisely on target, including those of two *coup de main* parties, one each from the 52nd and the Royal Ulster Rifles, which captured the Issel bridges.

In the accomplishment, the glider pilots again won high praise from their passengers. 'My admiration for their skill is beyond words,' was the comment of an officer of the Royal Ulster Rifles during a lecture on the operation in the following year. The men and freight, including quantities of motor fuel in some of the Hamilcars, delivered without loss is the more commendable because 284 gliders were hit by flak in descending though, fortunately, only 26 pilots were killed or wounded in the air, and 7 of the tug pilots.

As in previous operations, the glider pilots were soon drawn into the cut and thrust of the battle. The collection process was more rapid, however, than on former occasions. Whether led by Army or Royal Air Force officers, squadrons performed many functions in holding ground, in mounting or reinforcing several counter-attacks, and in the gathering of prisoners.

Still, when the link with the Second Army was completed and the widespread fighting of the first forty-eight hours had abated, Lieutenant-Colonel Chatterton ordered Lieutenant-Colonel Murray to withdraw through an established evacuation chain. The regiment had lost 38 killed and 77 wounded; 135 were missing. This was about a quarter of the flying strength.

On 29 March Major-General Gale sent a message to Field Marshal Sir Alan Brooke, their Colonel-Commandant.

Feel sure you would like to know that the Glider Pilot Regiment has done magnificent work for 6 Airborne Division. Their skill and bravery are spoken of by all.

Meeting Lieutenant-Colonel Chatterton a day or so later, he said, 'Well, we did get it right; and your boys got it right as much as anybody. We do know now how to put gliders down smack on the target. We can expect to do that every time in future.'

As it happened, however, they had just completed the final air landing operation in a short and distinguished period of service.

# Gunners in the Air

## II – 'The Air OP . . . has become a necessary part of gunnery'

# CHAPTER TWELVE

# 651 Squadron Takes Off

The formation of 651 Squadron and 1424 Flight in August 1941 was not quite the triumph some members of the Royal Artillery believed. For while it was true that the former ostensibly disposed an Air Observation Post for use within the field forces of the Army, it lacked an operational aircraft and was still subject to objections and obstructions by the Royal Air Force.

At the end of the year the position was this. The Army had stipulated a requirement for one squadron for each corps and field army headquarters, a total of twelve squadrons, exclusive of others to be formed by the Canadians for their own needs. The Royal Air Force had agreed to three and, as the burden of manning fell principally upon their resources, no more would be formed until and unless they made the necessary provisions.

On the other hand, the Air Ministry was helpful in the development and supply of aircraft, pursuing Major Bazeley's requests readily with the Ministry of Aircraft Production. A worthy pioneer in the whole scheme, he nonetheless delayed the final adoption of an adequate aircraft by pursuing an ideal model. The reported virtues of the Stinson 074, renamed the Vigilant I, charmed him.

Forty-eight Stinsons had been ordered to equip 651, 652 and 653 Squadrons with sixteen aircraft apiece as they completed formation, respectively on 1 March, 1 May, and 1 July 1942, when the training of Royal Artillery pilots to fly them would have been completed. It was probably fortunate that the first ten delivered had an unfortunate accident. When the merchantman carrying them from the United States unloaded at Liverpool it was discovered that, lying under 300 tons of cheese during a rough passage, five had been crushed beyond recovery. One hundred had been ordered, ten had been supplied, five reached the purchaser after fourteen months of waiting, with one reputedly following in another vessel. The Ministry of Aircraft Production was unable to obtain any date for further deliveries from the manufacturers, and later admitted the possibility that it had earlier cancelled the full order in error. For one reason or another, if the British Army had waited for the Stinson, they would have lacked an AOP capability throughout the war.

It could wait no longer. Hoping ultimately for the supply of Stinsons, it was accepted by Major Bazeley that they must introduce the modified Taylorcraft Model D.

When this decision was taken in March 1942, 651 Squadron had fifteen, which were in the process of being uprated from a 55 Lycoming to a 90 hp Blackburn Cirrus engine. This improvement went some way to reducing the take-off distance but increased the load carrying potential – the payload – by only 40 lb to a maximum of 530. The War Office asked for a 100 hp engine to be fitted to the production order of one hundred aircraft. But orders for the 90 hp engines had been made and associated specifications agreed. To avoid further delay in production, the latter had to be accepted for the time being.

Meanwhile, General Sir Alan Brooke, having assumed his appointment as CIGS, had begun to press for the formation of three more squadrons as a step towards the final figure of twelve. Unexpectedly, even before the chiefs met, the War Office discovered that the whole case had been conceded. In a paper addressing the whole question of Royal Air Force support for the Army on 1 April, the Chief of the Air Staff remarked, 'The Air Ministry have no comments on the War Office proposals for Air Observation Post Squadrons. The only difficulty is the supply of aircraft'.

The Royal Air Force no longer regarded the operation of the air observation posts as 'a pointless exercise . . . an expensive waste of time'. Air Marshal Sir Arthur Barrett, AOC-in-C Army Cooperation Command, placed this beyond doubt at a meeting called to discuss the organization, administration and equipment of AOP units on 25 April 1942.

> . . . The AOC-in-C went on to remark that, for his own part, he did not at first think that the AOP was a practical proposition but from what he had seen during the early part of the year he considered that it could do the job and, therefore, made a strong recommendation that it should be established. He wished therefore to dispose of the idea that the RAF as a body were in any way against the AOP concept.

By conviction and zeal, by persistence, by the adroit use of allies, and a wide knowledge of light aircraft, Major Bazeley had won his case against considerable odds. But this did not satisfy him. The flow of aircraft from Taylorcraft's workshops was inadequate, his fertile mind was continually conceiving improvements and modifications to the model under construction, and he was not prepared to abandon the search for a completely different basic model – the Miles 38/28 caught his attention in this respect; and the autogiro briefly showed its rotors again.

It was true that the Taylorcraft factory lacked sufficient design and production expertise, a deficiency recognized in common by the senior management of the company and the Ministry of Aircraft Production. The latter gave constructive advice on changes to be effected and combed through the industry to pick up skilled men to fill essential posts. But finding experienced managers and craftsmen took time; British aircraft manufacture was expanding rapidly from a very limited base to meet a huge number of demands.

These difficulties were exacerbated by the flow of modifications proposed by Major Bazeley. The fact that the Taylorcraft was, in his view, no more than an interim vehicle, did not suggest to him that multiple changes of specification, with all that involved by way of evaluation, checks for airworthiness, and procurement of materials, must delay production overall. These pursuits vexed some of his allies, including Major-General Lund, chief gunner in the Home Forces, but he continued to inspire their assistance in the search for a more suitable aircraft.

The search led nowhere. Even the Stinson was to prove unsuitable in trials. Production of the Taylorcraft was beginning, and to encourage its acceptance it received a British name in March, the 'Auster', Middle English for 'a southerly wind'. On 21 July 1942 the first production model reached 651 Squadron from intensive flying tests, the Auster Mark I. Seven more followed during the next few weeks, in the nick of time: at the end of August Major Bazeley was ordered to take the two equipped flights of his squadron to North Africa. On the basis that the aircraft would soon be under fire, Royal Air Force Army Cooperation Command found some armour plate which was fitted to the pilots' seats on a makeshift basis known to the service as a 'lash up'. Thus one of the outstanding Bazeley modifications was satisfied. It would soon be apparent whether it was worth its weight.

Operation 'Torch' opened on 7 November 1942. Under General Eisenhower's supreme command, ground and air forces were to land in French North Africa, to exploit eastwards rapidly, pinching out the enemy's airfields and ports in Tunisia, finally to provide a backstop for the drive westward by the British Eighth Army. Morocco and Algeria had been chosen for the landings. The readiness of the resident Vichy French forces to cooperate with the Allies was doubtful, but at least these colonies contained neither German nor Italian forces. Tunisia was occupied by Axis garrisons operating the line of communication to Tripolitania under the protection of strong air defences based locally and in Sicily.

The question was whether the key points in Tunisia could be taken rapidly by *coup de main*. To do this, the leading elements of Lieutenant-General Sir Kenneth Anderson's First Army would have to travel 500 miles to secure the Tunisian airfields and ports against entry by German reinforcements. Two task forces were put ashore at Algiers to dash eastwards: 'Blade Force', an armoured regimental group; and the 1st Parachute Brigade. These were to be followed as rapidly as possible by the greater part of the 78th Infantry and 6th Armoured Divisions.

Day and night fighters, and fighter bombers, were to land rapidly to provide for the advancing ground forces.

The task forces, supplemented by commando landings, were launched on 15 November. As many units of the 78th as had come ashore by that date were sent after them. Hard driving and marching carried them to the edge of success, but the Germans were just strong enough to hold them short of Mateur, Djedeida, and Medjez el Bab at the end of the month. The leading element was then only 30 miles from Tunis.

The winter rains began. Dry stream beds filled, the baked earth in the fields became mud. Cross-country movement became difficult. As the main bodies of either side hastened forward, the general line extended southwards, the First Army's British and American divisions confronted the Germans and Italians of the Fifth Panzer Army. On extended supply lines, the Allies struggled to extend their positions and, failing, fought to retain them until spring weather favoured further offensive action.

In the last week of November 1942 aircraft of 651 Squadron reached the Front as it formed close to Tunis. After a quick reconnaissance of potential landing sites and establishment of the squadron base the shop opened and attracted many customers. On the 25th, pilots were involved in the attack to capture the road junction and bridge at Medjez el Bab and, when this was driven back, directed fire onto the German supporting batteries. A week later the AOPs were drawn into a hot battle at Bou Arada as the German counter-attacks persisted. In a matter of days, the squadron engaged, somewhat at its own discretion, in trouble shooting across the volatile front.

The arrival of Lieutenant-General Sir Charles Allfrey with his V Corps headquarters brought them under close control, a change not immediately welcomed. The corps embraced all British forces in northern Tunisia. Its artillery organization assumed responsibility for all gunner regiments and independent batteries, and provided the control system whereby fire from all of them could be concentrated on any target within range. For while divisional field artillery gave first priority to supporting its own infantry and tanks, its guns were required to shoot on other fronts when occasion demanded. Medium and, when available, heavy batteries were controlled directly by the corps.

No. 651 Squadron was now directly subordinated to V Corps, which allotted its aircraft on a contingency basis. Lacking experience of their capabilities, the artillery commander and his staff were anxious for the safety of the pilots. Restrictions were placed upon their movements in the air above the battleline. They were to keep 1,000 yd or more behind the forward positions of infantry. They were not to fly above 600 ft – a measure of protection against attack by enemy aircraft. Individual sorties were to be confined to twenty minutes.

These constraints were well considered. Working previously with 78th Infantry Division, the squadron had been perhaps too bold in its inceptory response to the calls on its services. On several occasions the Austers had been well in front of the infantry lines or day tank positions in searching out enemy battery locations and were lucky not to have become targets for ground fire, not least because they stayed too long in view. Within the limits of fuel, time had not seemed to matter much. Equally the products of their work had been so valuable that they had received encouragement from ground formations to operate freely. Aside from the direction of artillery fire, pilots sent back incidental but valuable information to divisional headquarters, including the locations of friend and foe. Because operations were spread across scrub covered mountains, ground dispositions were sometimes in question. In late November, for example, an AOP report established the precise location of two British infantry companies previously believed by the divisional staff to be elsewhere.

This opening phase with 78th Division ended on 7 December 1942. It had included the provision of liaison sorties, a flying 'taxi' service of very considerable value in view of the stretched communications and the collapse of all but metalled roads.

In January, V Corps headquarters became less protective of 651 Squadron. For one thing, a good deal of their flying was again in close cooperation with the divisions – 78th and 6th Armoured – and the flow of general information they supplied was as much appreciated by the corps operations and intelligence staffs as those at lower headquarters. The number of local tactical reconnaissance sorties increased, and occasional evidence suggesting that a pilot had flown above a thousand feet or across the contact line in the identification of targets tended to be ignored. However, bids for Auster 'taxis' threatened to divert the aircraft from their intended roles. Corps headquarters limited this service.

Two months of battle transformed the squadron. The greatest change involved the binding of its members, an experience they shared with the many members of First Army and the Royal Air Force entering battle for the first time in those winter months. But in 651 Squadron the men concerned wore two uniforms. Pilots and supporting gunner drivers and signallers wore khaki, the squadron adjutant, aircraft engineer and technicians wore blue, with all that implied in difference of outlook on formation. A report of these times noted,

When we first formed the Squadron, and during the early months of training in England, it was very hard to explain to the airman just what we were trying to do. He seldom saw the [practice] shells fall or heard our orders over the R/T [radio telephone]. It was very hard for him to realise 'what it was all in aid of'. Many asked to be posted back to 'a proper squadron, sir, with proper aeroplanes!' By jockeying them along we persuaded them to give it a trial and they came overseas with us.

They were too polite to say they knew it would not work but it was easy to see what they thought. After three weeks in action their attitude was completely different. They had begun to see that their pilots were producing the goods, and they also realised that they could not do this without their help. But what really 'got' them was the fact that they were the most advanced R.A.F., that they were in real earnest soldiers and airmen in one. They had to fight as soldiers and maintain their aircraft as airmen, and their pride was terrific. Their brothers on an airfield just did not know what war was; they and only they were the 'real boys'. That our first two Immediate Awards were an MC for a pilot and an MM (an Army decoration) for an airman put the final seal on a wonderful team spirit, and their morale was sky high. . . .

Mobilized with two flights, further Austers arrived to fill out the third. During Torch, these three, A, B, and C, were able to operate independently as required and, similarly, any one of the four sections within a flight, a section comprising one Auster with the pilot-observer, one 3 ton truck with a driver who also operated the ground radio, a fitter, a rigger, and 100 gallons of aircraft fuel and a selection of spare parts, and one motor cycle with one despatch rider.

When detached, both flight and section needed support, chiefly the supply of fuel, rations, spares, mail and, more occasionally, the replacement of an aircraft or pilot. The flight commander was available as an immediate, temporary replacement pilot in an emergency, but squadron headquarters contained four aircraft and two pilots as first reserves aside from the squadron commander and his second in command, the 'squadron captain'. It also possessed a mobile maintenance party and a workshop manned exclusively by 'tiffys' – RAF slang for artificers – in a servicing flight. The section detachment worked principally with an artillery regiment using an airstrip as close to its batteries as possible.

Major Bazeley was recalled at the end of January to pass on his experiences. He reported his ideas as to the location of squadron headquarters in relation to his aircraft deployment and the overall artillery commander. He had been able to visit flights and sections frequently, using one of the reserve aircraft. Behind him he had been served by mobile and static RAF workshops for recovery and major repairs. He was succeeded by one of his flight commanders, Major R.W.V. Neathercoat.

On balance, 651 Squadron came to accept the restriction of twenty minutes for a sortie; it was reckoned that a pilot was able to conduct a shoot in about eight minutes providing that the guns responded to his instructions without delay. This rule of engagment was quickly adopted by the First Army artillery including the American elements. Air defence and ground artillery observers also came to recognize the need to warn the airborne AOP when enemy aircraft approached.

In January 1943, for example, a pilot of C Flight was involved in a second battle at Bou Arada. The village was then on the boundary between V Corps and the French (and American) XIX Corps. He reported,

While at 600 feet I received the warning 'Bandits', with the direction from which they were coming. I turned and saw about a dozen Ju. 87 dive bombers and several escorting Me. 109s at about 1,500–2,000 feet, coming towards me. I dived to ground level and flew evasively over low, dark wooded hills which I had previously chosen as best suiting the aircraft's camouflage. . . . I waited till I saw the bombs fall and after giving time for the raiders to clear off, returned to the landing ground. . . .

First Army signalled to the War Office, 'Air OP an unquestionable success despite adverse conditions and local air inferiority'. The only complaint was that there were too few of them. The Eighth Army, which had previously asked for an air observation element to complement its considerable artillery resources, represented its case again in January 1943. First Army had already asked for a second squadron to support IX Corps, about to take the field. In the latter connection, No. 654 Squadron was under embarkation orders for the Mediterranean.

Formed up under Major T.J.C. Willett RA on 15 July 1942, the squadron was, with 652 and 653, equipped with Tiger Moths while awaiting Austers. Two Mark Is arrived in November for training, but as a result of being selected for operations, 654 received the first Auster IIIs in January, powered by the 122 HP Gypsy Major I engine. The airframe had been strengthened and modified to take the larger engine, and flaps had been fitted under the rear-wing portion.

Carried by sea, the squadron reached Algiers on 4 March but had to take its turn while the Royal Air Force supply and engineering branches cleared the crated Austers and assembled them. They finally reported to Lieutenant-General Sir John Crocker's IX Corps on 4 April just as the action in First Army was shifting from his sector to that of V Corps. Targets were scarce at the tail-end of a successful ground thrust.

There were plenty elsewhere. By this time the Germans and Italians were fighting desperately to avoid being crushed between the First and the approaching Eighth Army. General Montgomery's leading corps was closing up to Enfidaville where, losing part of his armour to the First, he was to depend a good deal on the weight of his artillery to open the enemy defence line. Both 651 and 654 Squadrons were moved to his command to support this operation, in which they encountered for the first time a novel organization, an Army Group Royal Artillery (AGRA), the concentration of army artillery resources under one command, capable of being moved from one corps front to another as required.

They entered Eighth Army service within the AGRA. Impatient to acquire air observation facilities, its commander committed both squadrons to a succession of shooting and reconnaissance sorties. No. 654 lost an aircraft in the process when its pilot forgot the rules about flying over enemy lines. Hit by ground fire he survived a crash-landing to be taken prisoner. For a time also, the squadron supplied an air courier service between the two armies, circumnavigating the enemy by flying out to sea.

On 13 May Tunisia was finally taken. The guns ceased firing and the AOP squadrons concentrated. Equipment was overhauled. A leave programme began. All realized that another campaign was impending, and some were comforted by the reflection that they would enter it as seasoned warriors.

CHAPTER THIRTEEN

# Into Southern Europe

Some account has been given of the landings in Sicily and Italy during July and September 1943. Eventually, four AOP squadrons became involved in the latter campaign. Nos 651 and 654 accompanied the Eighth Army into Sicily by sea as the crossing from North Africa was well beyond the Auster's range. Each put aircraft into the air during the second half of the month and both were completely operational by the beginning of August.

Though they had claims to the status of seasoned warriors, they found themselves working and living in a markedly different environment to that of Tunisia. The island seemed to be filled by bare, soaring mountains. The exceptional flat and highly cultivated plain west of Catania was dominated by the lava slopes of Mount Etna. Elsewhere, olive trees abounded among small stony fields cleared among the narrow boulder-strewn lowlands.

This environment limited the number of landing sites. Reconnaissance parties were looking for advanced landing grounds (ALG) close to the guns. Few were found. As often as not, the nearest

An Auster 'dug in', just short just short of Cassino, Italy (*Museum of Army Flying*)

strip of suitable land might be at a distance of fifteen minutes flying time, an hour by road. Royal Engineer bulldozers would help to clear and level ALGs if they were close at hand.

The rules for operating heights had to be reconsidered. The pilots had developed a measure of cunning among the Tunisian mountains, bobbing up over crests when they were obliged to but discovering ways of edging round them to engage targets. In Sicily this was more difficult; the mountain ridges often rose in steps from the shoreline. Periodically, strong air currents swept through them to disrupt tactical flying. No. 654 flew its sorties among the landscape of cliffs and crests, supporting XXX Corps as it followed winding roads inland, looping west and north ultimately to encircle Etna. No. 651 Squadron supported XIII Corps along the coast.

In the mountains the Austers flew many contact sorties, reporting the movement of infantry and tank groups on remote tracks. The ground radios of these small columns were frequently screened by the high crests, and often AOPs were the only agents able to report their location to parent brigade and divisional headquarters. Sometimes single enemy self-propelled guns, sniping from defiladed positions, could only be seen by AOP pilots soaring over enemy territory to avoid ground fire. In the mountains and across the Catania plain, the German forces fought stubbornly in defence and the Italian artillery continued to fire impulsively.

On the coast road the registration of prospective targets and neutralization of enemy artillery and multi-barrelled mortars occupied 651 Squadron. For a time, the 6 in guns of warships on the sea flank provided support, but while this was effective it involved the relay of messages through two radios and AOP sorties extending to forty-five minutes. This was not prudent in daylight. The German Air Force continued to raid into Sicily from Italian airfields. Auster pilots diving to evade attack were sometimes forced over enemy territory into flak.

Night flying increased as the coastal and mountain corps fought doggedly to penetrate the enemy posts on cliffs and behind crests. At night, muzzle flashes quickly disclosed the positions of those enemy supporting batteries which had remained silent and hidden during the day against Allied air strikes. During one week, calls for night AOP operations almost matched those for daylight. The manpower and equipment of flights became strained.

Squadron commanders found themselves explaining that while many sorties were mounted at a few minutes notice, their ability to respond quickly depended on liaison with the cooperating regiments. In Sicily this sometimes involved a return road journey of two hours. Weather and meteorology had to be studied frequently, maps and air photographs scrutinized. The technicians had to keep sufficient aircraft serviceable to meet the demand for operations, and when they were not doing this they were engaged in guard duties. A section detachment was popular as much as anything because the battery or regiment in location provided all the sentries.

On 16 August the Germans and Italians finally conceded the island. The former had lost seven thousand prisoners but succeeded in withdrawing sixty thousand soldiers and airmen across the Straits of Messina. The latter were in the process of falling out of the war: Italy surrendered to the Allies on 3 September, as British forces crossed to the mainland. For a few brief days it seemed to General Eisenhower that southern and central Italy, even Rome, might fall to a combination of airborne and seaborne landings, but the Germans reacted swiftly to the Italian defection, and the Italians judged themselves incapable of frustrating their movements.

Still, the Fifth Army under General Mark Clark was put ashore in Salerno Bay on 9 September 1943 behind a strong sea and air bombardment while the Eighth captured Taranto and pushed up the Adriatic coast. Delaying the latter with rearguards, Field Marshal Kesselring, the German Commander-in-Chief, concentrated six weak but well equipped divisions to oppose General Clark. Seizing the mountains overlooking the semicircular farmland south of Salerno, these forces rapidly brought the beach-head of the Fifth Army under persistent shell and mortar fire. Thrusts by panzer groups drove the Allies out of several localities. For a time, indeed, it seemed that the American and British divisions would be swept back into the sea.

The advanced element of 654 Squadron was landed into this mêlée behind the assault wave. With them came three Austers, partially dismantled for the sea passage. Finding an advanced landing ground was not difficult: the ground was flat, many of the fields were large and bare in this autumn season. The problem was to find cover from the observation of the enemy artillery.

The detachment assembled the aircraft, completed a round of contacts and plans during the night of the 9th and began flying on 10 September. A Royal Air Force corporal rigger described operating conditions over the next few days:

> . . . enemy shellfire crept towards us, and just as we expected to be under the next lot, it would move sideways on to someone else. The [farm] buildings across the next field were hit several times, and on the second day something hit the road running down to the [farmhouse] we were using as our billet. A funny thing was, as we leapt into our slit trenches, out came several old Italians, who had been hiding in one of the barns. I think they were going to make a run for it but we persuaded them to stay where they were. It must have been their farm because they brought out some wine that evening for us. They knew the hiding place.
>
> After we [launched] the first Auster next morning, several groups of soldiers came rushing past us saying that the enemy was just behind them. Phil [a gunner] asked them where they were going and they said to the beaches. Well, the sea was only about 200 yards behind us. . . . We stood to but stayed where we were. No sign of the enemy.
>
> One of our trucks got held up that afternoon coming back with the rations. The trouble was that Jerry [the Germans] seemed to be firing everywhere. But we got the guns going. . . .

This was not a wholly false claim. Forward observation officers on the ground were directing shells at many targets but their view was limited because the coastal area was so flat. Olive groves, woods, and buildings obscured German infantry and heavy mortars. Enemy field and medium batteries were concealed in the foothills. The tactical air forces reconnoitred and struck at such targets when they found them, as they sought out similarly enemy headquarters or armour debouching onto the plain. But the guns and mortars were camouflaged, wholly so when not firing. The slow flying AOPs could search out battery positions where the recce or fighter pilots swept past in seconds. And the fall of enemy shot was apparent to the AOPs, offering them a bearing to the point of origin.

The process of striking targets was also slower than that of the Allied day fighters and fighter-bombers, but it was more precise and on the whole weightier. Once registration was completed, however, a variety of weapons was available to fire on the enemy marked: naval guns, American heavies, and the medium guns of the British X Corps.

The AOP was also able to bring fire closer to friendly positions than fighters engaged in ground attack and, still more, fighter-bombers. During close actions they worked with the field guns of American and British divisions. Several times they directed the fire of 3.7 inch anti-aircraft guns, using their flat trajectory to snipe at enemy armour.

The Fifth Army stood its ground. The enemy losses became insupportable under the intense supporting fire and the counter-attacks of American and British armour and infantry. Abruptly, the German high command broke off the containment battle. At this point, the main body of 654 Squadron opportunely joined its advanced detachment, bringing a sack of mail. While the maintenance flight checked comprehensively the aircraft coming out of action, four other Austers flew to Capodicino airport at Naples to support the Fifth Army as it moved northwards on 22 September.

By mid-October 1943 the Allied armies straddled Italy from the mouth of the River Volturno to Termoli on the Adriatic Sea, a line of 120 miles across the Matese mountains. No. 654 Squadron remained with the Fifth Army, 651 with the Eighth. Rainstorms began during this period. Drenched and often mired, infantry and tanks closed slowly to the southern end of the Apennines under the bombardments of guns and aircraft.

The engineers laid reinforced coconut matting for advanced landing grounds among the artillery. Flights and sections settled alongside them. In December the Allied advance came to a halt.

CHAPTER FOURTEEN

# 'There is a bloody war on in the Far East, you know'

Ⅰn December 1942 a senior staff officer from Army Headquarters, India, was visiting the War Office to press for reinforcements and equipment to bolster a counter-offensive into Burma. The Director of Staff Duties listened to him patiently and responded in what was meant to be a positive way. The First Army was engaged with the Americans in French North Africa and would soon join hands with the Eighth Army. When that was complete operations would open to end the war in Europe. After that, all aid would pass to India; twenty divisions would be sent for the reoccupation of Burma and Malaya. Meanwhile, several specialist units would be sent to assist the theatre. He mentioned three and remembered a fourth:

'Oh, and there's another body, a bit of a bonus: 656 AOP Squadron.'

'What's in an AOP squadron?'

'Sixteen light aircraft and about 150 soldiers and airmen. The officers spot for your artillery.'

'Is that the best you can do? There is a bloody war on in the Far East, you know.'

Fortunately, this dismissive remark was not passed to Major Denis Coyle who was forming up No. 656 to move to India after working up his mixed command. He recalled,

. . . we were warned for an unknown tropical destination and spent the last month collecting all the aircraft spares that we could possibly lay our hands on and packing them up as securely as possible in thousands of packing cases. Included among the cases but in very specially constructed containers were the instruments of our dance band which had been formed earlier and which had earned a lot of money for [unit welfare funds] by playing in the local village halls near Stapleford Tawney in Essex where we had been based.

. . . detraining at Liverpool . . . we met our first clash with authority because the RAF embarkation staff, seeing this mixture of uniforms, tried to separate the soldiers and airmen whereas we insisted in falling in by Flights. However the movement staff finally won because, when we found ourselves on board, the unit was split up into penny packets and we discovered that it was against RAF policy to send units overseas, only individual drafts. . . .

During the voyage they trans-shipped in Egypt and discovered that they were bound for India. Disembarked at Bombay, their composition again puzzled the authorities. Which reception camp, they were asked, should they be lodged in: Army or RAF? Major Coyle was now beginning to see the advantage of options. The RAF camp was clearly the better of the two, and he opted for it. It was also close to 'a very nice little airfield at Juhu'.

However, they had no aircraft; the Air Ministry had overlooked the requirement. Urgent reminders were signalled to London and, meanwhile, Tiger Moths were borrowed from the Indian

Air Force. They practised airborne shooting at the School of Artillery at Deolali, trained in jungle warfare and, as one honest officer remarked, 'had a very good time. Once or twice, I had to remind myself that we were actually going to war'.

The Austers – Mark IIIs – arrived in ships' holds in mid-January. Unloading sufficient for B Flight, detached for a special amphibious operation, the remainder were sent on to Calcutta. Notwithstanding the absence of their radios, the squadron entered battle in Lieutenant-General Sir Philip Christison's XV Corps on 25 January 1944.

On this date British and Indian forces occupied Assam following the wholesale reversal of Allied arms in Burma. But they had acquired a shrewd chief in General Sir William Slim and he did not intend to make the mistakes of his predecessors. His soldiers had also learned useful lessons. Of considerable importance, his air support included a transport force able to supply two or three divisions at a time from the air.

Having balanced his Fourteenth Army at the end of 1943, General Slim began a modest advance into the Arakan at the turn of the year, which continued deliberately against deeply entrenched Japanese defences. Recently reinforced, the enemy commander took this to be a good moment to open a counter-offensive, employing the previously successful method of circling the British and Indian positions and ambushing their occupants when they attempted to withdraw.

No. 656 Squadron began flying in support of the 5th and 7th Indian Divisions in XV Corps, chiefly in reconnaissance along their respective fronts, watchful for an active enemy air force. They were just beginning to pick up the pattern of the ground between the Kalapanzin river in the east and Maungdaw on the Naf estuary to the west when several strong Japanese columns made their presence known by capturing two of the three communications centres behind the divisions and ambushing traffic on a road leading back to the third.

Major Coyle had set up his headquarters on 'rather a useful area of cultivation' behind 5th Indian Division when he realized that the Japanese intended to capture it. For several days all hands were occupied in the struggle for survival – their route to the rear was cut.

At the same time Captain Rex Boys had established an advanced party from C Flight close to the 7th Division and set off on a reconnaissance sortie. He was shot down by Japanese fighters, made a crash-landing and was seriously injured, both his legs being broken in several places. Local villagers dragged him for some miles to a first aid post but the ambulance driving him back to a dressing station was halted by fire. Four days passed before he was rescued and reached a hospital.

Sergeant Roe and five members of C Flight were awaiting his return at a temporary landing site when, as Mr Reg Bailey, one of their number, recounted,

. . . a party of what appeared to be Burmese approached us, the leader made himself known to us as a British officer. He asked us who were were and what we were doing . . . no other units were within several miles of us. We explained who we were and that we were awaiting the return of our officer who had flown out on a reconnaissance. He then told us that there were 800 Japs following him down the valley. . . . This would of course mean that the 7th Division was completely encircled and he expected it to be closed within hours, or certainly by tomorrow. He then had a word with Sergeant Roe. . . . we should await the return of our officer and then move to within the posts of the division.

. . . We then took up our positions on a small hill and waited. It was one of the longest afternoons of my life. What I remember mostly was the heat and the buzzing of the flies and insects. We were straining our eyes up the valley to catch our first sign of the Japanese, but hoping not to. How long we lay there waiting I do not know. It was certainly several hours. The first heartening sight we saw was that of several columns of Sikh infantry moving slowly up the valley, presumably to meet the Japanese. However, they seemed pitifully inadequate in numbers to face 800 Japanese.

Hours passed exceeding the Auster's endurance.

. . . Sergeant Roe decided there was no point in waiting any longer and we packed our trucks and moved back into the 7th Division enclave.

They moved into the corps 'Administrative Box' containing supplies, spares, and medical facilities within a defended perimeter on which the forward troops could draw in just such a situation as was now developing. But the numbers to hold the defences were scant and everyone necessarily took a turn in holding some part of them. Several times the enemy broke in during darkness, once entering a field hospital to slaughter patients and medical staff. But all breaches were filled by counter-attack. Reg Bailey and his comrades occupied two posts and found that,

. . . the senses played tricks when one is in a high state of tension and small bushes and so on, seen in the gloom, all appeared to be Japanese crawling towards us. We often stood with grenades in our hands, pins drawn, holding the clip down ready to throw them. We were under instructions not to fire unless we were forced to because of giving away the positions. We also had a couple of loaded Sten guns [machine carbines] in front of our trenches. The plan as far as Tubby Charrington and I were concerned, who shared a trench, was that we would hurl all our grenades, then empty the Sten into them, and then take to our rifles and bayonets. As a last resort we had a machete laying at our sides. One thing was certain that we, like the rest of the people on that hill, never intended to be taken prisoner.

As soon as the road back to XV Corps headquarters was open, Major Coyle returned there. He converted the Austers temporarily into light air ambulances, leading eight into a strip within 114 Brigade on 18 February to evacuate casualties.

Unable to draw XV Corps out of its positions, the Japanese commander began to find himself short of supplies. His ambush parties were themselves increasingly ambushed, his attacking columns hemmed in. By the end of February 1944 the Japanese 55th Division was disintegrating, its remnants obliged to withdraw across country.

B Flight moved to the Fourteenth Army in March after marking time impatiently in India. Attached to IV Corps it was besieged within a few weeks in Imphal, its aircraft much in demand by the corps and divisional artillery. There were four divisions within the perimeter and each possessed at least one airstrip for use by day, but vacated by dusk because enemy patrols visited them at night. Thus the flight was stationed on the protected central strip. However, an assumption that the outlying strips would always be open after dawn was sometimes misplaced, as a review of 656 Squadron's war service noted.

. . . Captain Southern set off one morning to land on an outlying strip [infiltrated by the Japanese] dressed as civilians during the night. Southern landed as was his normal practice and taxied with no undue hurry into the temporary shelter of the splinter-pen. He was rather surprised that his ground-crew were not there to welcome him but he wandered over to the telephone which should have connected him to [divisional] Headquarters, Royal Artillery, and gradually became aware that all was not in order. Tanks of the 3rd Carbineers started firing into the wood alongside the strip, while grenade discharges and mortar bombs started falling on the strip itself and small arms fire. . . . Southern dived for the plane, swung its tail around and pushed it on to the strip. Poking his head into the cockpit he flicked the petrol and switches on and in his haste put the throttle setting at about half open. Luck was still with him for the engine fired at once but, being at half throttle, the Auster moved off on its own in a hurry. He ducked under the wing and dived in and, if the spectators watching from the safety of their slit trenches are to be believed, the aircraft took off with his feet still hanging out of the door. . . .

It was not, thankfully, an everyday occurrence. But there were plenty of other adventures awaiting the squadron; for while all eyes were on Imphal the Japanese sent a large force to capture Kohima, and Dimapur, the rail-head for operations. All flights were involved in one or another of the threatened sectors, squadron headquarters withdrawing essentially to Dimapur for a time. Major Coyle spent many hours in the air visiting his detachments, separated by hundreds of miles. Navigation became difficult for all pilots as the monsoon developed.

As the enemy was everywhere thrown back, the effects of the prolonged rain, driven often by winds gusting to 70 mph, grossly inhibited flying, and indeed the preservation of aircraft on the ground. Picketing the Austers was extremely difficult because winds were so variable in direction. The Fourteenth Army artillery commander arranged for No. 656 to withdraw to Ranchi to refit with Auster IVs and Vs, and to welcome their first reinforcements from the Indian Army flying training scheme.

# CHAPTER FIFTEEN

# Across Three Continents

A requirement for twelve squadrons had been agreed between the War Office and Air Ministry in 1942, and all had formed up by the end of 1943. Some account of the five squadrons at or en route to war in that year has been given. The remaining seven squadrons were destined for north-west Europe.

For those who had spent the war years at home, there was a tendancy in 1944 to think that the return to France constituted a resumption of hostilities on land discontinued at Dunkirk in 1940. It was not seen like that by the forces who had pushed back into Burma, or those who had been fighting in Africa and were then engaged in Sicily and Italy. Broadcasting and press references to 'D-Day' from 6 June 1944 caused the troops on the Italian front to style themselves with good humour as 'the D-Day Dodgers'.

The four AOP squadrons then in Italy had as good cause as any to smile wryly at the suggestion that the real war for the soldiers was about to begin in north-west Europe.

No. 655 and 657 Squadrons had embarked for the Mediterranean in August 1943, the latter under Major J.R. Ingrams, who had raised the squadron, the former under Major D.B. Oldman whose predecessor had recently been killed in a flying accident. Both squadrons were equipped with the Auster III.

Oldman had served as a flight commander during the Algerian and Tunisian operations, and he was thus able to exercise 655 over some of the ground covered during the First Army operations. But air and ground elements in both squadrons grew impatient as weeks passed without orders to enter operations. Some of the waiting time was passed in planning to fly the Austers to Italy rather than crating them for a sea passage. Much thought was given to fuel dumping and the accessibility of distant airfields across the water.

No. 655 was called forward first. Early in December 1943 the sixteen Austers began island hopping across the Mediterranean narrows, first to Pantelleria, then to western Sicily where they were briefly accorded special honours by the United States Air Force as they unwittingly landed in the air stream carrying President Roosevelt. Finally, outrunning their rations, they spent Christmas Day eating corned beef with hard tack and were flooded by a storm on New Year's Eve. Thanks to a mighty effort by the Squadron Warrant Officer, Mr Dust, and the ground crews, the squadron was made ready for battle by 3 January 1944.

B and C Flights were at once involved in searching for targets in the open ground between the Maiella massif and the Adriatic shore. The Germans had brought forward in November and December a number of guns to harrass the British, Canadian and Polish forces in the line. Shifting position frequently, German heavy and medium guns in small groups found hiding places behind villages and towns, and within the valleys of numerous streams flowing to the sea from the Maiella eastern watershed. Along the mountain edge, German self-propelled guns crept forward to snipe singly at the Allied positions. Their ground observers found eyries among the mountain heights to direct fire on the supply routes leading through such towns as Lanciano and Castefrentano, and to discover the Eighth Army's field and medium batteries in this sector. In positions below Monte Maiella and its outcrops, the Allied artillery relied upon their Air Observation Posts. B and C Flights of 655 found full employment in action with their comrades in 651 Squadron and the Canadian AOPs, taking off and landing from muddy airstrips, watching for sudden snowstorms which, from time to time, blinded pilots, sometimes fatally.

On the day the squadron entered the line, A Flight under Captain W.G. Gordon was detached to join 1st British Infantry Division, making ready for an amphibious landing at Anzio.

In the western sector of the Italian line General Clark was manoeuvring in January 1944 to capture Rome. The direct route lay past the mountains behind Cassino and up the Liri valley, ground chosen for its defensibility by the Germans. This was the western end of the Gustav Line. Generals Alexander and Clark recognized that making a breach here would be costly, but planned nevertheless to strike into it with the dual aim of weakening the enemy positions on the shoulders of the Liri valley and drawing in enemy reserves. With these engaged, the VI Corps under an American commander, Major-General J.P. Lucas, was to be landed on either side of Anzio and Nettuno – Operation 'Shingle' – to advance across the flat Pontine plain to Rome, seizing the roughly circular Alban hills – Colli Albani – on the way to secure their right flank. Such a thrust would surely oblige the enemy to withdraw sharply from the Liri Front. Such was the reasoning and the plan.

In intermittent snow and sleet the French corps began the offensive on 12 January 1944. South and west, Americans and British joined the assaults, supported by 654 Squadron, which had advanced from Salerno via Naples. Despite some progress the two sides were once more locked after nine days. But the action had clearly drawn in German reserves. No less importantly, Field Marshal Kesselring's headquarters had not the slightest idea that an Allied amphibious force was about to land at 02.00 on 22 January. By the following evening the 1st British and 3rd United States Divisions were ashore with special forces and the corps artillery. Naval guns fired supporting salvoes. The tactical air force sought to deny the approach of enemy reinforcements.

Unhappily, in spite of clear instructions to the contrary, the corps commander busied himself with securing the bridge-head instead of thrusting inland. Two German battalions and a few coastal batteries were then opposing the landing of VI Corps. When, eventually, Major-General Lucas attempted as the result of several injunctions to advance, he discovered that elements of eight enemy divisions barred the routes to Rome. Moving at night on the basis of a planned reaction, these forces concentrated rapidly.

Released too late by Major-General Lucas, the advancing British and American armoured cars, tanks and infantry found every road to Rome blocked. Among a host of problems was the identification of German positions within the southern spurs of the Colli Albani and the deep beds of the rivers which flowed south from them.

Captain Gordon's flight operating in parallel with an American detachment was sent to search them out, despite uncertainty as to the precise line of contact on the ground, and the frequency of German air intervention. For the greater part of the fighter and fighter-bomber resources of the *Luftwaffe* in Italy were employed against the Anzio bridge-head in late January and through February; Kesselring was under orders not simply to contain the bridge-head but to destroy it. Gordon noted in his diary on 16 February,

Boche attacked all along the front with very heavy air. John Foster and I had a field day with 80th [Medium Regiment] against tanks. He got one on fire, I saw three smoking. . . . All pilots flying during [air] raids, but I all but had it at dusk. Saw four down to LAA [light anti-aircraft].

On the 17th: Had a party round the gun positions with two ME 109 [German aircraft]. Boche attacking hard, now up to [Rome highway] flyover (about 10,000 yd from the sea). Bill Barber chased by ME which was shot down by a sergeant with a Bren [light machine-gun]. Hugo Walter got a hostile battery. . . .

The battle continued into the spring. The requirement for AOPs was so crucial to the use of the artillery ashore and the naval guns standing off, that C Flight of 654 Squadron was sent to join A. Generally successful in dodging enemy air attacks, both flights lost pilots killed in these encounters. By May, David Oldman's 655 Squadron was transferred entirely to the western sector: B Flight and his headquarters joined Major Willett and the rump of 654 working the mass of guns assembled to weaken the defences at Cassino and along the heights enclosing the Liri valley. This was important work in preparation for a break-out and link with the Anzio forces, reinforced and under a new, enterprising commander, Major-General L.K. Truscott. On 25 May Captain R.A. Fortnum of C Flight returned from his Anzio base to the contact zone at 08.30 and was,

. . . astonished to see that a large convoy of armoured vehicles had appeared and were stationary, but pointing north west. There was about 800 yards between the leading vehicles of their column and the leading vehicles of our own recce [reconnaissance] column, both columns being held up by blown bridges. I called up [the artillery regiment he was supporting] and asked if they knew anything about them. They reported 'No,' and asked me to find out who they were. I flew back and then down the column very low, and I could see that they were American armoured cars. I still had no means of communication [with them], and so decided to land. I chose a field by the road and, offering up a quick prayer that there would be no mines, landed there. An American lieutenant came running across to me, and informed me that they were the 91st Reconnaissance from Terracina. He reported that the coast was clear of the enemy, and asked me to inform the Anzio forces. I took off again . . . and reported . . .

The struggle was at last bearing fruit. Rome was taken on 4 June. Across the whole Front the Allied line moved forward as the Germans extricated themselves to fall back under the pressure of the Allied air forces and pursuing ground columns to the Gothic Line, some 200 miles to the north. Well forward, the four British AOP squadrons hit and harrassed enemy rearguards. No. 657 Squadron earned a form of commendation from two enemy elements operating on its front at this time. The commander of *Kampfgruppe*, von Zangen, observed in July,

Enemy [that is, Allied] artillery was frequently directed by air observation. With the aid of artillery observation planes, the enemy were able to kill off strong point after strong point with concentrated fire.

95 Artillery Regiment reported,

> Whenever arty/recce or AOP aircraft are seen by Battery OPs they sound the alarm. Firing stops and camouflage is replaced.

Most importantly, the long battle had drawn in ten divisions from other Fronts.

Passing the news to Marshal Stalin on 5 June 1944 that Rome was taken and the Gustav Line broken, Mr Churchill added that,

> . . . I have just returned from two days at Eisenhower's headquarters watching the troops embark [for Normandy] . . . With great regret General Eisenhower was forced to postpone for one night, but the weather forecast has undergone a most favourable change and tonight we go. We are using 5,000 ships and have available 11,000 fully mounted aircraft.

Among those aircraft were the seven AOP squadrons which had yet to enter battle. Launched as part of the Second Tactical Air Force, they were disposed within two of its formations: 83 Group was responsible for 652, 653, 658, 659 and 662 Squadrons; 84 Group for 660 and 661 Squadrons. The Overlord order of battle lists the Austers with the Typhoons, Mustangs, and Spitfires flown by their colleagues in the Royal Air Force, the Royal Canadian Air Force, and aircrew from Czechoslovakia, France, Norway, and Poland. Nos 652 and 662 Squadrons led the way among their peers, landing their reconnaissance parties on D-Day, 6 June 1944.

In addition to the artillery organic to each division landed on 6 June or in the subsequent build-up of forces, the Royal Artillery and Royal Canadian Artillery comprised the following equipments, whose maximum ranges are indicated:

| | | |
|---|---|---|
| six heavy regiments | either 155 mm guns | 25,000 yd |
| | or 7.2 in howitzers | 19,000 yd |
| | | |
| twenty-four | principally 5.5 in guns | |
| medium regiments | firing 80 lb shells | 18,000 yd |
| | firing 100 lb shells | 16,000 yd |
| | | |
| eight field artillery | 25 pr gun/howitzers | 13,000 yd |
| regiments | towed or self-propelled | |
| | 105 mm 'Priests' | 12,000 yd |

A proportion of these provided the corps artillery, the remainder being disposed within six Army Groups, Royal Artillery (AGRAs).

The enemy were so close to the landing site first selected for A Flight that Captain M. Loveridge, its commander, chose another at Beny-sur-Mer. En route the ground party became involved in a fire fight with enemy defending a radar post. LAC [Leading Aircraftsman] Sissons was wounded in the action.

German aircraft appeared occasionally but without any warning to the AOP units; the radio link at the Anti-Aircraft Operations Room rarely worked. Captain Eric Pugh of A Flight was shot down and killed by five Focke-Wulf 190s on 8 June. C Flight lost Lieutenant L. Vann and his observer, LAC Atkinson, on the 13th.

On that day also, Captain R.L. Munro of 653 Squadron.

> . . . was lucky enough to catch a column of vehicles and brew them up. Twelve sorties in all were made, chiefly tactical reconnaissance, or Tac/R. LAC Graham was rear observer in seven sorties, LAC Sellick in two, and AC [Aircraftsman] Lewis two.
>
> The need for rear observers was shown the next day when a swarm of Me 109s took advantage of cloud cover and beat up the beaches and everything else they saw on the way.

The squadron was flying Auster IVs with rear seats fitted. An observer looking back through the rear window was thus able to comment on ground targets or flak unseen by the pilot and, even at this comparatively late stage of the war, the appearance of enemy aircraft. Some of the flights in Italy had used observers since 1943, though there was neither training nor official status for those performing it. They were drawn from volunteers among the ground crews. Eventually, after repeated recommendations, a half wing was permitted to be worn on the left sleeve, and specialist pay of one shilling a day (half the pilot's rate) was awarded to those 'regularly engaged in duties as observers'.

The ground reconnaissance party of 662 Squadron reached the beach opposite Le Hamel at H plus 1 hour on D-Day and became involved in the struggle to push inland. An advanced landing ground was established that same day in a field liberally marked with German warning signs, '*Achtung Minen*', but a French farmer, paid to plant them, advised that no mines had been laid in the area. Checks confirmed that the ground was clear. A message was at once despatched to call forward the first flight.

Unfortunately, the communications vessel offshore was hit by enemy fire before it could relay the signal to England. A day was lost before the omission was discovered and the squadron did not reach the beach-head until D plus 2, and was thus inadvertently late in performing its first task of directing naval gunfire. Captain R.H.C. Woodman described the flight across, escorted by a Walrus amphibian aircraft of the Fleet Air Arm:

> After about forty-five minutes the mist cleared and I saw the others ahead. Down on the starboard side 2,000 feet below, saw streams of ships coming and going from the beach-head along the lanes swept by the mine sweepers. We had orders to keep fairly close to them in case we were attacked. . . . After about an hour the French coast materialised, Le Havre to the left, the Cherbourg Peninsula away to the right! As we passed over the protecting screen of warships at 2,000 feet (to be clear of the balloons) the Navy opened fire at us with Bofors. One shell burst between Alec and the Walrus! Someone fired the recognition signal and the Navy shut up. We passed over the coast at Arromanches, which looked a bit of a mess. Everywhere seemed to be on fire and an occasional shell kept bursting in the water amongst the thousands of large and small ships which were hurrying to and fro. The Walrus flashed 'Good luck' in morse and turned for home. Alec Hill in front turned due west and began to lose height. I looked down and there was a winking green Aldis lamp coming from a field

near a small village. I was the last to land and did a very 'ropey' landing. Field only about 120 yards long!

No. 659 Squadron began to deploy into Normandy from 14 June. Its task was to support VIII Corps, foremost in the movement to bypass Caen. Eagerly pursuing targets as the corps entered the line during the remainder of June, it lost several aircraft, and a pilot, Captain Heard, shot down by a pair of Me 109s.

No. 658 Squadron was hard on their heels. Its first aircraft flew over on 18 June to support XXX Corps, but a brief period of bad weather reduced flying opportunities. Within a month, however, the whole unit had settled into operations and on 17 July its commander controlled a shoot which demonstrated the power of the British and Canadian artillery in the field. Forty enemy tanks – actually part of II SS Panzer Corps – were said to be in the area of Ste Honorine du Fay – Aunay. Low cloud prevented flying for some hours but Major A. Lyell was in the air at 16.00 when he spotted movement and dust in the area. On reporting his readiness to fire for effect, he found himself directing 600 guns, the artillery of three corps and three AGRAs. The

Royal Tank Regiment officer briefing a pilot, of 655 Squadron, in Normandy, 1944 (*Museum of Army Flying*)

weight of shell descending devastated the German armour reinforcing a thrust into XXX Corps left flank.

Nos 653 and 660 Squadrons expected to be called forward from the middle of June; they were committed to formations expecting to lead the break-out from the bridge-head. But while the latter was firmly established before the end of the month, the run of battle, the nature of the country, and the inexperience of some divisions delayed the advance into north-eastern France until the latter part of July. This delay meant that landing grounds were becoming hard to find. Space close to the beaches was increasingly taken up by supplies and service units. Still, 653 moved across on 26 June, and 660 was allowed to send its advanced party on the 28th. The squadron followed on 12 July to join II Canadian Corps artillery.

All identical in establishment and marks of their Austers – IIIs and IVs – the individuality of the squadrons, apparent during training, developed more fully on the battlefield.

No. 652 Squadron benefited at once from its internal arrangements to produce air photographs rapidly, and generously helped others for a time. Following prior contacts, 662 used the photographic services of a Royal Air Force reconnaissance wing. No. 658 Squadron had also struck up a friendship with RAF units in its group and established a private link with the group fighter operations centre, from which it received warnings of enemy aircraft intrusions. Counter bombardment tasks were handled by several methods within squadrons, the commonest being the use of squadron headquarters as a CB flight formed from reserve aircraft, though this enterprise had to be modified as Austers within flights were lost or severely damaged in action.

Certain of the early operations could scarcely have been conceived in training schemes. For example, 660 Squadron found itself maintaining what was termed 'Auster cover'. It was discovered while the British forces were involved in the grinding operations round Caen that the appearance of an AOP in the air was sufficient to persuade the German artillery to cease firing. Thus an Auster was kept almost continuously in the view of their observers.

A unique operation followed the marking of a bomb line close to Caen by RAF pathfinders. An aircraft of C Flight, 652 Squadron, observed that the first wave of bombers were dropping bombs on to and inside the markers, endangering friendly positions. The rest of the flight took to the air,

An Auster of 652 Squadron flying over field battery, 1944 (*Museum of Army Flying*)

Major Cobley the squadron commander among them, to warn off the next wave. Ascending, firing Very lights, flashing Aldis lamps, pilots and observers successfully shifted the line of the bombers' run to the enemy side of the line.

Caen fell on 9 July. The Americans took St Lô on the 18th. The break-out was beginning. As General Patton's armoured forces raced away, the First Canadian Army thrust south east from Caen to Falaise where the air forces began a fearful destruction of the remaining enemy concentrations. The artillery continued it, aided by C Flight of 661 Squadron which had just arrived in France to support 2 Canadian AGRA.

A prolonged pursuit followed across the Seine towards Belgium and Luxemburg. The Front was wide. There were insufficient supplies to support the whole of 21 Army Group and thus some corps were held back as the summer passed. Their AOP squadrons remained with them. The records of the latter contain entries such as 'Air Taxi Service began'. The Austers were used to convey formation commanders and staff officers to headquarters increasingly separated; and the more they were used, the more this facility came to be regarded by headquarters as a regular function of an AOP squadron. Aside from the provision of this service, flight and squadron commanders practised skills and techniques worked up during operations, and all took advantage of the opportunity for intensive maintenance of aircraft and associated equipment, notably radio sets.

Forward, 658 and 662 Squadrons supported XXX Corps as it crossed into Belgium, preceding it indeed on one occasion at least.

To 'B' Flight, 662 Sqn, fell the honour of being the first Allied aircraft to land in the Belgian capital for six years – and the rather unenviable distinction of choosing for this purpose a field in the city, surrounded on its sides respectively by a tall factory, factory chimneys, high trees and a main road with overhead tram cables . . . quite the smallest field the flight landed in during the campaign!

It was something of an anti-climax when early the next morning a German Tiger tank, with some either [sic] Germans astride it, came trundling down the main road, passed within a few feet of where the aircraft were parked, put a round through the wall of the factory where the flight personnel were quartered and disappeared down the road to meet a somewhat sudden end at the hands of an alert anti-tank gun crew.

Later in the day, the squadron commander of 662, under pressure from XXX Corps headquarters to find a landing ground near to their headquarters in the palace grounds, found the runway and control buildings of Brussels airport apparently deserted. He ordered forward B Flight of 658 attached to his command.

The four Austers appeared over the Brussels housetops. They put their flaps down and then suddenly the fun started. A battery of 88's exactly 1,100 yards from the edge of the drome who had been lying doggo opened up. The aircraft ignoring all danger of mines landed and taxied like maniacs behind the derelict hangars. Only one aircraft was hit – a miracle. The situation was now that behind two very seedy looking hangars were four aircraft, four pilots, the C.O. in a jeep. A battery of 88's firing over open sights at us . . . An undamaged aerodrome worth its weight in gold and no guns that we could call on for an hour or two. At this moment small arms fire broke out in the buildings on the far side of the drome and the Squadron H.Q. transport arrived from the Brussels entrance and were greeted by a hail of fire. We had to get some help as quickly as possible both to save our skins and the airport. A message (couched in rather excited terms) to Corps produced the answer – sixteen armoured cars and a company of guards – and by night fall the guns had been captured.

In late September 1944 the grand advance came to a halt west of the Rhine. German forces had mustered sufficient strength to hold the advancing Allies on a series of waterways, including the Rhine at Arnhem.

In this latter connection, 'Air Taxi' services operated along the American sector of the airborne carpet. Major Lyell had come under fire attempting to land in Arnhem on 17 September. Turned back by fire he saw the Guards Armoured Division in action on the road north. That same day, he remarked,

Charles McCorry of B Flight . . . flying a Major Hazell from Nijmegen to Tac Army with an urgent message that supplies that had been badly needed by our troops at Arnhem had been dropped into German hands. Mac's aircraft was shot down near Uden. . . . Mac had got his first aid kit out . . . and was administering morphia to his passenger when they were both killed by enemy fire. . . .

At about the same time, James Stunt . . . with the BRA (Brigadier Jack Parham) and Harry Salter with the Chief of Staff Second Army were flying north along that road and were also heavily engaged by a 20-mm and small arms fire between Uden and Veghel. James and the BRA managed to get through with only minor damage to their aircraft but Harry's was so severely damaged that he had to crash land a few hundred yards from the wreck of Mac's aircraft. . . .

While the British Second Army swept forward from Caen to Brussels, First Canadian Army moved deliberately up the Channel coast, clearing German garrisons from ports and airfields needed to sustain the momentum of the advance, and destroying coastal batteries and radar installations. Nos 660 and 661 Squadrons served the Canadian artillery from division to AGRA. One flight was on call continuously to provide a taxi service. They reached Belgium just as it became apparent that the port of Antwerp could not be used until the German garrison on Walcheren island had been removed. No. 661 spent many days supporting amphibious operations to clear this territory. No. 662 moved on with II Canadian Corps through Nijmegen, where it added to its roles the provision of a radio link with underground forces in Holland.

Otherwise, in the winter of 1944/5, the AOPs closed up to serve the artillery demands of a static line, when often the matter of greatest concern was the state of the airstrip and what new measures could be employed to hold back the mud oozing across it. Rain and sleet, occasional snow, and residual ice restricted flying. Flights were grateful for the shelter of buildings however derelict beside their bases. Christmas approached. The Ardennes offensive burst upon the American forces and then the British. Artillery action which had settled to periodic harassing and the occasional call for defensive fire against German raiding parties revived to the full range of its power. This required intensive flying by the Austers in the direction of fire, in local reconnaissance, and in satisfying as best it could a high demand for aerial taxis.

They did not revert to winter quarters and customs when the offensive was finally quenched. General Eisenhower's determination to open his own 1945 offensive across the Rhine before the spring involved considerable preparatory work. The west bank of the river had to be cleared – Operation 'Blockbuster' – in which elements of 652 and 661 Squadrons joined 662. The event of crossing by 21 Army Group involved the greatest Allied artillery fire plan of the war to destroy enemy infantry, armour, and enemy batteries, complementing the tactical air offensive.

AOPs were employed at every level, registering and directing divisional, corps and AGRA fire.

There was great difficulty for an AOP pilot during the first few hours of the operation [one of their number reported], since with a thousand guns from 40-mm to 9-inch firing on a long programme, and with the close proximity of the enemy light flak in front of our own bridgehead, there was very real danger of being brought down by one of our own shells. This was, in fact, the cause of three AOP pilots and their RAF rear observers being killed that day, while another pilot had a 5.5 shell pass through his rudder without exploding or altering the trim of his aircraft.

When 6th Airborne Division was delivered by air on 25 March 1945, a pilot of 658 Squadron considered

. . . it incredible that the Airborne would ever reach their DZs through the heavy battle smoke which rose to a height of 2,000 feet and rolled over the German rear areas. . . . At this stage it was the Air OP job to try to neutralise the flak batteries, still very active after the 'milk round', and we carried out a number of quick shoots on some very aggressive 20-mm positions.

The Austers advanced over the landing zones to identify enemy threats to their ground deployment, and were at several points too ardent. Four were damaged or shot down, one to the east of the Diersfordter Wald. Fittingly, the pilot was rescued from no man's land by glider pilots.

The German Army, caught now between massed forces approaching from the east and west, was on the edge of defeat. One after another its towns and cities, its river lines, its fields showing the shoots of spring grass and grains, passed to the control of the Russian armies and those of the Allied expeditionary force. The fire direction role of the AOPs fell away. Reconnaissance and taxi work took precedence as the enemy's capability to resist was exhausted. On 7 May 1945 the war in Europe came to an end.

It had ended in Italy a shade earlier, formally on the 4th. But a few days before a New Zealand patrol crossing the Po suddenly found itself accepting what seemed to be the surrender of the whole German Army on the river line. The collapse spread across the entire Front. Three of the four AOP Squadrons were active on that day; the fourth, 657 Squadron, had passed in March with I Canadian Corps to north-west Europe, to serve for just a month in that theatre prior to the armistice. Throughout 1944 and the months of combat in 1945, three of these four had been continuously in action, occasionally all four together in the advance to the Gothic Line and the operations to break it open.

Four 658 Squadron Austers whose pilots accepted the surrender of Kiel airfield in 1945. Four others are immediately following (*Museum of Army Flying*)

In Burma 656 Squadron was extended to its limits as the tide of victory flowed for Fourteenth Army. In central Burma and along the coast, flights worked with the corps in contact. One discovered incidentally that the enemy had vacated Akyab island and saved the civilian population there from the perils of a mighty bombardment from air and sea. Mandalay was taken on 20 March, Rangoon occupied on 3 May.

The sights of the South East Asia Command were now fastened on the recapture of Malaya. No. 656 Squadron was redeployed in the middle of June to join the invasion force and was under orders to sail with it when the war ended on 14 August 1945. It was not denied the extension of its travels, however; the force landed in Malaya to accept the surrender of the Japanese forces there. After flying past in the victory parade on 14 September, the squadron moved piecemeal to the counter-insurgency operations in the Dutch East Indies. But that is another part of the AOP story.

Twelve squadrons, formed belatedly, had made a remarkable contribution to the war in three continents, Field Marshal Montgomery noted in a despatch on 4 September 1946,

> The Air OP . . . has become a necessary part of gunnery and a good aeroplane is required for the job. Very good RA officers are required for duty in the squadrons. It is not difficult to teach them to fly. . . .

Their continuance was to be challenged in the decade that followed, but they had made a mighty case for the retention of the Army in the air.

# The Struggle for Separation

CHAPTER SIXTEEN

# The Struggle Begins

T  he day the war ended, the British government was beset by a prime difficulty: it was strapped for cash. National expenditure had to be abated as a matter of urgency. In the autumn of 1945 the budgets of the three armed services were inevitably prime targets for reduction; the host recruited for war was being demobilized and there were high expectations that national service would be brought to an end within a year. The residual regular forces, it was calculated, would be maintained for a decade by the huge reserve stocks disposed in service depots.

These were broad theories canvassed during the post-war general election. They were flawed. The new government discovered that it was not only acutely short of funds for the recovery of national prosperity but it was also inescapably committed to extensive military deployments. Occupation duties involved large numbers of soldiers.

Some of these commitments were discharged within two or three years, but as one fell away another took its place. British forces withdrew from the occupation of Japan, the struggle for the Dutch East Indies and Trieste, the mandate in Palestine, the civil war in Greece and, greatest of all, the old Indian empire. But the government found itself obliged to propose and provide substantial forces for the NATO alliance, to assert British determination to defend Hong Kong, and to counter Chin Peng's insurrection in Malaya. Out of the blue, a strong British contingent was sent to join the United Nations forces in Korea. All these contingencies arose in the years 1945–50. Thus, while considerable reductions were made in the manpower of the armed forces during this term, the Army was maintaining field forces equating to eight divisions.

In that period of five years, a struggle developed for the survival of British Army aircraft in the air. The opening round began on 21 September 1945, shortly after the armistice with Japan was concluded.

The Director of Air advised the VCIGS that,

The Paper [enclosed] states the case for the Army taking over full responsibility for all light aircraft employed in meeting purely domestic Army requirements.

2. There has been a strong case for this for some time, but in order not to prejudice existing arrangements, I thought it better to leave things as they were while fighting was still in progress.

3. Now that the fighting has ceased I feel that we should delay no longer in carrying out this much needed reform. To miss the opportunity now is to saddle ourselves with the present unsatisfactory system for an indefinite period, at a time when every trend of development points to it being more and more of an anachronism. . . .

5. . . . in spite of very strong support from DRA [Director, Royal Artillery] and D. Sigs [Director, Royal Signals], the issue has always been defeated on manpower grounds by DMP [the Director of Manpower Planning].

6. I realise how acute the manpower situation is, and will continue to be, but we are concerned here with a major matter of principle concerning the future efficiency of the Army. . . .

Taken in isolation, the timing and wording of this covering note seem odd. They were prompted, however, by the experience of the war and recognition that the services were about to be simultaneously reduced and reorganized.

As Director of Air, Major-General Crawford had often been conscious that the AOPs, scattered across the overseas theatres of war in minute numbers and lacking any chain of direct contact with himself, operated truly 'on a wing and a prayer'. Letters and informal reports from squadrons overseas had made it apparent that some commanders felt keenly the lack of a command, or at least a base structure looking after their interests in the field; a regimental or wing headquarters. The Royal Air Force looked after the technical requirements of squadrons, and the artillery staff coordinated their employment. The Royal Artillery manning system filled regimental vacancies in their establishment. But some commanders missed the presence of a senior pilot – a staff officer or, better, a commander – in the theatre who would judge the moment to pull a unit out of contact after a prolonged or intense term of operational flying, develop ideas about flying tactics, and hasten spares overdue.

In the United Kingdom the Operational Training Unit – 43 OTU – provided a centre to which informal reports of squadron activities were sent, and from which in cooperation with the Director of Air's staff a monthly newsletter was circulated to remind the distant squadrons that they were not alone in their trade, or forgotten. But the OTU had neither the authority nor the means to afford depot or headquarters services such as those provided by Headquarters, Glider Pilots.

There was also dissatisfaction as the war continued with technical procurement and supply. Reports from the field detailing serious faults or recommendations for modifications were rarely dealt with promptly or effectively within the RAF command chain. Nos 651 and 654 Squadrons themselves devised several simple changes to engine equipment to reduce overheating and excessive piston wear because the group engineer failed to attend to them. No. 658 Squadron reported in February 1945,

Auster 4 spares are still not available with the result that only by taking parts from crashed aircraft can operational aircraft be kept serviceable. . . .

Of course, within the overall organization for the supply and repair of aircraft, the Austers were less than minnows; very small fry lacking that senior pilot within theatres to represent their needs at a high enough level to secure a remedy.

In all, the causes of dissatisfaction with the system differed from squadron to squadron, but whatever the weighting accorded individual items, all commanders believed that AOPs should operate entirely within the Army command, procurement, supply, and maintenance structure.

A second ground for the Director of Air's representation was the growth of the demand for light liaison flying, the carriage of commanders and staffs on reconnaissance but, most frequently, aerial taxi work. From every theatre, corps and divisional commanders had commented on the value of the Auster as a light transport, saving road journeys to meetings, making it possible to visit distant units. Royal Air Force communications flights were established to provide this facility but the numbers of aircraft were too few to meet the need. In practice, only army or army group commanders were able to secure a flight at short notice and, in any case, the aeroplanes in service were unsuitable for visits beyond the fighter strips because of their landing and take-off requirements. Hence the use or, rather, as corps and divisional commanders confessed, the misuse, of the only aircraft under Army control, the Austers of the Air Observation Post squadrons. The case was pressed for the early introduction of an Army air transport facility which would include a capability to extricate casualties from isolated positions – after the manner of 656 Squadron in Burma – and to provide a signals despatch service.

Third, the Director of Air apprehended that, with the war over, money and manpower would be sharply reduced. Seeking the preservation of front-line squadrons, the Air Ministry would be looking widely for economies elsewhere. The airmen and facilities involved in Army flying would be ripe for sacrifice.

Having read the full case, the VCIGS commented on 26 September 1945:

I agree it is desirable for us to take over the responsibility for light aircraft. The manpower aspect does not impress me – if the need is there the men must be found.

But unless I am mistaken there will be strong opposition from the Air Ministry and I think our chief problem is what tactics to adopt to obtain our objectives. It may not be desirable to contact the Air Ministry on a directors level because this may give them an opportunity to consolidate opposition. . . .

The upshot was a letter from the CIGS – Field Marshal Lord Alanbrooke – to the CAS on 15 October:

My dear Portal, Now that we are in the process of formulating the shape of the post-war Army, this seems to be the appropriate time to consider whether, in future, the Army should assume the responsibility for manning and operating its own aircraft for certain specifically Army functions.

It is certain that, as time goes on, movement by air will become an increasingly normal thing, and more and more both in and out of the Services will learn to fly. It seems logical, therefore, that the Army should, in the near future, be prepared to operate such aircraft as it will require for its own domestic needs.

You will remember that, in the later stages of the Burma campaign, a large number of light aircraft was used for exclusively Army purposes and they were found to be absolutely essential. I feel that Army commanders will, in the future, expect to have at least a minimum number of such aircraft at their disposal and will want to control their employment. . . .

The Chief of the Air Staff replied on 31 December:

. . . I would say that I think there are strong arguments against departing from the 'major user' or 'agency' principle. There are arguments in favour of aircraft that can only be of use to the Army coming under Army control, subject to the operational advice of the Air Force Commander, but to divide the control of aircraft and pilots that have uses common to both services would militate against flexibility and economy. If division of control were followed by division of responsibility for maintenance and training, there would be further loss of economy.

. . . The Air Observation post is predominantly an Artillery requirement, and there is a case for the Army assuming responsibility for manning and operating its squadrons. It would, however, be uneconomical, I suggest for the Army responsibility to extend to that of training, maintenance and supply behind the Squadron, because that would lead to duplication. . . . We would of course always prefer to man these squadrons completely with R.A.F. personnel in order to have single control over flying discipline, and other matters, but we recognise the importance gunners attach to their connection with the A.O.P. Squadrons. On the whole I think that the existing compromise is the best practical solution, at any rate until we see the trends of new development. . . .

Inter-communication for Commanders and Staffs in forward areas is recognised as a requirement of growing importance. Single engined, unarmed light communication aircraft used for this purpose would not strictly violate the 'major user' principle, but here again we come up against the fact that so long as aircraft remain comparatively expensive to build and maintain, and pilots' training involves big overheads, the proposition of handing this responsibility over to the Army would not be economical in the national interest. Another point which we must bear in mind is that the complete air superiority we had everywhere towards the end of the war has given everyone a false impression of the freedom with which the air can be used in forward areas. . . .

He agreed that Army commanders and staff officers 'must have aircraft immediately available for inter-communication'. Where the Air Force had no common interest in this, special arrangements would have to be made. At a later stage, 'when light aircraft are as easy and as safe to handle in all weathers as cars, when their cost in money and manpower is considerably less', the Army might well run its own light aircraft 'just as the Air Force runs its own staff cars'. But,

The Air Despatch Letter Service and casualty Air Evacuation I consider can only be regarded, now and in the future, as 'common user' services which should be controlled by the Royal Air Force.

These arguments, sound in theory, did not persuade the CIGS or his senior colleagues to change their minds. In practice, they knew, a facility run entirely by the Royal Air Force became primarily an air facility. Over the war years it had become apparent to the Army staffs in joint army/air group headquarters that the air commanders and their staffs, nominally sharing communications aircraft on equal terms, were accorded first call on them because the supplying squadron or flight was in the Royal Air Force chain of command.

Still, the CIGS wisely decided to discontinue an action which he could not then win. He proposed that they should 'leave things as they are for the present', a decision in which Portal's successor, Marshal of the Royal Air Force Lord Tedder, concurred at the beginning of 1946.

One conseqence of the exchange was that the Royal Air Force made no attempt to scrap or change their contribution to the fielding of light aircraft. In so far as their commitment to train glider pilots to fly and to provide tugs for continuation training was concerned, this seemed to be waning of its own accord. The 1st Airborne Division was disbanded in 1946 and, after a tour in Palestine, the 6th was reduced to a regular brigade in 1948, when the number of glider pilots diminished proportionately. One Territorial Army airborne division was retained for a time. The question as to whether airborne forces would be viable in future conflicts was argued periodically but, in any case, it was agreed that the glider as a battlefield delivery vehicle had had its day. It only remained to decide when to wind up the Glider Pilot Regiment after its short but valiant history. Fortuitously for those officers and NCOs still present and anxious to fly, a solution was at hand.

In parallel with the reduction in the Army Air Corps, the twelve wartime AOP squadrons were reduced to four by 1948:

651 Squadron was posted to Egypt in 1945.
652 Squadron remained in Germany.
656 Squadron, disbanded but reformed, was in Malaya.
657 Squadron was brought home to England in 1945.

This total was based on the AOP support required for a notional number of AGRAs and divisions on mobilization, backed, from 1949 to 1957, by five units in the Royal Auxiliary Air Force, 661, 662, 663, 664, and 666 Squadrons.

The experiences of the war suggested that there should be two types of flight, A and B, the former operating with the guns, the latter occupied with aerial photography, located with squadron headquarters. But in the five post-war years in regular service, these ideas were eroded and, finally, abandoned. The fact was that there was insufficient demand to justify the retention of four squadrons solely for artillery purposes. The Austers were therefore used regularly for reconnaissance and communications – 'aerial taxi' duties – at home and abroad, and were in considerable demand in the succession of campaigns great and small, in which the Army was the principal operator.

This happy arrangement which satisfied Army needs without offending RAF sensibilities might have continued indefinitely but for the technology factor. The Auster fleet was ageing, approaching its limit to absorb further modification beyond the highly rated Mark 9 under development. New aircraft were needed for the Army, models conceived in the light of post-war technology, or maturing after long development, such as helicopters, of which a handful had been passed to the Army for trials. But the Army had no direct communication with the aircraft procurement department, now in the Ministry of Supply. Its agent – indeed, the arbiter of its requirements in aircraft – was the Air Ministry, and the forum *inter alia* for the evolution of general requirements the Land/Air Warfare Committee.

From 1946 the Director of Air (restyled Director of Land/Air Warfare) was charged to embrace the whole spectrum of the Army's inter-operation with air forces. As a means of reaching decisions jointly in this field, the War Office and Air Ministry agreed to nominate officers from corresponding departments to the committee, which was of sufficient importance to be chaired alternately by the Vice-Chiefs of the General and Air Staffs.

In June 1949 the principal subject for discussion was 'Light Aircraft Requirements for the

Army'. The War Office proposed the procurement of a fixed-wing model for AOP work, and two helicopters: a small two-seater for reconnaissance, and a four-seater for casualty evacuation. Later in the month, the committee published Policy Statement No. 9 as a reflection of joint agreement. What is remarkable about this document is not that the two services agreed on the forms of aircraft to be sought, though they did so, but the wording of the opening paragraph:

1. The purposes for which the RAF agree to provide light aircraft for the Army, and the types of aircraft now in use, are as follows:

|     | *Purpose* | *Aircraft at present in use* |
| --- | --- | --- |
| (a) | Air OP, including limited photography | Auster Mk 6 |
| (b) | Training of Air OP pilots | Auster Mk 5 |
| (c) | Local reconnaissances by Commanders and Staffs | Auster Mk 5 or 6 |
| (d) | Evacuation of casualties from forward areas | NIL |
| (e) | Intercommunication by Commanders and staffs | Auster Mk 5 or 6 |
| (f) | Air Despatch Letter Service (not implemented in peace time) | Auster Mk 5 or 6 |

All the duties regarded by Lord Portal as 'common services', with the exception of casualty evacuation, were accepted tacitly as the work of Army pilots.

The proposal included statements of essential payload: 440 lb for the fixed and light rotary-wing models; 650 lb for the larger helicopter. For the time being, it was concluded, the Auster Mk 6 would serve for the AOP, but commercial models should be purchased for the helicopters in the absence of suitable service models. In the longer term, fixed and rotary-wing aircraft should be developed to satisfy specific operational functions. Again, all the aircraft were to be supplied to and piloted by the Army.

The Air Ministry agreed to these proposals without demur. In September 1950 the committee considered organizational matters arising from the enlarged prospectus. Scales were discussed in terms of numbers of aircraft to serve each division, corps, and army or army group headquarters extant in peace or formed on mobilization. The numbers likely to be required for the air despatch letter service – ADLS – and casualty evacuation were assessed on a calculation of daily sorties. Opinions were expressed as to the suitability of fixed and rotary-wing models for the different roles.

For the first time, a light aircraft wing headquarters was mooted for incorporation within the army/tactical air group command level, to be activated on mobilization, and a light aircraft squadron headquarters at corps level in peace and war, subsuming the AOP squadron headquarters in being. Thus the Army would institute in war an overall command structure embracing all light aircraft functions. Behind the corps area, casualties from the casualty clearing units would be evacuated by Royal Air Force aircraft.

Requirements for pilot skills were set out. The servicing and maintenance of aircraft and associated equipment would be continued by Royal Air Force tradesmen. Six regular light aircraft flights were to be formed as soon as possible, backed by twelve in the reserve forces. These would be in addition to the five Royal Auxiliary Air Force AOP squadrons then in being.

The Army proposed to raise the numbers seconded to flying duties, opening for the first time this specialization to officers and NCOs from all arms, including essentially a number from the Royal Signals for ADLS duties, and the Royal Army Service Corps for casualty evacuation. Immediately, however, they had pilots in hand: the remnant of the Glider Pilot Regiment, five officers and forty-nine senior NCOs.

The War Office put these proposals formally for implementation to the Air Ministry in April 1951, together with a request for procurement of the new aircraft, within a defence budget inflated by the demands of the Korean war and inceptory commitments to NATO to a level of £4,700 million over the following three years. This focused the attention of the Royal Air Force on the full implication of Army expectations.

The Vice-Chief of the Air Staff put the matter to his colleagues in the Air Council in January 1952, making the following comments on the provision of pilots:

16. Despite a decision promulgated in a L/AW Committee Paper that the Army should fly all light aircraft operating in the forward areas, I consider that it would be preferable that aircraft in the proposed Light Liaison Flights should be flown by RAF pilots. I consider that it would be uneconomical to train Army pilots to the standard required for safe operation at night and in bad visibility. Furthermore, there are certain to be numbers of RAF pilots either resting from operational flying duties, or who have medical categories which restrict them from flying modern high performance aircraft, who could be used for this purpose. While final decisions on this are being made I have agreed with VCIGS that the following represents our views on the desirable time table and organisation:

(i) We should aim at getting a Light Liaison organisation set up in Germany as soon as possible. It should include an experimental helicopter Flight (from aircraft already available).
(ii) The organisation to be commanded by an airman, and run through the normal channels by 2nd Tactical Air Force; it would be at the disposal of [the] British Army of the Rhine, who would notify their requirements in an agreed manner.
(iii) The units should be ultimately manned by RAF pilots, but in the interim, suitable Army pilots to continue; details to be worked out by the staffs. It was agreed that [RAF] pilots selected for this work should be employed for a full tour of two to two and a half years. . . .

With due deliberation, some ten months after the War Office proposal had been made, the Air Council discussed this matter on 7 February 1952. Members then expressed predictable views. The Secretary of State, for example, clearly worried about items likely to add to his ministry's budget, questioned the urgency of the case. His under-secretary 'suggested that light liaison flights might well be improvised when the need arose'.

The Chief of the Air Staff [Marshal of the Royal Air Force Sir John Slessor],

. . . said there was a current need for liaison flights in Malaya which was being met, by no means satisfactorily, by misemploying AOP aircraft. At the same time, he was far from satisfied that the present UE [unit scale of equipment] of AOP aircraft could be justified: he doubted whether the aircraft were ever used in their designated role and, indeed, whether there would be a firm requirement for AOP in a future war. In the last war, they had been introduced in conditions of air superiority and, without further study, it could not be taken for granted that they could be used in other conditions. . . .

These remarks may be excused, perhaps, by the circumstances of the time. The British contingents in the Korean war continued to absorb considerable funds at a time when the Royal Air Force was seeking to modernize and reinforce its forces committed to NATO. As an emergency measure, agreement had been given to the formation of a light aircraft flight to join the 1st British Commonwealth Division in Korea, where it joined an AOP flight sent from Hong Kong. Otherwise, as often before, the provision of light aircraft seemed to the Royal Air Force irrelevant to the needs of the times.

The War Office was now pressing for a response, however, and thus the Air Council approved the immediate requirements, but sanctioned the formation of four rather than six light liaison flights, while reserving their position on the expansion of the Royal Auxiliary Air Force. Changes in the AOP organization would not be required, they concluded, because light liaison flights should 'in due course' be manned by RAF pilots. This communication reached the War Office on 8 April 1952 where it was received by the Deputy Chief of the Imperial General Staff, responsible for Army organization and equipment. He did not like the proposal but instructed his staff to examine it in detail, considering at the same time whether the Army could take on itself the servicing and maintenance of the aircraft involved.

He pursued also the surprising concession by his former colleague, the Vice-Chief, who had by that time vacated his post, that Army pilots would not be able to fly safely at night and in bad weather. Somewhat as he expected, records manifested that the night flying record of the AOP pilots, in war and peace, and similarly their capabilities in all weathers, showed that this opinion was groundless. Among a host of examples was the transportation of Brigadier 'Hammer' Matthews, a nineteen stone commander, Royal Artillery, on numerous occasions in poor visibility.

All this took some months. On 25 November 1952 he passed the following comments to his colleagues in the Army Council:

4. Acceptance of the Air Council's counter-proposals would inevitably result in control of light liaison flights becoming merged with that of the existing communication flights in the headquarters of tactical groups. Operational control would, therefore, then pass from the Army to the RAF. . . . The Air Council's counter-proposals are, I suggest, unacceptable.

Even so, the Army budget could not provide funds for a wholesale takeover of the ground staff posts manned by the Royal Air Force. To gain their main point, that Army officers alone should pilot light sorties in the tactical contact zone, concessions would have to be made to the Air Ministry point of view.

They should agree that casualty evacuation and army headquarters liaison duties remained a responsibility of the Royal Air Force. Reductions in aircraft would have to be accepted in the formation of regular and Royal Auxiliary Air Force flights, and in the number of aircraft within AOP flights from five to four. These changes would reduce an overall complement of 175 aircraft to 112, including those allotted to the four regular independent light liaison flights.

It was these four small units that the Royal Air Force proposed to take over completely, replacing the commander and other pilots' places. The DCIGS proposed a way of circumventing this intention.

They should disband the light liaison flights, reorganizing the Army pilots and the small number of Army other ranks within them to form individual sections. These would not be viable technically or administratively, so they should be grafted on to the existing AOP organization. In view of the reduction in aircraft overall, the sections would not be distributed evenly among regular squadrons but disposed to meet operational need, as in Malaya.

The War Office put all these proposals to the Air Ministry on 11 December 1952. The economies projected would benefit both services, leaving but one Army requirement in the matter, as the War Office letter concluded:

> . . . the Army Council would be grateful for confirmation that it is the intention of the Air Council to replace with helicopters those fixed wing aircraft used for Light Liaison purposes.

On the whole, the Air Ministry accepted the War Office counter-proposal as regards organization. Army pilots were found to be capable of flying light liaison aircraft. But the Air Council was not at all ready to provide the Army with a fleet of helicopters, and was alarmed to learn that the latter were studying the economics of introducing large cargo helicopters to replace part of its ground transport. In this its judgement was better informed. The air staff figures for purchase and maintenance were fuller and more accurate than those of the Army. Even so, when the Air Council Standing Committee considered policy in July 1953, it took a realistic view of options. Referring to an air staff refusal earlier in the year to consider the supply of helicopters to light liaison flights, the Vice-Chief of the Air Staff doubted,

> . . . whether the line taken was sound or could be maintained. There might be cases in which, under special conditions, such as existed in Malaya, the use of helicopters would represent an overall economy, though in themselves they were an expensive form of aircraft.
>
> 2. CAS agreed. The increasing use of helicopters not only by the Services but by civil aviation would probably in time reduce the cost of development and production. He felt that, notwithstanding the present high cost, it might be necessary on grounds of policy to consider the provision of helicopters for the Army, possibly at the cost of a cut in the unit establishment. He would be reluctant to see any steps taken which would give the Army grounds for demanding the provision of their own helicopters outside RAF resources.
>
> 3. CAS referred to the Working Party set up by the War Office [under Brigadier G.E.R. Bastin] to consider the use of helicopters in the Army, which was about to present its report. It appeared from the minutes of a meeting recently held . . . that the Working Party was likely to recommend that heavy freight helicopters with a range of some 150 miles would serve a useful function in restoring mobility to ground forces. . . . It was essential that the Air

Ministry should be ready to consider the Army's statement of its requirements in a constructive light. . . .

Unaware of these views and frustrated by what appeared to be the intransigence of the air staff, the Director of Land/Air Warfare – Major-General G.S. Thompson – proposed to the CIGS on 6 August 1953 that the time had come for the Army to take full responsibility for its own aircraft:

> . . . Owing to the present system, we are failing, increasingly, to make proper military use of helicopters, already assessed at their proper value by the Navy, Civil operators and American Services. The helicopter would probably be of greater value to the Army than any other Service or organisation. . . .

With this the Army Council agreed, including their Secretary of State. Full responsibility for light aircraft without conversion to helicopters would add £300,000 to the War Office budget for maintenance and 220 men for the regular and reserve Army units concerned. New Austers would cost about £3,000 each (actually, £4,000). Considering the working party's report at the same time, it was noted that the cost of a 'cargo' helicopter was believed to £30,000. Even so, at the end of the summer, the council proposed to man, maintain and administer entirely its own light aircraft, and to form an experimental unit to investigate the feasibility of operating 'helicopters (or other aircraft capable of landing in a confined space as cargo and troop carriers and as ambulances) . . .'.

Such ideas, intolerable eighteen months before, were becoming acceptable to the Royal Air Force. Here is a note from the Vice-Chief of the Air Staff to his Air Council colleagues on 12 April 1954:

> 4. We all, I think, have at the back of our minds the fear that the War Office, with their enthusiasm for air transport and their tendency to underestimate its cost and to overestimate its utilisation possibilities, may want to spend an undue part of the defence budget on helicopters and light aircraft. They are in a fairly strong position to do so, since the effect of the Radical [Defence] Review is to tend to put their other requirements for expenditure on a falling curve. We may also fear that the War Office may underestimate the vulnerability of these aircraft and depend on them to a dangerous extent.
>
> 5. On the other hand, it is difficult to deny the units in question are not simply supporting, or operating with, the Army. They are, as the War Office points out, virtually a part of the Army. . . . I find it very difficult to see any convincing arguments we could produce against the principle of the War Office's case in respect either of the AOP and light liaison aircraft or of heavy helicopters. The dangers in the latter case are more serious than in the former, simply because, if the idea of extensive use of heavy helicopters comes to anything, the commitment will be much larger and more expensive. But it is with the heavy helicopters that the War Office's arguments are strongest. It is difficult to deny that the War Office is in the best position to decide how far it is efficient and economical to substitute this form of transport for normal transport in the field.
>
> 6. It seems to me that if we concede to the War Office the responsibility, subject to

overriding control by the Chiefs of Staff, etc., of determining these requirements, which are of such intimate concern to them, we shall be in a *stronger* position to keep them on the rails, as their proposals come forward, than under the existing system. Under the existing system, when we fail to meet their requests we give them the impression that we are influenced by selfishness or inertia rather than by the merits of the case. . . .

When the Air Council discussed 'RESPONSIBILITY FOR FLYING UNITS DESIGNED TO MEET THE NEEDS OF THE ARMY' on 6 May 1954, the Chief of the Air Staff agreed with the Vice-Chief's contentions,

3. . . . he agreed . . . that in modern conditions it was wrong to forbid the Army to buy domestic transport aircraft and to make them rely on the good-will of the Air Council. At present the Army had too few aircraft because air funds had to be spent on projects of greater importance to air defence. That was hardly logical, since the need for Army aircraft should be considered against the background of the Army's transport problem and the need for mobility in the field, not as part of the war in the air. On the other hand, there was the fear that VCAS's proposals might prove to be the thin end of the wedge, leading in time to pressure by the Army for wider functions in the air – and certainly the Army would never give up any air responsibilities that they were allowed to acquire. He would not pretend that such fears were unfounded. His own view was that the Royal Air Force was now sufficiently well established to resist any attempt to whittle away its functions. . . . As regards the financial aspect, he had no doubt that Army Votes [of finance] should in future bear the cost of Army aircraft and that it should be for the War Office and not the Air Ministry, to deal with the Treasury. . . .

Close to acceptance, the Army's case effectively passed into suspended animation due to political intransigence, financial stringency, technical difficulties, and resurgent assertions of Royal Air Force prerogatives.

Politically, the case was pressed first by Antony Head, then John Hare, successive Secretaries of State for War in Mr Churchill's and Mr Eden's Conservative governments, and opposed by Lord de L'Isle and Dudley and Nigel Birch, Secretaries of State for Air in the same period. The latter, as a junior minister in the Air Ministry was a prolonged opponent of an Army air force of any description beyond the AOP organization. Curiously, the fiercest battle was fought between ministers on the arrangements for the establishment of the Joint Helicopter Evaluation Unit (later retitled the Joint Experimental Helicopter Unit, conveniently abbreviated as JEHU), charged to discover to what extent the larger helicopters could enhance the mobility of the Army's field forces and replace their ground transport.

Lack of finance was a persistent factor inhibiting the introduction of helicopters into operational service within the Army and Royal Air Force. The Royal Navy played its hand more skilfully in gleaning funds for its own needs and those of the Royal Marine Commandos in this period, made the more confident in the value of rotary-wing aircraft to many of its operations after seeing the extensive work performed by United States naval and marine corps helicopters in the Korean war.

The Army as a whole was neither as confident in the reliability nor, in consequence, as eager to procure these machines as the other services, though this may be explained by the growing division of the Army into two bodies.

The first was what may be termed the 'heavy metal' element, stationed in Germany and comprising the greater part of British armour and artillery including anti-aircraft artillery for 'hot war', a substantial component of the NATO Allied Command in Europe confronting the massed armies and air forces of the Warsaw Pact. Air Observation Posts were regarded as essential to artillery support in its major field formation, the 1st British Corps. In peace, their capability to operate reconnaissance and aerial taxi services was taken for granted, even before the arrival of light liaison increments. But when it was apparent that funds for armoured, artillery, and heavy equipment might be reduced in order to purchase helicopters for this work, opposition was expressed by commanders at almost all levels.

The other part of the Army was deployed in what was later termed 'out of area', meaning outside the NATO theatre, on active service in Malaya and Korea, subsequently in Kenya, Cyprus and Port Said. Commanders, staffs, and units involved were familiar with the extraordinary advantages of possessing aircraft capable of vertical take-off and landing in operations, and in the evacuation of casualties. Light aircraft – the Auster and the Royal Air Force Pioneer – were highly valued in these roles. Helicopters manifestly offered a new dimension. The only complaint was that, in Korea, the British Commonwealth forces possessed none and were thus reliant on American generosity, and in the other theatres there were never enough of them.

JEHU was formed on 1 April 1955 at Middle Wallop, at which Army pilots were trained to fly under Royal Air Force command. From the outset its work was constrained by insufficient resources, particularly in the full range of aircraft, and the realization that there were insufficient funds to develop their prime target, a helicopter capable of lifting a tonnage over a given number of miles per day equal to that of fourteen 3 ton trucks. By 1 March 1956 the Secretary of State for War was obliged to tell parliament in the debate on the Army estimates that,

> . . . I do not wish to deceive the House. I do not believe it is realistic to think that we can have these [helicopters] to replace the vehicles in the Army.

The Land/Air Warfare directorate had not given up the struggle, however. When it became known in the previous November that development of a 'heavy load-carrying helicopter' was to be discontinued, they investigated the cost of purchasing a suitable model from the commercial market. But this was one item among a number. Overall, they were looking towards an overall fleet of five hundred aircraft – fixed and rotary wing – comprehending logistics, AOP and light liaison. What were termed 'freighter aircraft', and 'long range personnel carriers' would be the responsibility of the Royal Air Force but to a scale jointly agreed with the Army. The remainder would be wholly run by the Army. Excluding provisions made by the Air Ministry for major transport aircraft, the capital cost over five years was estimated at £63 million.

This scheme was inadvertently disclosed to the Air Ministry by the War Office while it was still under discussion. The air staff did not much care what stage it had reached: the ideas it projected were alarming. A group-captain briefing his superior remarked, 'The Army's gone mad! Where do they think they will find the money?'

The Air Ministry concluded, with good reason, that it would be found at the expense of the

Early helicopters: Sikorsky R6 – the 'Hoverfly 2' (*Museum of Army Flying*)

Early helicopters: Bristol 'Sycamore' in 1906 Flight (*Museum of Army Flying*)

Royal Air Force budget. As before, diversion of their cash from 'the front line' of combat aircraft to Army interests concentrated the minds of the Air Council on the control controversy, suspended by diversionary pursuits.

Air Marshal Sir Ronald Ivelaw-Chapman, Vice-Chief of the Air Staff at this time, proposed a means on 27 June 1956 of evolving a policy to satisfy both services. He reasoned on these lines. The Army's claim to run its own aircraft entirely remained unanswered. They should now concede it on the lines proposed by his predecessor; that was, within limits. The concession should embrace the Austers and light helicopters in service with the AOP and light liaison organization. It would oblige the War Office to come to terms with the financial implications of this responsibility, at the same time relieving the Air Ministry from negotiations on their behalf with the Treasury. This would leave open the matter of providing and controlling the heavier aircraft such as the fixed-wing Pioneer and Twin Pioneer and the heavier helicopters, hitherto excluded from the Army's formal proposal.

> . . . It could be argued that to make an offer on these lines now might weaken our position in arguing against the major plan for logistic support aircraft which the Army will put forward. On the other hand it could be argued that we should be strengthening our hand by so doing and put the Army in a difficult position whilst at the same time leaving ourselves entirely free to fight the major issue. . . .

Having shown that it was not pursuing a purely obstructive policy, the Air Ministry should secure agreement on the following bases:

> (i) The Army should assume full responsibility for purchasing, manning, maintaining and operating unarmed aircraft used solely for its own purposes in the AOP and light liaison roles. The maximum all up weight – the weight of the aircraft plus whatever load was to be carried in flight – would not exceed 4,000 pounds.
> (ii) The Air Ministry in conjunction with the War Office would remain responsible for formulating specifications.
> (iii) In the field, Army aircraft would be subject to the overall direction of the air force commander.

The first, and key, limitation, as the Vice-Chief pointed out, was that only two of the aircraft in service or currently planned would fall to Army control, the Auster and the Skeeter two-seater helicopter. Despite the objections of the Secretary of State when the Air Council considered this advice on 5 July 1956, and the ruffling of his feathers when the Army's proposals were once again prematurely disclosed by the War Office, the Ivelaw-Chapman scheme was put to the latter.

A longstanding calumny should now be dismissed. The successive Directors of Land/Air Warfare in 1956 and 1957, Majors-General R.C. Bray and R.K. Exham have been held responsible for accepting the 4,000 lb limit, the one from lack of interest, the other from lack of knowledge. The minutes of the Army Council's meeting on 26 November 1956 show this to be wholly false:

The Secretary of State [John Hare] said that, since the Council's last meeting, he had heard from the Secretary of State for Air [Nigel Birch], who was now willing to agree that the Army should control and operate its light aircraft on certain conditions. The main condition was that the Army would be restricted to unarmed light aircraft of a maximum all-up weight of 4,000 lb.

In discussion the point was made that, while so severe a restriction was perhaps a pity and one which the War Office might later wish to alter by negotiation, taking on light aircraft would present the Army with new maintenance problems of considerable magnitude, and there was therefore much to be said for starting in a small way and expanding later if necessary. There was no intention of entering the field of light cargo aircraft, which was being considered by [Admiral Bingley's] Committee [covering all three services]. It was therefore agreed that the Secretary of State should inform the Secretary of State for Air that he did not wish to quarrel with the conditions proposed, though he must reserve the right, if developments justified it, to propose that slightly larger aircraft should become a War Office responsibility. He could, however, give an assurance that this was suggested purely in the interests of flexibility and that the Army had no intention of starting up an Army Air Force or an Army Transport Command. . . .

This view was passed from Mr Hare to Mr Birch that same day, and was acknowledged on 29 November 1956. The latter returned what the War Office considered to be a helpful comment:

. . . it is only reasonable that you should suggest some flexibility [in the all-up weight]. The time may come when there will be no suitable aircraft with a weight under 4,000 lbs.

The issue was at last settled, and at a time of turmoil and ministerial changes in the service ministries as the Port Said operations came to an inglorious end. The Eden government was dissolving. A new Minister of Defence, Duncan Sandys, with a remit to make yet more economies in the armed forces, took office in January 1957, and one of his early tasks was to give formal approval to the agreement to transfer light aviation lock, stock, and barrel to the Army.

Whatever people may tell you now, [General Hull, the DCIGS of the day, was later to say], we didn't really expect to get final agreement in 1956. And when it came, although I had been told that all the preparatory work had been done, scarcely anything was settled, let alone on paper. The REME [Royal Electrical and Mechanical Engineers], for example, were expected to take over the RAF technical work in a few months. But one thing I thought there would be a lot of argument about was easy: the new name. Everyone I asked seemed certain that it had to be the 'Army Air Corps', the revival of the old airborne title. Several years later, I was put right on the matter. The old hands weren't looking back at all. They were picking up the title of a much-envied and admired organisation, the American Army Air Corps!

CHAPTER SEVENTEEN

# Gunners and Glider Pilots

There were arguments later as to who founded Army aviation in the post-war years. Claims were staked by the Royal Artillery and the Glider Pilot Regiment. It is true that AOP squadrons continued in service continuously from the victory over Japan to the re-formation of the Army Air Corps, as often as not with a flight at least involved in almost every operation. But the glider pilots had worthy evidence to adduce. Like 651 Squadron, they were in Palestine for three years from 1945 and maintained their flying skills in light aircraft, though the AOP pilots undoubtedly flew the greater number of counter-terrorist sorties in the territory. But when India was partitioned in 1947 the balance was reversed: British glider pilots flew light aircraft extensively in the absence of AOP squadrons. At a time when Hindu and Muslim mobs were slaughtering each other's refugee columns, Tiger Moths and Austers often provided the only safe and sure means of local travel. Cricket grounds were much in use as improvised strips. The following year, when the Berlin airlift began, the Glider Pilot Regiment at home offered its aircrew unsuccessfully as loadmasters, and was thus the more delighted when, unexpectedly, the Royal Air Force selected some of their number to be second pilots on York four-engined transports. With the demise of the first Army Air Corps in 1950 (the Parachute and Glider Pilot Regiments passed to the infantry) glider pilots assumed the light liaison role, operating in Malaya and Korea.

In Malaya the Royal Artillery AOP led the way in light aircraft support from 1948, as the largely national service army in the peninsula was drawn into the demanding task of defeating Chin Peng's Communist revolutionaries. Early misdirection of troops into civil police duties and a futile policy of speculative 'sweeps' were replaced by integrated ground and air operations though, curiously, it took the infantry some months to appreciate the extent to which the Austers could enhance their activities. Naval Sikorsky 55 helicopters were made available. The Royal Air Force complemented its Sycamore light helicopters and fixed-wing Pioneers with another version of the S55, the Whirlwind, built by Messrs Westland. Fighters and bombers intervened as required. The Commonwealth air forces dropped supplies at remote jungle sites from a variety of transport aircraft.

No. 656 AOP Squadron, located in Asia since 1943, operated Austers principally from three sites in Negri Sembilan, Pahang, and Perak, from which they flew often over mountains covered by lofty trees and dense undergrowth. The original members had long since departed on rotation. Those who took their place, glider pilots among them from 1950, learned quickly to cope with monsoon weather: lightning, high turbulence and heavy rain were seasonal hazards, but clouds and persistent ground mists were a greater danger. The aircraft had no blind flying aids. With the onset of low cloud, a pilot had to fix precisely his position on the map and proceed by dead reckoning to the nearest airstrip. His only long-range radio was a high frequency Army No. 62 set tuned to the more powerful No. 19 at the flight base. If the calculations were faulty the aircraft crash landed, at best in cultivation. The weather was consistently the most formidable enemy.

Major L.J. Wheeler RA, commanding 656 Squadron inspects an RAF Dragonfly, one of only three helicopters in Malaya as terrorist operations began (*Major L.J. Wheeler*)

Occasional mechanical faults also claimed lives. One lucky pilot survived the discovery of a poisonous snake rearing behind his seat.

Progressively, the demand for light aircraft extended from taxi services to reconnaissance, shadowing terrorist movements, fixing infantry positions in deep jungle, and assisting in survey. From 1952, 656 Squadron under Major Lionel Wheeler worked up a system of marking deep jungle targets – most productively, guerrilla camps – with smoke and subsequently anti-submarine flares racked under the Auster wings. VHF radios were essential for communication between aircraft, however; the markers had a limited burning time, so the bombers had to follow the Austers closely – but the Austers had to have time to escape. The following pilot memoir illustrates the problem:

> . . . Just below, another glimpse of the stream bed and the site of trodden earth marking the bandits' parade ground . . . A tug on the [release] toggle and a brilliant light as the flare ignited, swinging down to the trees on its parachute. [From above the leading bomber captain calls] 'Marker – this is Sixgun. Got your flare. Bombing in 45 seconds.' Now for the getaway: six Lincolns up above with fourteen 1,000-pounder iron bombs, which they could release in one salvo. I opened the throttle wide, counting the seconds. Before I had covered a

Fitting a flare to an Auster, 656 Squadron (*Major L.J. Wheeler*)

mile the sky lit up behind me and in my rear vision mirror I could see the jungle taking to the
air in the flashes of the bombs. Seven seconds later the shock wave hit my Auster. It was as
though it had been hit across the tail with a giant crowbar. . . .

The greater range of activities extended working hours. Yet, for all the mists, sudden rains,
persistent mosquitoes, occasional ground attacks or ambushes of their supply vehicles, most of
those in the detached flights found their occupation rewarding. They made themselves tolerably
comfortable in a few tents or under bamboo thatching. Every few months flights rotated to
another site. Every week two or three would depart on local leave, or embark at Singapore,
homeward bound in the ship which had brought out their replacements. In the twelve years of its
residence the squadron contributed 171,241 flying hours to the campaign.

In Korea the Austers of 1903 AOP and 1913 Light Liaison Flights joined the 1st British
Commonwealth Division as it established itself in defence along the lower Imjin river. They shared
a strip close to divisional headquarters. The former, an essential eye of the artillery in
mountainous country, picked out by patient observation precise targets among the enemy caves
and bunkers for bombardment. Both flights became adept at dodging the considerable capacity of
Chinese air defence weapons, no mean skill at the low speeds and heights implicit in their work.
Losses were consequentially low, though many Austers returned to base with bullet or shrapnel
holes.

Setting up a static aerial at an unmanned strip prior to the evolution of the 'trailing aerial'. The radio in the Auster is a No. 62 Set (*Major L.J. Wheeler*)

The light liaison pilots of 1913 – officers, warrant officers and sergeants still wearing their Glider Pilot Regimental badges – reconnoitred, dropped leaflets, and partnered the AOP in air photography. They carried commanders and staffs as much along the line as in taxi work behind it, though the carriage of large passengers in the Auster 6s was never comfortable. Captain Peter Downward, the first flight commander, was grateful for the loan of a relatively spacious American L–19 Bird Dog to ease the discomforts of his tall divisional commander.

Lacking helicopters, 1913 Flight was unable to lift Commonwealth wounded from forward positions, a task borne universally by the Americans. It was a lamentable situation; British Army helicopter pilots, qualified during 'trials', were available, and the United States Army was ready to loan rotary wings to the British contingent. The War Office showed no interest in such an arrangement.

The light aircraft flights were the only units operating under Royal Air Force colours in Korea. Soldiers and airmen jointly launched their pilots throughout the swings of the peninsular climate from winter ice to sub-tropical summer, often accompanying them as observers.

Contrast these conditions in the Orient with challenges of quite another kind: an AOP squadron relearning some of the lessons of war among the open farmlands and wooded hills in the British defence sector in Germany.

Major Peter Mead, newly appointed to command 652 Squadron in 1950, took it out on the annual corps' exercise,

> . . . withdrawal from one river line to another, and with the preparation of a counter-stroke. The enemy was a token . . . force, but it contained the greater part of the R.A.F. in Germany and they appeared to have been briefed to eliminate our Air O.P.s. Had we known this, I doubt if it would have worried us much; we did not believe the jet fighter pilot could come down close to the ground and 'mix it' with us, nor did we believe that he could detect our well-concealed fields and strips. In theory, our pilots carried 'rear observers', but in practice they were rarely carried. . . . in theory pilots flew low, in practice they flew at about a hundred feet. In theory they observed from behind the line of their forward troops and by climbing only briefly from ground level, in practice they flew boldly enough to get the information their commanders wanted. In theory they used Cato [Concealed Approach and Take-Off] techniques; in practice a quick circuit of a local wood was often the only precaution they took. We were in for a ripe surprise.
>
> . . . As the withdrawal started, so the enemy fighters started to beat us up. One pilot reckoned he had been 'shot down' as he took off from his strip, another as he landed. After three days . . . only one of our pilots was left alive.
>
> . . . I called for a volunteer to be my 'rear observer', and worked out a hasty drill with him. The engine noise, and the primitive radio arrangement in the Auster allowed of no speech; all the rear observer could do, sitting back to back with the pilot, was to strike him on the thigh – once if he should turn to starboard, twice for port. . . .
>
> . . . back to the new squadron strip which was well south of the [River] Leine. My Cato was not up to much, but I pressed on with the final approach. Down went full flap and then – bang – bang on my right thigh from LAC Bull the rear observer. . . .

At the end of the exercise we had a tremendous squadron post-mortem, in which we worked out the implications of air inferiority on our battle drills and our training. . . .

Experiences such as those of Major Mead's squadron raised questions of AOP viability in the Army as well as the Royal Air Force, though the AOP and light liaison pilots tended to the view that they would survive by applying greater thought and practice to evasion. As it happened, none had to put this theory to the test of war; though it seems likely that the Auster would have had a fair chance of survival against attacks by the massed aircraft of the Warsaw Pact flying at speeds considerably faster than the Focke-Wulf 190s and Me 109s often evaded during the Second World War. Another solution in the opinion of many experienced pilots was that helicopters, possessing the ability to descend rapidly and to fly very close to the ground, and to hide in farmyards and copses, would be more likely to survive than fixed-wing aircraft in a hostile air environment. But in 1950, as noted, the Royal Air Force had no intention of providing the Army with helicopters.

The Austers continued therefore to serve exclusively as the Army's transport and eye in the sky until 1956. Among its adventures in this period, 1910 Flight was detached from the Suez Canal Zone to Eritrea to assist in the suppression of banditry. The five Austers flew in the service of government and police rather more than of the Army, daunting savage foes, rescuing imperilled officers, asserting political authority, subscribing their dues to membership of the Biggles club in much the same way as RAF colleagues had done in the Near East desert between the wars. They dropped supplies to friendly forces and leaflets on the marauders; and evacuated casualties on

Flight of 656 Squadron Mark 6 Austers on a former wartime grass landing site. Few of the bases were as open as this, but the surrounding forest was common to all (*Major L.J. Wheeler*)

both sides including those of the Shifta, most lawless and numerous of the robber bands. These adventures occupied 1950–2, when the flight returned to the Canal Zone.

In the immediately following years, the British government agreed to withdraw from Egypt and the Suez Canal, creating a new base for its forces in the Middle East in Cyprus. One effect of this was to encourage a faction among Greek Cypriots to unite their people with Greece – enosis. Archbishop Makarios and Colonel Grivas were their leaders. In the second half of 1955 it became apparent that terrorism was their weapon.

No. 651 AOP Squadron was in the process of being disbanded as intelligence reports disclosed the political dangers approaching. Clearly, there would be a requirement for the services of Army aviation in complement to the Royal Air Force. 1910 Reconnaissance Flight was retained in service, and joined by 1915 Light Liaison Flight, newly formed, at Lakatamia – immediately south of Nicosia airport – on 4 April 1956. By this time the slender island garrison had been reinforced by the equivalent of two brigades, and more were to come. Grivas had established five terrorist groups in the Troodos mountains and the western Kyrenia range. Urban cells were widely distributed. Political moonshine and terror were rife as a means of persuading the Greek-speaking community to make the island ungovernable.

Tactics progressed beyond a replication of the early errors of the Malayan campaign to practice of its triumphant principles. But intelligence gathering was slow and depended as much on overt measures, including reconnaissance by light aircraft, as clandestine material. Isolating gangs from food and weapons sources, widespread across the countryside, proved impracticable. On the other hand the mobility of the ground forces was immeasurably greater as helicopters arrived, chiefly Royal Navy Whirlwinds expropriated from their anti-submarine warfare role in the Mediterranean fleet, and RAF Sycamores. The only inconveniences of these valuable reinforcements was that there were too few of the first, and the second were flown by skilled pilots who were absolutely ignorant of ground requirements.

Then, in July 1956, a new problem arose in the Mediterranean for Britain and France: President Nasser of Egypt arbitrarily nationalized the Suez Canal. The British and French governments made a secret deal with Israel for the reoccupation of the waterway and destruction of Egyptian military facilities. The Franco-British operation was named 'Musketeer'.

Political and military misjudgement put ashore a force which, among a variety of omissions in the ground and air, failed to make use of more than a fraction of the parachuting and helicopter potential. JEHU temporarily mobilized as the Joint Helicopter Unit with six Whirlwinds and six Sycamores, supplemented 846 Whirlwind Squadron, Royal Navy. Between 06.10 and 08.40 on 6 November, these small numbers put ashore a Royal Marine commando with all its light vehicles, support weapons, ammunition and stores. By 10.30 the majority were available to move other troops southwards along the canal for completion of the next phase of Musketeer; but this option was not pursued by the army staff. The opportunity was lost. Three weeks later 1903 Recce and 1913 Light Liaison Flights, partners from Korea, were landed at Port Said airfield without any clear requirement for their numbers except a capability to direct naval artillery during the British withdrawal, for which the recce flight would have amply sufficed.

Experience in Malaya and Korea notwithstanding, the Army as a body in 1956 lacked a professional precept fot the tactical use of helicopters and, indeed, Austers beyond AOP and taxi work. Few had seen a helicopter in a military environment.

# CHAPTER EIGHTEEN

# All-up Weight and 'Integration'

Although Army pilots had been advocating an independent air corps for years, when it was finally authorized, as General Hull discovered, 'scarcely anything had been settled' as to its form and substance.

This is not surprising. Views had been uttered for years about how Army aviation should be run. Advocacy in and out of the crew room was one thing; setting it down on paper within the War Office budget was another. This burden now fell upon the L/AW staff, to whit, the single general staff officer dedicated to aviation policy in the directorate in 1956. This was Major R.A. Norman-Walker. Suddenly, the formation of the Army Air Corps became his responsibility. As he was to write later,

> For the GSO2 L/AW(d) the actual planning of the AAC was a piece of cake. From the official position of Junior Voice Crying in the Wilderness he found himself translated to the post of Major Prophet with a congregation yearning to be led into the paths of righteousness. There was no one else in the War Office qualified – or at least licensed – to lay down aeronautical law. He was lucky to get plenty of urgent admonition and expert advice from Middle Wallop – then the Light [Army] Aircraft School, RAF – Lieutenant-Colonel Colin Kennedy and Majors Maurice Sutcliffe and Bob Begbie were particularly helpful. With their guidance and to his own gratified astonishment the GSO 2 found himself making plans and writing establishments with which everyone agreed. . . .

On the basis of meeting the entire manpower bill for the training centre and flying school at Middle Wallop, fielding three squadrons of varying sizes and four independent flights, the Army Council allocated 1,500 officers and men. No specific sum was granted for other costs – and for the best of reasons. Attempts to calculate a figure foundered. Reviewing insistent arguments that a specific figure must be put to the Treasury, the Permanent Secretary remarked,

> . . . there is no point in pursuing this for the moment. It is an extraordinary case. I should think that we are experiencing the same problems as the Royal Air Force when it came into being. All the equipment is in service, the men are in service. There will clearly be adjustment expenses but we are unable as yet to put a figure on them because it is far from clear where they will arise. . . .

Given a base and flying units, an early question was who should man them? All existing posts were filled at that moment but one or another arm had to assure replacements as these were vacated when tours ended or occupants left the service. The Royal Air Force aircraft engineers and artificers would be replaced by REME officers and men, the technical storemen by the Royal

Army Ordnance Corps. The Royal Signals, Royal Army Pay Corps, and Army Catering Corps would man posts appropriate to their specialities.

The greater number of pilots, and non-technical ground appointments, were subscribed by the Royal Artillery, and for this reason it was initially proposed that the arrangement should continue, but the idea was rejected. The Director Royal Artillery apprehended that this considerable commitment might threaten the manning of his regiments. Equally, General Hull among others foresaw that the Army Air Corps might become 'a gunner preserve', an outcome which would discourage secondment from other arms.

As a compromise it was agreed that ground posts other than those established for technicians and specialists would continue to be manned by the Royal Artillery. Pilot posts would be filled by officers volunteering from the Royal Armoured Corps, Royal Artillery, Royal Engineers, Royal Signals, and the infantry, and warrant officers and sergeants from any arm.

These volunteers would be joining a small permanent cadre of forty-five pilots, maintained for continuity of skills and standards, which included the residue of the Glider Pilot Regiment. The latter was finally to be disbanded. Certain stipulations were made. All volunteers must be under thirty years of age for a first tour with the Army Air Corps. Officers must have completed three years at regimental duty, other ranks two, with their parent regiment or corps before applying.

The field organization was to be modified, reflecting changes previously denied by the Royal Air Force, notably, the introduction of a wing headquarters in a theatre containing air units at every level. It was made clear that the squadron was a self-accounting unit and not a sub-unit of a wing; a unit disposed, as a matter of scale, for each division in the field, and containing three light aircraft flights and a supporting workshop.

Two forms of Flight were to be maintained: Reconnaissance and Liaison. Each would contain three fixed-wing aircraft and three helicopters.

The Reconnaissance [Recce] Flight was structured to support a brigade group. With seven pilots drawn from the fighting and supporting arms, it subsumed the duties of Air Observation Posts – extended to include the spectrum of tactical reconnaissance – and was to be capable of conducting traffic control, aerial telephone line laying, courier and mail services.

The Liaison Flight was established for 'communication and liaison duties, particularly to assist the exercise of command'. This meant in practice that the prime duty was to provide air transportation both for point-to-point journeys behind the contact zone and reconnaissance by formation commanders within it. Supplementary tasks included the collection of casualties from forward areas, movement of urgently needed 'tactical stores', and signals support functions in common with the recce flights.

Independent flights were to be capable of all these duties, while supporting themselves in the field for indefinite periods.

The fixed-wing aircraft were already in squadron service: Austers Mark 6 with the Mark 9 to come. For a few glorious months after the historic settlement of the control issue between War Office and Air Ministry, it was believed that the early provision of a helicopter would be assured either by introduction of the Skeeter or by purchase of a model from the international market. The French Alouette seemed to have every capability the Army Air Corps desired. There was, however, no option: for the present, it was the Cierva Skeeter or nothing.

Cierva was that same small company which from 1928 had produced autogiros of sufficient promise to maintain Royal Air Force interest until abandonment after the Second World War. It then developed helicopters. The Skeeter was designed for the civil market at moderate cost – about £3,000 – with running costs equating to a 20 hp car. Unfortunately, the engine and airframe were mismatched. Modifications led to a second mark notable for high resonance on the ground, a failing which broke it up on 26 June 1950. Due to this and the failure of another project, Cierva went out of business. Its assets were bought by Saunders-Roe.

Looking towards the Ministry of Supply's requirement for an AOP helicopter to enter service in 1957, the new owners persisted with the development. Fairey Aviation, the most promising contender for the contract, fell out of the competition on the matter of pricing. A Mark 6 Skeeter showed some promise during a brief trial at Middle Wallop in January 1956, and two Mark 10 were delivered again in January 1957. Major Begbie put them through trials on Salisbury Plain and in Germany, a process which proved adventurous; pilots and helicopters were dented in minor accidents due principally to lack of power. Finally, Saunders-Roe installed a 215 hp Gypsy Major engine which earned the aircraft a limited flight clearance. They had reached Mark 12: Hobson's choice. The first production model of sixty-four was delivered to Middle Wallop in August 1958.

By that time the Army Air Corps had formally returned to the Army order of battle in its new form. Vesting day was 1 September 1957. At Middle Wallop command passed to Brigadier P. Weston, a soldier who had seen considerable service in RAF Army Cooperation Command before and during the Second World War. The station was renamed 'The Army Aviation Centre', which included the Army flying school. Squadrons at home and abroad retained their former titles but flights were renumbered by dropping the first two digits previously used; 1903 Flight RAF, for example, became simply 3 Flight AAC.

Celebrations apart, the transformation was not at once apparent to those working at flight level. Khaki and blue uniforms continued to work in partnership; RAF technicians remained as REME replacements were still under training. Asked later how the reorganization affected him personally, Gunner Norman Langley with 651 Squadron said,

> Before [the change] I was wearing my regimental badge, doing a bit of driving, aircraft handling, signalling, jack of all trades. Afterwards, I was doing the same thing. In between we had a parade and congratulations all round.

Months were to pass before the institution of the Army Air Corps began to impinge upon the junior officers, NCOs and men who were founder members. There were immediate consequences, however, at the higher levels of activity.

In the War Office Major Norman-Walker had completed his tour of duty, and was replaced by five officers. Colonel Peter Mead, formerly observed under notional air attack in Germany as commander of 652 Squadron, was one of them. His team – L/AW 2 – was discovering that its range of work was wide.

It was extended by the new defence policy introduced in 1957 by Duncan Sandys, Minister of Defence, devised to make further economies over five years. Atomic weapons would be relied upon chiefly to daunt the Soviet Union in Europe. Strong reserves would be maintained in the United Kingdom, and these, rather than static garrisons overseas, would respond to future emergencies, moving to the locations concerned across the world in the expanded air transport fleet entering

Royal Air Force service. National service would be brought to an end within five years to reduce the training establishment and the excessive turnover of men in units.

The Army Air Corps was not suited to this concept. Reinforcement ranges envisaged were far in excess of light aircraft capabilities, indeed of all helicopters. Germany could be reinforced by staged flights across the Channel, but units required further afield would have to be transported in air freighters. A very large freighter, the Belfast, would in due course provide such a capacity. But theatre commanders insisted that they needed light aircraft support permanently. If their local field forces were to be reduced, there was a greater need for the watch and ward facilities which light aircraft provided. Knowledge of local flying conditions and territory would be particularly valuable to reinforcements as they arrived. This contention argued for more light aircraft and hence more men.

As the Royal Air Force had foreseen, the old order of Army aviation had relied upon a number of its services in addition to technical maintenance. From 1958 these had to be provided from AAC manpower. The 1,500 men allotted to formation were, in any case, insufficient to meet operational demands. Plans for the introduction of new aircraft, most importantly a 'utility' helicopter to carry an infantry section or an equivalent cargo load, depended upon additional manpower. Applications to the War Office manning branches failed – didn't they realize the Army was being reduced in numbers? Back door appeals to arms directors to surrender fractions of their strength to the Army Air Corps were rejected. Thinking caps grew threadbare.

In the matter of uniform caps, however, at the domestic end of the staff responsibilities in L/AW2, there was progress after minor skirmishing. In the early months of 1957 a new uniform was proposed for all serving with the AAC. Finance officers rejected this, except for those in the permanent cadre. So did colonels of regiments. There was nonetheless a wish among the aviators and ground staff for some distinctive item of dress. A coloured beret was an obvious solution, and Major Maurice Sutcliffe, commanding the remaining glider pilots, pressed for the adoption of the airborne maroon. This did not suit the AOP majority. They looked for innovation. Numerous proposals for a light blue beret received strong support, which explains why so many proponents claim to have originated the idea.

A badge was a necessity. Brigadier Peter Mead (such he eventually became) recalls that Major King-Clark selected the eagle from the Natural History Museum, but Brigadier Norman-Walker tells us that while he was still the sole Major Prophet in L/AW(d),

> The AAC eagle was first produced by Bob Begbie in early 1957 – a drawing on tracing paper. . . . The present eagle may not be identical but I think that Bob has the right to claim it as his own.

A strong rearguard of colonels of regiments and corps sought to resist this innovation no less than a uniform. Their protests were fired at various targets, one being the Adjutant-General, General Sir Hugh Stockwell, who had just been appointed Colonel-Commandant of the Army Air Corps. They could legitimately object to the badge, he ruled as Adjutant-General, but not the beret, citing airborne forces as a precedent. So the light blue beret was worn by all, embellished by the badge of the individual's regiment or corps. The permanent cadre adopted the eagle.

Four uncertainties persisted, however; some in one form or another into the 1970s. They were as follows: aircraft and roles; manpower and organization. The first involved a matter of crucial importance: the all-up weight of Army aircraft.

The Skeeter, described by an experienced sergeant pilot as a 'maverick', entered service as a stopgap. Though it was judged in time to be 'highly manoeuvrable' by some of its pilots, many students and occasionally instructors at Middle Wallop had unnerving reminders of its eccentricities in full view of their peers – a sudden upward tilt of the nose being one. On the whole the beast was mastered as much by instinct as intellect. 4 Recce Flight at Hildesheim was the first to become equipped with it entirely in March 1961. Disposal to European airspace was due to the Skeeter's inability to obtain clearance for tropical flying. In high temperatures it could not meet the vertical climb rate stipulated.

A possible successor had been in sight since 1956, the Saunders Roe P 531, a speculative development to meet the Army's requirement for a liaison helicopter. It had four passenger seats, 1,000 lb of payload, and a climb rate of 700 ft per minute 'outside of ground effect', all to be operative in universal climatic conditions. These were exacting specifications. From the basic design – a 'super Skeeter' – the Scout emerged in 1959, and, as a naval variant, the Wasp. The all-up weight exceeded 5,000 lb.

This was clearly above the limit articulated by Air Marshal Ivelaw-Chapman and adopted by the Air Council in 1956 to marginalize Army aviation. So, too, was the proposal for the fixed-wing replacement, the Canadian 'Beaver'. This consideration did not inhibit the Land/Air Warfare director and staff, however; they trusted in the final exchanges between secretaries of state in 1956 that the figure of 4,000 lb was not absolute.

Two other contenders vied with the Beaver: the Edgar Perceval 9 and the Pioneer. All three took part in the 1st British Corps annual exercise in August 1958. The Beaver alone satisfied Army Air Corps prerequisites. In January 1959 meetings were held to consider choice of both a fixed-wing model and a helicopter.

The L/AW 2 'desk officer' in charge of the programmes was Major T.A. Richardson, a former AOP pilot. The Army wanted the Beaver so, following the most direct route, he asked the Ministry of Supply to procure it. This was not the usual procedure. A department was expected to specify desired characteristics of an aircraft to the Ministry, when its experts would commence a development or sanction purchase in the open market. Much to his credit, the principal negotiator accepted the L/AW approach, proposing that the Army should write a specification which the Beaver alone would satisfy.

Two models competed for the helicopter choice. Brigadier Weston favoured the Alouette. It did not meet the standards articulated by the Army but it had shown itself to be a reliable work horse in French military service in Europe and North Africa, and it was available. It was, however, foreign, a circumstance which made the Ministry of Supply uneasy. The L/AW preference for the Saunders Roe P 531 was therefore welcomed. Mutual confidence was expressed in its potential for improvement well beyond the status of a super-Skeeter.

Inexperience now led the soldiers concerned into error. They canvassed the greater part of the War Office and the Air Ministry for ideas as to what these improvements should embrace. The sum of responses suggested a perfect machine, able to carry an immense variety of loads, auto-stabilized, capable of navigation through the thickest clouds at night in the lowest and highest, the wettest and driest conditions known to man. The engine and associated components, REME proposed, should have an operating life of 1,000 hours with limited servicing.

The Skeeter Mark 12 enters service, 1958 (*Museum of Army Flying*)

Most of these ideas had to be abandoned, not so much to contain costs and weight, though both were of importance, but to maintain the prospect of delivery within eighteen months, if at all. Development was initiated.

In the inceptory stages the Royal Air Force gave invaluable advice. As the projects moved onwards, however, the air staff became uneasy. The introduction of the five-seat liaison helicopter was acceptable, despite its all-up weight. The Beaver was not. Its capabilities included supply dropping and troop transportation which were defined as RAF functions. If procured, the Air Ministry insisted, the aircraft must be flown by RAF pilots. The disagreement ascended to secretary of state level.

An argument was already in progress between their offices on the future of JEHU. The Royal Air Force was proposing to take sole charge of the trials because the 1956 agreement recognized its supremacy in the troop and freight carrying roles. If the Beaver was piloted by soldiers, it would be trespassing on RAF preserves. It would, moreover, inhibit an Air Ministry aim to offer 'air policing' to the Colonial Office in the manner of the 1930s, though this consideration was withheld from the debate.

Discussion began in March 1959. From the outset the uniformed members of the Air Council were at a disadvantage. Their Secretary of State, George Ward, was inclined to agree with his War Office colleague, Christopher Soames, that they were considering a light liaison aircraft, not a troop transport. He was not convinced by the Chief of the Air Staff that a concession on the Beaver would lead to claims by the Army to control all its supporting air transport. In February 1960 a compromise was tried by the air staff: the Army should fly the Beaver in Europe and the Arabian Peninsula, where the liaison requirement was paramount; the RAF should fly it in the Far East where, in Malaya, 'the two Services worked side by side'. Harold Watkinson, Minister of Defence, did not agree. Accepting the expressed role of the Beaver, he decided that the Army should fly it without prejudice to the RAF responsibility for air transportation.

Despite late political lobbying to introduce a competitor from Scottish Aviation, the Beaver was adopted to replace the Auster. Thirty-six – of forty-two finally delivered – were ordered from de Havilland of Canada. The first entered service in 1961.

These decisions provided for immediate requirements, or, to be accurate, provided for them on paper and in terms of finance. Problems with the Scout development necessitated the purchase of seventeen Alouettes between 1958 and 1961 to fill the utility role, and many members of the AAC came to the view that greater numbers of Alouette should have been procured to permit rectification of the design faults before the Scout was fielded. Operational imperatives also facilitated the procurement of a light helicopter both to replace the Skeeter in Europe and to function in hot, high, and humid conditions. The light aircraft fleet was thus growing steadily in numbers and variety of equipment. These factors militated for increases in manpower.

REME finally assumed responsibility for servicing and maintenance in September 1958. The shortfall in its numbers at Middle Wallop was met temporarily by the attachment of a number of aircraft technicians from the Royal Navy. Bearded men appeared among the soldiers on parade. A small increase in pilots and ground staff was permitted, but it was only a palliative. Perversely, as the War Office manning staffs pointed out, numbers applying for pilot training were falling away; regiments and corps were reluctant to second officers and NCOs. A manning crisis was foreseen.

It loomed as Major-General Weston became Director of Land/Air Warfare in 1960. Believing that major problems were best solved by radical solutions, he decided to 'integrate' Army aviation with the field units of the Army.

A climate of opinion seemed to favour it. Certain reconnaissance, infantry, artillery, and engineer regimental commanders were beginning to see the extensive advantages of helicopters for reconnaissance, fire control, the visiting of distant detachments, and the carriage of weapons or men, including wounded, in the whole spectrum of operations. It was their view, however, that when a unit needed a helicopter it was needed at once and should therefore be under their control. This suggested the formation of 'air troops' or 'air platoons' as sub-units under their command. Given this facility it was logical that the regiment should provide the pilots and non-technical ground crews, be supported by regimental signallers and transport, and administered by the orderly room and quartermaster. On this basis manpower problems would be solved, for the scheme assumed that the regiment or corps concerned would find the pilots and ground staff by surrendering posts within their respective establishments.

Warming to his idea, General Weston began to broadcast it within the Army with this conclusion: light aircraft would eventually operate entirely on the new system, and the Army Air Corps would disband.

Brigadier Mead was so alarmed by this disclosure that he asked General Stockwell to a private meeting at Middle Wallop with General Weston, himself and his deputy, Colonel Denis Coyle, wartime commander of 656 Squadron in the Far East. He described later in his book, *Soldiers in the Air*, how he outlined,

> . . . in a few words my objections to the idea being circulated that the Army Air Corps was obsolescent. Without awaiting any further statement of my views, Hughie [Stockwell] came down emphatically and unequivocally . . . on the side of his Army Air Corps. . . .

General Stockwell's judgement was in no way swayed by proprietorial considerations. Some years later he reviewed the points he made to the DCIGS – then General Sir P. Pyman – in objecting to total 'integration'. Disbandment of the Army Air Corps would cast away all the aviation experience amassed and preserved which were manifest, for example, in the qualified flying instructors, and circumscribe the single-minded development of new ideas and techniques. Regiments and other corps would feel no obligation to man the Middle Wallop centre. It would be staffed by pressed men, discarded by commanding officers. Spirit and standards would wither.

Still, the idea had merits. Some degree of integration would undoubtedly offer benefits to field force units and they should be prepared to pay for them by giving up established posts to provide manpower. However, he considered that,

> . . . this should be done selectively, and be backed by various levels of flights and squadrons to provide for the many other people requiring light aircraft from a pool. . . . I didn't know whether it was the answer for the long term but saw that it was probably the best way of coping with the difficulties just then.

'Integration' proceeded on that basis. On 11 November 1964 the Army Air Corps began to implement a five-year plan to deploy light aircraft down to unit level, expanding in the process from an establishment of 140 aircraft, half of which were helicopters, to 356 aircraft in 1969, of which 95 per cent would be helicopters. The principal operational element would be the brigade flight of four Scouts, commanded by a major, who would also supervise the aviation standards and requirements of 'air troops' or 'air platoons' within selected units. A lieutenant-colonel would be appointed as 'commander, divisional aviation (and a numbered squadron)' supervising, similarly, subordinate elements and controlling the divisional headquarters Beaver flight.

The rearrangements were not standard throughout the Army. For example, provisions for 1st British Corps headquarters did not apply elsewhere. Some theatres lacked a divisional structure. Flights were tailored to meet the needs of theatre headquarters, engineers, signals, and service corps.

Distant from high policy making, squadrons in the Middle and Far East were becoming engrossed in active service.

# CHAPTER NINETEEN
# Hot and High; High and Humid

The tribes inhabiting the deserts of sand and mountains of the Aden Protectorate occupy the greater part of their time in two pursuits: subsistence farming and feuding. The first involves herding livestock, and tilling the thin soil between the precipitous ridges of their territory. It is hard work. The second engages them in guerrilla warfare, mostly fought at long range with rifles, a test of manhood, a periodic excitement in an otherwise hard and humdrum life. This is preferred.

Sometimes, tribes fight one another. What they enjoy most is fighting the government. In 1963 the newly formed federal authority began to collect taxes from Yemeni caravans travelling to Aden which, by custom, had been levied locally. The Radfani peoples cut the road in protest. It was cleared by the Federation Regular Army – the FRA – supported by Austers and Beavers, but cut again as soon as the troops drew back. Reinforcements were accumulated from Britain and the Persian Gulf to assert government authority.

The Austers and Beavers belonged to 653 Squadron, brought to Aden from Cyprus in 1960 by Major Bill McNinch, where it had been disposed, unappreciated, on a bare site, operating out of aircraft crates. A new Army commander changed all this. By 1964, 3 Wing under Lieutenant-Colonel Francis Graham Bell was stationed in a dedicated base at Falaise airfield in Little Aden. His helicopters – Alouettes – were detached to Kenya. But two Scouts arrived aboard HMS *Bulwark* on 23 March for 653 Squadron, and the reinforcement plan would bring three more by air in May.

. . . Funny thing [a trooper in 13 Flight wrote home in April], everyone in Germany told me nothing ever happened in Aden. In the last few weeks, we've been working flat out. . . .

The squadron was launching frequent reconnaissance and liaison flights, the latter for the FRA and civil government, throughout March and April. At the same time the Scouts were busy with pilot conversion and 'hot and high' flying trials. Sorties north of the Radfan airstrip and base at Thumeir were targets for small arms fire from the end of April.

In the final week of the month Special Air Service groups were inserted by Scouts close to the Yemen border and into the Jebel Halmain, a difficult task. At this range landing sites were under sniper fire by day. Night landings were impracticable among the cliffs and boulders. Suppressive artillery and armoured car fire assisted these deliveries at last light. Returning across the dry bed of the Wadi Taym the fuel tank of Graham Bell's Scout was clipped and a bullet passed through the tail rotor of a second piloted by Captain Claude Surgeon. All landings were made hazardous by dust clouds.

Brigadier C.H. Blacker's 39 Infantry Brigade opened operations on 25 May, advancing by night an FRA battalion, 45 Royal Marine Commando, and a company of 3 Para to dominate the Dhanaba Basin, 2 miles north of Thumeir. A Scout reconnoitred the area next morning prior to resupply sorties by Beavers and Royal Air Force Belvederes.

A Beaver of 653 Squadron, piloted by Major John Dicksee over Little Aden, 1961 (*WD Official*)

The main body of 3 Para Group entered operations in June to clear the Bakri ridge, the Jebel Haqla peak and the heart of the Wadi Dhubsan, which contained the principal Radfani grain stocks. The commanding officer scanned the ground from a Scout, set his engineers to advance the guns of I Battery and a road-head, and seized in darkness half the Bakri ridge. Next morning, supplies, essentially water and mortar ammunition, were delivered to his force. In this process one Army Air Corps Scout delivered in small packets thrice the load in an hour of a Royal Air Force Belvedere, a twin-rotor helicopter with six times the carrying capacity. Moreover, the Belvedere pilots chose arbitrarily the point of delivery in a unit area, whereas the Scout would land or hover at a point indicated. The former took the view that one locality was as good as another in a battalion area but failed to realize that this was not so; it involved a recovery journey up hill and down dale on the recipients' backs.

One day of this convinced 3 Para's colonel that Scout service alone should carry him to the Wadi Dhubsan. Lieutenant-Colonel Graham Bell responded. Major Jake Jackson had just arrived as a relief pilot from trials work at Boscombe Down and identified himself with the group's fortunes. The doors and back seats were stripped from his Scout, which shuttled to and fro with supplies, equipment, and casualties including the odd wounded tribesman, as the parachutists cleared the ridge and jebel. When the demand was heavy a second Scout was committed, flown often by Major Jimmy Nunn, acquired as a relief pilot from Kenya. By this economic means 3 Para Group were supplied day by day to the head of the Wadi Dhubsan.

Scout and Royal Tanks scout car cooperating in the Radfan, 1964 (*AAC, Museum of Army Flying*)

Reinforced, and advancing again by night, the battalion swept the adjacent heights and grain stocks in the Wadi bed. After dawn an attached company reported an advance of 10,000 yd, a claim so questionable that the commanding officer set off in Major Jackson's Scout to investigate it. Shortly, tribesmen were seen on either side, firing delightedly at this aerial target, and before evasive action could be taken the helicopter was hit a number of times. One passenger was wounded. Fuel began to stream over the canopy.

Landing under these weapons was out of the question. Major Jackson turned about and managed a descent close to 3 Para's outposts on the stony Wadi bed. The Scout was secured against capture but not fire; for while the parachutists ejected the Radfani force, sniping persisted for some hours. It was essential to recover the aircraft as rapidly as possible.

Corporal Carcarry, a REME technician, came forward to examine the aircraft. The rotor head and blades were undamaged and he decided that replacement of the non-return valve and low pressure fuel pipe would put the helicopter back in the air. Another Scout lifted him to Thumeir, an Auster to Little Aden. Spares and tools were redied and checked. Before nightfall, Lieutenant-Colonel Graham Bell delivered these loads, 40 gallons of fuel and, essentially, Corporals Carcarry and Hustwith, to the damaged helicopter. Working by torchlight under a blanket they laboured through the night.

Scout of 653 Squadron landing at Thumeir during the Radfan operations, 1964 (*Trustees of the Imperial War Museum, London, ADN 65/355/80*)

Early next morning Major Jackson turned the engine over. It fired, ran easily under test, and to the relief of all about, rose into the air to land at Thumeir. All operational tasks completed, 3 Para withdrew in naval helicopters.

The land force commander, Major-General John Cubbon, sensibly regarded this mishap as a fortune of war. The squadron, fired by their success with 3 Para, supported 1 Royal Anglian and 45 Commando in succeeding operations, though they wisely cancelled plans to employ Beavers as bombers when the RAF protested that they were being put out of business. It was just as well. Over following weeks the squadron was pressed to meet its proper functions. Pilots near (at the base) and far (in Kenya) needed no encouragement to join operations but their other duties could not be wholly neglected. Visiting pilots were pressed into service, among them Major-General Napier Crookenden, making an inceptory tour as Director of Land/Air Warfare. When the expedition ended there was scarcely a height round Thumeir which had not been served with picquets or supplies by the Scouts. Austers and Beavers flew to support them by day and night.

By July 1964 government authority had been restored. It was not the last security operation before the British withdrew from Aden but potentially the most challenging. It earned 653 Squadron the best of reputations, the high confidence of those it supported.

· · · · · · · ·

Beaver fitted for supply dropping (*RAF, Aldergrove*)

Meanwhile, a new campaign was running in the Far East. In December 1962 a half-baked revolutionary attempted to seize power in the Sultanate of Brunei, the tiny oil-rich state between British North Borneo and Sarawak. To the vexation of President Soekarno of Indonesia the coup was rapidly defeated. He had expected to exploit it as a means to annexing Brunei and the two British colonies. In this connection he had made common cause with some thousands of Communist Chinese settlers in the territories.

Sarawak and North Borneo were about to pass to Malaya from British control with the agreement of the United Nations. Soekarno made the error of believing that, having recently concluded a long internal security campaign in Malaya, the government in London would withdraw rather than underwrite another in Borneo. Without British support the former colonies might be persuaded or terrorized into expressing a wish to become a part of Indonesia.

He was wrong. Although no state of war was declared by either side, hostilities developed along the border between Indonesian and British Borneo, a distance of 1,300 miles, principally along a mountainous centreline. As in Malaya the extensive tree cover rose 200 ft above tangled undergrowth. Roads and random clearings marked timber extraction. Itinerant Dyaks and Ibans burned patches for cultivation. Along the coasts, up broad rivers, there was trading and farming. But for the most part, the rain forest spread unbroken inland. There were only sixteen towns throughout the territories.

The mobility of forces thus depended upon helicopters. In December 1962 No. 656 Squadron was based on the grass airfield at Kluang in Malaya. Two flights plus the air troop of the Queen's Royal Irish Hussars contained helicopters; a fourth, Austers and Beavers. During 1963 sections rotated to the scattered forces in Borneo, reinforcing a handful of RAF Sycamore helicopters, single and twin Pioneers. Navigation was difficult; maps of the territories showed coast and river lines and a few mountain peaks. Otherwise, they were blank. Fortunately, similar problems of access delayed the deployment of Indonesian forces. Early raids across the border were shallow and short lived. Still, they alarmed the indigenous peoples who began to believe the intruders' boast that they would return in overwhelming strength.

As often before, the political and military authorities underestimated the magnitude of the task. A wholehearted military challenge would have wrecked rapidly the Indonesian raiding capability. As it was the trickle of naval, land, and air reinforcements from Malaya and Singapore was insufficient throughout 1963 to daunt Soekarno. British and local forces just held their own until it became clear that the federation of the colonies with Malaya (what was to become Malaysia) would founder unless Indonesian operations were defeated.

By 1964 this outcome could no longer be ignored. Border posts defending civilian settlements were being attacked. Permanent brigade headquarters were established in Kuching and on the Rejang river, in Brunei, and Tawau, at the south-eastern extremity of Sabah. Australian and New Zealand units entered operations. Two squadrons of naval Wessex and Whirlwind helicopters alternated with Royal Air Force Whirlwinds to move platoons, companies, occasionally battalions in and out of the jungle fastness and supply their major needs. Argosys, Beverleys and Hastings provided long-range air transport and major supply drops. Royal Air Force air defence and ground attack aircraft were on immediate call.

By the middle of 1964, 656 Squadron had been reinforced with sixteen Scouts and an additional flight. The commanding officer, Lieutenant-Colonel Begbie, was then able to increase his operational contribution to two helicopter flights and a fixed-wing detachment in Borneo under Major John Dicksee. This rapidly enhanced watch and ward along the border.

The fixed-wing aircraft offered the most economic means of reconnaissance, and local passenger transportation between bases. The latter was no less dangerous than the former. On his second sortie in operations, Sergeant Thackeray was carrying a padre on his Christmas Eve rounds from Lundu to Kuching in 1963 when his Auster was hit by anti-aircraft cannon fire. His passenger was mortally wounded. On his second sortie in operations, Sergeant Thackeray's left arm was broken and bleeding heavily. He realized that he was losing consciousness. There was no airstrip nearby but a helicopter pad offered an entry point among the trees. Using his knees and right arm to operate throttle, flaps and control stick he contrived a stalled landing.

The helicopters were stationed at Kuching, Brunei, and, remotely, at Long Pa Sia in a border fort among the high peaks of Sabah. Friday was important in that outpost; the weekly supplies arrived then by parachute. This support apart, the Scouts provided all other air services, inserting or recovering patrols, evacuating casualties, shuttling light freight, or watching movement across the border. Sometimes they were fired upon from positions just inside Indonesia, which the pilots countered by fitting machine-guns. When artillery was deployed forward, 656 Squadron pilots revived their AOP capabilities, and were reminded that shots falling through the tree canopy were extremely difficult to spot.

Sergeant [later, Major] A. Markham, had to switch roles abruptly in 1965. His task was to carry members of parliament by Scout round company bases in southern Sarawak. In flight, he noticed 'day-glo' [fluorescent] panels laid in a deserted helicopter landing site – an HLS – to convey a distress signal. Landing his passengers, he asked the infantry hosts if they had any troops close to the clearing. They had none. Refuelling against emergencies, Sergeant Markham excused himself and departed to the HLS. 'I circled cautiously until I was sure there was only one soldier in the clearing, and he was one of ours. . . .' He had found the survivor of an Australian Special Air Service patrol, dispersed in a night river crossing. A search party was needed.

At full speed Sergeant Markham made for Kuching, returning with an SAS party half an hour later. The back seat and doors were stripped from the Scout to accommodate men and equipment. He then resumed border taxi work.

As ever, jungle and weather menaced light aircraft journeys exceeding a range of 50 miles. Aircraft at Kuching required for periodic workshop inspection had to be flown 450 miles across mangrove swamps to Brunei, refuelling on a coastal sandbar after 150 miles. Through the greater part of the journey, radio contact was confined to passing civil aircraft. 'If you're going in [emergency landing]', one pilot confided, 'it's comforting to know that Malaysian Airways had a fix on you at some point.'

Pilots practised emergency drills regularly, though sometimes these were insufficient to avoid disaster. Sergeant 'Doc' Waghorn, a Royal Army Medical Corps pilot, assisted a Gurkha detachment to run down an Indonesian patrol in the south-eastern corner of Sarawak. After nightfall he set off by Scout with a prisoner and escort for Kuching. The route was well known: at 3,000 ft, the lights of Kuching were manifest 20 miles away. But the monsoon was approaching. Farmers were burning the dry undergrowth before the rains; smoke obscured the horizon. Sergeant Waghorn, his passengers and Scout were never seen again.

In July 1965 Sergeant Markham carried a reconnaissance party to a mountain top clearing on the Sarawak border. Its capacity to accept a troop of guns had been discussed and the Scout was bearing away when, as he recorded,

> . . . the engine wound down. We were not very well placed . . . below the level of the HLS. My only chance was to set range auto rotation speed and head away from the jungle covered . . . slopes.
>
> The jungle stretched all the way to Padawan, and as the ridges loomed, I flared wildly, at the same time milking the rotor [revolutions], and cleared them by a close margin . . . [repeating] the performance at the next ridge. I put out a Mayday [emergency] call on VHF but couldn't risk letting go of the controls to change to the [local] company tactical frequency. . . .
>
> I suddenly realised that an area of a different, lighter shade of green had come into range, and also that I couldn't jump the last ridge to Padawan. I turned for the light patch which was in a small bowl area, where water must have collected, but the vegetation, looking much more inviting than the 200 feet primary [jungle], seemed quite dense.
>
> I decided to flare off all forward speed and let the aircraft crumple the tail boom to cushion the landing. The aircraft was going to get bent no matter what I did. I timed the flare so that maximum nose was up as I entered the trees, and the blades began chopping wood. There

was even a small amount of buffeting and it started going dark as we came to rest on an even keel on the jungle floor, with all four blades on the same side of the aircraft.

We had made it. . . .

They were found and winched out by a Royal Air Force Whirlwind, alerted to search when the Scout became overdue. Last out, Sergeant Markham searched the Scout and discovered an operation order disclosing the impending plans, left by one of the officers. He returned it when they reached base and was passed two large gins in quick succession. More formal thanks were returned by his passengers some weeks later in the form of a clock.

The campaign ended in 1966. President Soekarno was deposed, discredited as much by failure in Borneo as elsewhere. While not underrating the prime contribution of the troops who trod the jungle floor, British Commonwealth and Malaysian success in arms was due, perhaps more than anything else, to the presence and cooperative use of helicopters. Recognizing their potential, the successive joint force commanders, Generals Walter Walker and George Lea, were insistent on the forward deployment of these aircraft throughout 1964–5 to whatever level was most productive. In the case of the Army Air Corps, this extended at one time to seven sites, north to south. The growth of numbers, including an RASC Beaver flight, and types – Siouxs joined the Scouts – drew the remainder of 656 Squadron under Lieutenant-Colonel Peter Collins to Borneo and the establishment of a theatre headquarters – 4 Wing.

Though all the soldiers entering the operations were regulars, following the end of conscription, some had never seen helicopters previously and many had never worked with them. One young infantry officer said later, 'Helicopters had become so much a part of our working lives that it was quite a shock to find when we returned [to Britain] that our training resumed as if they didn't exist'.

The Director of Land/Air Warfare was striving to correct that omission.

# A Fighting Arm

CHAPTER TWENTY

# Decisive Factors

Obliged to modify his plans for decentralization of the Army's aircraft, General Weston bore no grudges. He threw his many talents into implementing the modified scheme and the pursuit of additional aircraft.

When General Napier Crookenden succeeded him in January 1964, the new organization had been officially agreed. Selection and training of the first pilots for regimental air troops and platoons – air squadrons for reconnaissance regiments – was in hand, and courses had been arranged at the Army Aviation Centre for the training of regimental aircraft handlers. The Ministry of Defence was ready to select a replacement for the Skeeter from three competitors: the Agusta-Bell 47G–3B–1, the Hiller UH 12–E–4, and the Hughes 300 – joined at a late stage by the Brantley B2. Funds had been allocated to acquire two hundred of the model chosen.

In March 1964, following considerable political indecision, the Army's preference for the Agusta-Bell prevailed. It was named the Sioux. The first fifty were to be supplied by the Agusta plant in Milan, the remainder by Westland at Yeovil. General Crookenden noted that,

> The reason for this absurdly complicated plan was to sell Rolls Royce aero engines to Italy, but it certainly caused endless complications in the development and improvement of our version . . . and in the supply of spares. All correspondence had to go from [Middle] Wallop to the Ministry of Aviation to Milan to Fort Worth [Texas] and back again.
>
> We had bought this aircraft in the belief that it was a 'Ford' car of the air with thousands of hours behind it. . . .

This was not true of the delicate high inertia twin rotor blades and tail rotor, or the turbo-charger on the Lycoming engine, which required five minutes idling before shut down. Fifteen man-hours were required for an engine change against eleven predicted. It was underpowered. Even so, the Sioux had many virtues, including an advanced radio fit, it was delivered on time – from June 1964 – and with the patient skill of the REME aviation engineers under Colonel McCulloch many of its maintenance problems were overcome by July 1965.

With hindsight, the British Army expected too much of its helicopters entering service. It looked for a simple, robust machine – such as the Alouette – withal high powered, fuel thrifty, economic in maintenance, and operationally versatile. First marks of helicopters from whatever source, including the pioneer workshops in France and America, were invariably underdeveloped. The best models were those which had the potential for rapid or, at any rate, steady correction of errors or omissions in basic design. British helicopters and their service clients had also the disadvantage that they were latecomers to the industry.

The Scout exemplified these weaknesses and strengths. Its engine passed through a series of design changes informed by squadron reports on failures and fatalities. The original Nimbus designed by Turbo-Meca passed to Blackburn and Bristol Siddeley to Rolls Royce. Yet the Scout was a good workhorse through the operations of the 1960s and came to be considered a paragon as it passed thirty years of continuous service in northern and southern Europe, the Middle and Far East, central and South America. Cold and high, cold and wet, hot and high, high and humid – whatever the climate, the Scout coped.

The needs of Aden and Borneo in 1964–5 delayed deliveries due to the British Army of the Rhine. Curiously this stimulated briefly a lobby for the retention of the Auster in Germany on the basis of its economy, and reliability in war. But this passed as the Scout arrived.

It was welcomed as a true utility helicopter which included a capability to fire the British Vigilant and French SS11 wire guided anti-tank rocket. The NATO divisions in Germany were then faced by the superior armoured strength of the Warsaw Pact. An airborne anti-armour weapons system, the Army Aviation Centre suggested, should redress the limited capability of 1st British Corps to hold and destroy the prospective enemy onslaught.

The wish was father to the thought. It had been a longstanding aspiration among the light aircraft pilots of the Army to operate in a fighting role. The Air Observation Post pilots were not dissatisfied with direction of the guns, though many had wished, like Charles Bazeley in 1942, to arm their Austers with light machine-guns to extend combat capacity. Their ascendant use as air taxi drivers while the war continued had thus been disagreeable; it demeaned their skills, suggesting perhaps that they had no stomach for the fight.

This outlook abated in peace but, carried forward by gunners, took root naturally among helicopter pilots. Pilots from administrative corps were of the same inclination. Sergeant 'Doc' Waghorn of the RAMC in Borneo or his colleagues from the Royal Corps of Transport and Royal Army Ordnance Corps preferred running down the enemy with a machine-gun attached to their skids to carrying visitors, military or civilian, round the Radfan or Borneo posts. Tank hunting – tank destroying – fired the pilot's ambitions. Advances in technology were to fuel the aspirations of the young Turks in aviation, and indeed many in middle age.

Use of helicopters as tank destroyers was opposed by those who believed the tank, as the decisive weapon system in armoured warfare, had prime claim on Army developments in this field, and by the Royal Air Force. In February 1965 the RAF surprised the other two services by proposing the reassumption of all flying responsibilities. The Defence Secretary, Mr Denis Healey, having acceded to direct control of the Naval, Army and Air Departments, asked Field Marshal Sir Gerald Templer to chair a committee with Admiral Sir Caspar John and Air Chief Marshal Sir Dennis Barnett to investigate the merits of the bid.

The Royal Navy and Army entered an alliance.

The Director of Naval Aviation, Captain George Baldwin RN, came at once to see me [Napier Crookenden recorded] and our six officers in L/AW 2 set to work. Weekly meetings . . . followed in London, Wallop, and Lee-on-Solent. . . .

Our chief [Army] arguments included the need for pilots to be soldiers first and pilots second, and here our air troops and platoons gave us a convincing case. Then there was the need for the Army to command its own reconnaissance . . . We stressed the economy of our operation. We ran half as many aircraft as the RAF with a fraction of their manpower and our second and third line maintenance was already rationalised with the Navy. We made Brian Blunt our principal author and leg man and very well he did it.

Major-Generals Crookenden and Victor Balfour, the Director of Military Operations, gave their evidence before the committee on 24 March 1965 and, with the Royal Navy, won their case.

> . . . One of the RAF's biggest arguments was that the transfer of all helicopters to the Air Vote would free Army funds . . . for tanks and missiles. The whole exercise was a complete waste of time and did nothing except embitter our relations with the RAF.

In standing their 1965 budget philosophy on its head, the Air Board exposed the weakness of its case, but it must be said that the Army had, in part, inspired the challenge. Contrary to assurances by the former War Office that the Beaver would not be used primarily for the transport of troops and freight, special flights by the Royal Corps of Transport had been formed for this expressed purpose. Then, air commanders in Aden and the Far East reported that Army aircraft were usurping RAF functions – Beaver bombing, for example. The Skyvan short-range transport was under consideration for the Army Air Corps; and DL/AW was lobbying to take over RAF helicopters on the basis that the latter had no requirement of its own for them apart from search and rescue.

This inter-service dispute was put aside temporarily as other matters pressed for attention. A successor to the Sioux had to be considered and, if the Whirlwind and Wessex were to elude Army control, a larger Army utility helicopter. A procurement alliance was struck with the French company, Sud Aviation, for the Gazelle and the Lynx. Exercise HELTANK in Germany advanced ideas about anti-tank operations, a popular topic at the annual Army Aviation convention at Middle Wallop in 1966.

In the following year the policy of decentralization surfaced again. The permanent cadre of the Army Air Corps understandably resented their relegation within the field army to a largely advisory capacity. But this aside, its senior officers cited two factors arguing for abandonment of the scheme: a drop in safety standards; and a rising strain on REME resources. The first of these was debatable. It was based on the judgement that, as the first generation of regimental pilots came to the end of their tours, their replacements were unable to maintain requisite standards. The supporting statistics were questionable. True or false, the counter-argument ran, safety and skill could be assured by staggering the replacement programme. Units of the fighting and supporting arms with integrated helicopters were clearly more effective in the field than those without them. For example, the light armour of a reconnaissance regiment, complemented by its air squadron, discovered that its operating ranges were extended, communications assured, and the quality of its information was greatly enhanced. Battalion helicopters accelerated significantly the deployment and redeployment of armoured infantry in Germany no less than marching infantry in mountains, desert or jungle. The Royal Artillery enjoyed once more the undivided services of AOPs. Royal Engineer pilots maximized field squadron and troop operations.

Evidence of this sort to the Templer Committee provided the Army with its most powerful argument against RAF predators.

Yet, valid as they were, these contentions were insufficient to counter the second contrary argument of the Army Air Corps' officers. The complexity of Army aircraft systems was growing and would continue to grow. If money was no object, REME manpower could be expanded indefinitely to support flying at all levels. But funds were decidedly limited. The Gazelle and the

Lynx were in view, and with them new anti-tank weapons and surveillance devices. All these would be replaced by yet more advanced systems. Innovation over the remaining years of the century would overburden REME capacity; the aircraft engineers had twice required inter-service assistance since 1958 to cope with unforeseen contingencies such as faulty engines. Beyond this the rising cost of new equipment, irrespective of inflation, would prohibit its deployment to regimental level.

Major-General Frank King, who succeeded General Crookenden in 1967, believed that this factor was decisive. He put the case for recentralization to the Army Board.

Wisely, General King prescribed a staged conversion, a policy supported by the Colonel-Commandant of the day, General Sir John Mogg. Exercises at home and in Germany included trials of a new organization based essentially on a revived squadron command. Operational commitments had to be met, meantime, as change proceeded. NATO had first call on British defence resources. 'Out of area' obligations were diminishing but government continued to adopt others, deemed politically inescapable. Residual tasks were spread across the world from Hong Kong and Brunei through Commonwealth forces in Malaya to a declining garrison in the Persian Gulf, and rising support to Muscat and Oman. There were United Nations peacekeeping duties in Cyprus. Security duties closed in British Guiana but opened in Belize. All these involved Army aircraft. In October 1969, as reorganization was effected, Bernardette Devlin raised the Republican torch in Londonderry and Ulster began to smoulder.

Step by step, formation and regimental resources were pooled to provide the following structure:

| | |
|---|---|
| In the United Kingdom | Army Aviation commander and staff, Headquarters, Strategic Command |
| | 667 Squadron |
| | 3rd Division Aviation Regiment – |
| | 653 Squadron |
| | 663 Squadron } Brigade |
| | 664 Squadron } support |
| | 665 Squadron } units |
| | 666 Squadron – 24 Brigade unit |
| Allied Command Europe | Mobile Force – Flight |
| British Army of the Rhine | Theatre Army Aviation commander and staff |
| | 131 Independent Flight |
| | 7 Independent Flight – Berlin |
| | 1st British Corps – |
| | 655 Squadron |

1st Division Aviation Regiment –
651 Squadron
657 Squadron
658 Squadron

2nd Division Aviation Regiment –
652 Squadron
659 Squadron
660 Squadron

4th Division Aviation Regiment –
654 Squadron
661 Squadron
662 Squadron

| | |
|---|---|
| Near East | 12 Independent Flight (Libya) |
| Land Forces | 16 Independent Flight (Cyprus) |
| Persian Gulf | 668 Squadron |
| Hong Kong | 656 Squadron |

The new order of battle comprised eighteen squadrons and five independent flights – twenty squadron equivalents including special detachments and resources at the Army Aviation Centre – totalling, in sum, 2,771 officers and other ranks. Compare this with the 1,500 posts provided in 1957. REME accounted for 68 officers and 1,263 men in squadrons or independent flights, light aid detachments, aircraft workshops, and headquarters staffs. The availability of resources for this expansion must be credited to General Weston's initiative and the modified decentralization scheme.

A second outcome of that scheme was the articulation of tasks performed by junior ranks in ground crews, essential in the assumption of these tasks by regimental soldiers in the air troops and platoons. They comprehended aircraft marshalling, handling and refuelling; fire and crash services; and assistance to senior ranks in local air traffic control. As in past times, observers were found from their numbers and, now, in the course of recentralization, air gunners also, reflecting the adoption of aircraft armament.

From the outset of reorganization, it was plain that the permanent cadre pilots and those serving with them on secondment in squadrons and flights would be insufficient to man the new structure. The balance was to be found by annexation, temporarily but compulsorily, of the regimental pilots and, no less essentially, their ground crews. This incensed colonels and colonels-commandant. A number fired letters at Napier Crookenden, who was quite the wrong target, accusing him of a breach of faith.

The Army Department believed that this furore would evaporate. An assurance was given that all those extracted from regiments and battalions would be returned at the end of their tour, a promise underwritten by directions to each arm to provide a quota of replacements. With the adoption of this expedient, the executive staff branches occupied themselves with other problems. Manning difficulties were rife in that period, the first part of 1969, due to defence cuts. A number of regiments were nominated for amalgamation or disbandment.

In the search for economies it was proposed that arms representatives should move to their respective centres outside London and, although the Land/Air Warfare branch was not wholly in this category, its removal to Middle Wallop was mooted to Major-General R.D. Wilson, Major-General King's sucessor as Director.

Departure would terminate the longstanding L/AW responsibility for airborne forces, but much of the work had passed to other branches. Light aviation engaged the greater part of the Director's time and his staff. All things considered, the decision to move or stay depended on whether that preoccupation would be served better close to the executive general staff and Royal Air Force technical branches in Whitehall, or, as General Wilson put it,

> where the needs of [the organization] could be identified and the best experience tapped before formulating proposals for changes, research and development. . . .

He opted to move to Middle Wallop, and to reflect the realignment of his responsibilities from 1 January 1970, his appointment was retitled as 'Director of Army Aviation'.

In that year the numbers volunteering for flying were declining significantly, a consequence of regimental huff. In 1967, 378 officers and senior NCOs had applied, of which 164 had been

Soldier and airman: training of a junior NCO of the Army Air Corps at the Depot Regiment, Middle Wallop (*Museum of Army Flying*)

accepted. In 1970 the numbers were 187, 78 being accepted. The forecast for applications in 1971 was 150 (actually, 157). The supply of soldiers with the qualities to fill vacancies as air gunners, observers and non-technical ground crew was dwindling, proportionally, at a greater rate. If the trend continued, squadron strengths would be halved by 1976.

Since inception the permanent cadre of the Army Air Corps had been enlarged to 200 officers, warrant officers and sergeants, of which about 150 were in pilot appointments. There were 405 pilot appointments in the new establishment. In 1970 the requirement for air gunners was foreseen as 110. There were only 38 and all were filled by secondment. Major-General Richardson, once occupant of the future policy desk in L/AW 2, was confronted by this situation as he became Director of Army Aviation in 1971. There were many senior members of the permanent cadre available to suggest solutions to the manning problem. They included Brigadier Denis Coyle commanding the centre, soon to be succeeded by Maurice Sutcliffe; Colonel Dicky Parker at Rheindalen and, later, Peter Collins; Colonel Alan Stepto at Wilton, Strategic Command Headquarters. Their advice was unanimous. The permanent cadre should be enlarged to include a greater proportion of pilots and embrace all non-technical ground staffs.

This was hardly surprising; most senior members of the AAC had been horrified by the principle of decentralization and their concomitant removal from the chain of executive authority. Recentralization had restored and to an extent improved the aviation structure and professional environment, but they were anxious to consolidate both.

Some of the general staff branches regarded the advice as 'empire building'. The Army Air Corps was said to want to dominate Army flying. But why should they not? The permanent cadre had been created to provide professional continuity. Its senior members were speaking as much for their soldiers as the officers. A high proportion of ground crewmen, for example, including many of those acquired on loan from regimental air platoons and troops, wished to make a career in aviation duties. It was highly desirable that they should do so; continuity was needed no less in their work.

This last consideration clinched the matter, despite the expectation that the numbers of Army aircraft would decrease in the approaching decade as Alouettes, Skeeters, and Scouts were replaced by a smaller number of Gazelles and Lynx. However, it seemed certain that the latter would require a pilot and crewman. Soldier posts saved in the first development would, on balance, be required for the second. General Richardson initiated the process of representation.

It was a long business. Detailed proposals had to be prepared for scrutiny by a working party comprehending all interested branches. Their findings were considered by the Standing Committee on Army Organization and, securing their support, a formal proposal was put to the Army Board. The latter adopted them as service policy. Two years elapsed from the first marshalling of facts at Middle Wallop in 1971 to initial implementation of the proposal on 1 October 1973, eight years to completion in 1979. But the result was doubly a triumph. The permanent cadre extension was secured; and the Army Air Corps was instituted as a Fighting Arm joining, in this capacity, the Royal Armoured Corps and the Infantry.

Among the changes effected for future manning, several principles are notable. Secondment would continue to ensure a flow of fresh ideas between Army aviation and the remainder of the Army, but the ratio between seconded and cadre pilots, formerly 2:1, was to be reversed. The cadre would, initially, be extended by voluntary transfer from seconded pilots, but direct entry would be opened to officers and other ranks. Regular and short-service officers would enter from the Royal Military Academy. A number of special regular commissions would be open to other ranks. Commissioning opportunities for the highly experienced warrant officers and sergeants employed as qualified flying instructors were increased. They were to be designated Technical Aviation Instructors.

Soldiers would enlist either for general or clerical duties. Non-commissioned pilots would be selected from their number and take their place on a separate roll when qualified. Men selected to be air gunners or observers – to whom special half wings were already awarded on completion of their respective courses – would remain on the general duties promotion roll with non-technical ground crews and those employed in domestic administration. A third promotion roll would be maintained for clerks. A new title was chosen for the private soldier on enlistment: 'Air Trooper'.

Gunner Langley, a driver-signaller, aircraft handler, refueller, jack-of-all-trades in a ground crew in 1957 had followed in the tradition of those devoted men who had launched, recovered and secured the AOP Austers with their RAF comrades the world over in war and the campaigns that followed. Some had flown as observers, unpaid and unrecognized in this role. Year by year the range of their tasks had become more demanding as the Army's capabilities in the air were diversified. Not before time their contribution to flying operations was formally acknowledged in the Army.

CHAPTER TWENTY-ONE

# Testing Times

The Army Air Corps was categorized as a Fighting Arm because it had been equipped with primary direct fire weapons, specifically, anti-armour missiles. Yet, in the 1960s, many sections of the Army doubted the viability of the helicopter in 'hot' war; the Russian air defence array was formidable. Moreover, it was contended that the aircraft would not provide a stable platform for missile launch and control.

Those who took the contrary view supported it with data from American operations in Vietnam and British forces in Borneo, but these were scarcely applicable to the north German plain. British and American operability trials in Europe and the United States indicated that the helicopter had a higher chance of survival than a tank in general war but, it had to be owned, the encounters informing this view had taken place free of battle stress. Still, the drift of evidence apparently rattled the opposition. When war games conducted by the Army Operational Research Group concluded that the helicopter system offered the most economic means of destroying tanks, the general staff suppressed their publication for many months.

However, the cumulative evidence could not be ignored. The operational requirement for anti-tank helicopters in Germany was established and funds were earmarked for final development and procurement.

As noted the Vigilant was mounted on the Scout experimentally in 1962 and trials began with the French SS11 in 1964. Commercial and trades union interests combined to displace the latter with an inferior British system, but Roy Mason, Secretary of State for Defence, supported the Army's preference for the SS11. All these systems were 'semi-automated': the operator guided the missile manually to a target by transmitting corrective signals via wires trailed back from the missile base. Success depended on innate skill combined with training and experience. This limited the availability of operators.

Fully automated systems appeared which obviated the requirement for coordination of eye and hand. The operator simply had to hold the target in his sight. Movement of the sight automatically corrected the missile's course. Of the options available on the market in 1977, the Army chose the American model, TOW – Tube-launched, Optically-tracked, Wire-guided.

It was cleared for use by both Gazelle and Lynx. The former had entered service in May 1974 with 660 Squadron at Soest and, apart from an indifferent performance in hot climates, was exceptionally free of the introductory problems which dogged other British helicopters. The Army Department planned originally to order 569 to replace the Sioux and swell the light observation fleet, but the 1974 round of defence cuts reduced this to 212, which included nine for the Royal Marine Commando Air Squadron. With five seats, and a range of 310 miles at a cruising speed of 120 knots, it rapidly became a utility helicopter.

Its companion, the Lynx, was late in delivery, underdeveloped, and underpowered when deliveries began to 651 Squadron at Hildesheim and 654 Squadron at Detmold at the end of

Sioux over Londonderry, Northern Ireland. The Army Air Corps has served throughout the province in regimental strength since 1970 (*Museum of Army Flying*)

1977. Ordered as a utility helicopter it was, by this date, designated as the prime British anti-armour helicopter, operating in partnership with the Gazelle as its target spotter. Lynx and TOW would take over from the Scout and SS11. The 1974 economies had reduced the production order from 162 to 100 aircraft.

This was the uprating programme as planned and introduced, to be completed in the early 1980s. It was intermittently disrupted by internal security operations in Northern Ireland.

The civil rights movement there in 1969 was carried forward by the Provisional Irish Republican Army – the IRA – in 1970 as a basis for terrorism. The 17th/21st Lancers' Air Squadron, located with the Royal Air Force at Aldergrove, provided reconnaissance and liaison sorties at the outset to the Royal Ulster Constabulary, and the Army as it was committed to the struggle. But the pilots of the cavalry Sioux could not cope with the demand as disorders spread. 8 Flight – four Scouts and two Sioux – was sent from England to the RAF Station at Ballykelly to support the Londonderry area. A Beaver flight entered operations. A second reconnaissance regiment arrived with its air squadron.

With the successful reduction of urban rioting in 1971, terrorism spread across the province. Border and traffic watches, the carriage of pickets and other tactical detachments, the provision of reconnaissance for commanders at all levels, and casualty evacuation were roles familiar to those who had operated 'out of area'. The growth of an air taxi service was borne patiently by the AAC and seconded pilots, and was balanced by the periodic insertion and extraction of clandestine patrols by night, notwithstanding the rudimentary nature of their navigation instruments.

The Islander replaces the Army Air Corps Beaver (*Museum of Army Flying*)

During the first decade of deployment to Northern Ireland, flying continuity was maintained by the flight rather than the squadron. These were the years of Gazelle and Lynx entry, and of reorganization. The selection of detachments for Ulster thus had to ensure that equipment changes did not inhibit operational availability, and to provide a sufficiency of experienced air and ground crews to sustain the full range of operations.

Equipment development was not confined in these years to Germany alone. Helicopters came under fire in Ulster from 1970, though often pilots were unaware of it until bullet holes were discovered by ground crews. A warning device was developed and, in 1974, Major-General Roy Dixon, the first Director, Army Air Corps, tested it,

> . . . flying in a Scout fitted with such a device up and down a small arms range between the firing point and the butts while a marksman fired rifle shots beneath us. I was not entirely confident and expected at any moment to feel a searing pain somewhere in my anatomy. . . .

With the completion of reorganization in 1979, a resident AAC regiment was established in Ulster comprising 655 Squadron, operating nine Scouts and six Gazelles, reinforced by a second squadron rotating from Germany every four months. A fixed-wing flight from 7 Regiment – Beavers initially, Islanders later – was added to the resident units. As the Lynx element of mixed squadrons from BAOR accumulated specialized anti-tank equipment, the time spent in stripping

Scout on the Helicopter Landing Site at Bessbrook, Northern Ireland, one of the busiest centres of aircraft operations in the province (*B.G. Price*)

and refitting it at the beginning and end of tours became excessive. In 1986, 665 Squadron was re-formed in Ulster with a complete establishment for Lynx and Gazelle, manned on a trickle basis of roulement from units in Germany. On this basis light aircraft operations have continued day by day. New equipment, new methods have been brought into service in these following years, widening the scope of helicopters in counter terrorism. When this long-running task ends and, to an extent, security imperatives recede, the Army Air Corps' part in the campaign will be told in a dedicated volume.

Notwithstanding the considerable strain of this standing commitment on a corps numbering less than two thousand, all ranks, excluding REME and Other Arm technicians and specialists, the main body of the Army Air Corps, took a full part in trials, training and operations elsewhere through the 1970s and '80s.

In England the 3rd Division at intervals under Majors-General G.C.A. Gilbert and R.M. Carnegie exercised as an airmobile formation employing AAC and RAF helicopters. Infantry armed with Milan anti-tank missiles were moved by air to seal enemy penetrations or exploit flanks. Other arms were similarly moved by helicopters as occasion required.

A Scout winches up an infantryman on border patrol in Hong Kong (*Museum of Army Flying*)

While directing one of the exercises, General Gilbert alighted from a Scout when the rotors, slowly coming to a halt, fell off the head one by one. But apart from necessitating remedial action in the Scout fleet, the mishap did not restrain the testing of the British airmobile concept, a variant of that adopted by the United States Army.

Three comprehensive trials reached a common conclusion by 1975: airmobile forces offered an economic means of extending the viability and enhancing the enterprise of 1st British Corps. The difficulty was that neither the Royal Air Force nor the Army Air Corps had sufficient helicopters to support a division in this role. The project was shelved pending the introduction of the Chinook medium lift helicopter, on order for the Royal Air Force from the United States.

Far from trials, too far from home to contribute to Northern Ireland operations, two independent flights have provided light aircraft facilities in Cyprus discretely since 1964.

Sometimes, we think in the flight they've completely forgotten us. Do you know we were flying Alouettes long after they were put into museums? But never mind. We work in a

Lynx in Northern Ireland rigged with the 'Heli-telly', a surveillance device, one of many specialist equipments which facilitate counter-terrorism (*MOD (Army)*)

Gazelle landing flight teams into the Grunewald, Germany, October 1990. Although this was part of an annual operational test, it illustrates the ability of the Gazelle to drop/pick up patrols in cover (*Museum of Army Flying*)

Captain Froelich, RCT, flying a Sioux in the United Nations Flight in Cyprus (UNFICYP), resupplying Finnish troops in the Kyrenia range, June 1970 (*Museum of Army Flying*)

wonderful climate – almost perfect for flying. I'm always worried when we get visitors from Wallop that they will close everything down and bring us home. . . . I mean, they're actually paying us to serve here; it can't go on forever. . . .

These are the words of a pilot in the 1990s, serving in the United Nations Flight, but they might equally have been uttered by a comrade in 16 Flight, supporting the garrison of the British Sovereign Base.

The British battalion group serving in the United Nations Force in Cyprus keeps the peace along a section of the 'Green Line' which separates Greek and Turkish forces and communities, aiming to pre-empt friction between them or the occasional clashes contrived by the opposing soldiery. The helicopter flight makes an important contribution to this work. Aerial observation affords the quickest means of spotting civilians gathering, hellbent on righting some perceived affront by those on the other side of the wire fencing, or the deployment of local troops for a sortie. Eyes in the air, with a radio, provide the only means of observing all movement in the battalion sector simultaneously.

In 1979 a different form of peacekeeping occupied 656 Squadron, brought home at last from the Far East. Attempts to secure a political settlement in [Southern] Rhodesia appeared to be close to success early in November. There was to be an election on the basis of universal suffrage. But the state was engaged in civil war between government forces and guerrillas supporting the two

Gazelle in UNFICYP returns to base, 1985 (*Museum of Army Flying*)

Rearming the Lynx, Salisbury Plain (*Captain Sharpe*)

major opposition parties. It was clear that, without a cease-fire and the voluntary containment of all military forces, voters would be coerced. A Commonwealth Monitoring Group – CMG – was established under Major-General Sir John Acland to gather the guerrillas into sixteen Assembly Places – APs – and to monitor the government forces while the elections were held and the result was made known. CMG detachments had to be placed in the bush to guide, assemble and observe the guerrillas. They would depend upon aircraft for supply and communications.

Frugality of resources has long been an inceptory feature of British expeditions. No. 656 Squadron was ordered on 15 November to prepare a detachment of three Gazelles for the Rhodesian operation, codename 'Agila'. Late political heel dragging delayed their despatch. 'Five weeks and fourteen plans later', Major S.R. Nathan, the squadron commander, remarked, 'we actually deployed'. By this date it had become obvious that the spread of Rhodesian territory and lack of roads required more helicopters. Three Scouts accompanied the Gazelles on 22 December and within seventy-two hours the case for whole squadron became irresistible. Working with RAF C–130s, engaged in long haul and local supply dropping, and Pumas, the Scouts began work from Gwelo, the Gazelles from Salisbury, on Christmas Day.

The guerrillas assembling to observe the cease-fire had been living in the bush for years. Armed with a variety of modern weapons, they distrusted the white AP observers on the ground and the helicopters which brought supplies and mail every two days, weather permitting.

. . . [The guerrillas] were never entirely relaxed when we were in the air [Major Nathan continued]; at all locations they covered our approach with at least one AA machine-gun and, whilst the aircraft were on the ground, with small arms and RPG 7 [rockets]. . . in the first few days we gave away hundreds of cigarettes . . . and showed many of them round the helicopters in order to create some kind of trust. What else can you do when armed with a 9-mm. pistol and surrounded by hundreds of [rifles and rockets]?

Thunderstorms were frequent. Low flying was desirable to reduce target options for suspicious guerrillas but was abandoned due to navigation difficulties and ground hazards – a Royal Air Force Puma crashed after hitting wires on 27 December.

Despite rumours of breakdown, the cease-fire held throughout January and February 1980. The elections were successful and the Commonwealth Group dispersed. When the squadron returned to England with its REME and RAOC supporting elements on 19 March 1980, all were rapidly caught up in other demands. Their accomplishments involving 2,200 flying hours began to recede. But, as Brigadier John Learmont, deputy commander of the Commonwealth Mission, reminded Major Nathan in a letter,

In the early days you and your pilots were literally the lifeline for the soldiers at the rendezvous . . . it was a magnificent performance and it will never be forgotten by those you supported. . . .

As this demanding 'sideshow' ended successfully, one among the run of contingencies falling to the British services year by year, another was brewing.

Argentina had long pressed a fallacious claim to the Falklands dependencies. On 2 April 1982 her forces occupied the islands by *coup de main* and, at once, a British joint task force was assembled to recover them, operating at a range of 8,000 miles.

Preceded by warships, amphibious craft and civil transports sailed for the South Atlantic during April and May, reliant on a single carrier for air cover. The islands were within range of Argentine bases containing over 100 fighters and ground attack aircraft, supplemented by 20 Pucara with the 10,000 troops occupying East Falkland. In the distant autumn season, the weather was generally clear. Daylight hours were short. In these circumstances, 3 Commando Brigade, reinforced by two parachute battalions, was to be landed to begin recovery operations. 5 Infantry Brigade was to follow. The Royal Marine Air Squadron and 656 Squadron AAC formed part of the task force.

The story of this operation, 'Corporate', is told elsewhere: how the ships were attacked from the air in the ocean and within the Falkland Sound, how the landing force made a lodgement, secured tactical features, defeated outlying Argentine strongpoints, suffered and survived air raids, and finally surrounded and overcame a numerous and well-armed enemy. Naval and land forces all contributed essentially to the victory. None more so than the two light helicopter squadrons.

The Royal Marines embarked nine Gazelles and six Scouts with the landing force, taking under command an advanced element of No. 656 Squadron with four Scouts. Because the enemy had numerous air defence weapons it was decided to provide the Scouts with internal machine-gun mountings for 'self-defence'. The SS11 was added 'because the enemy is believed to have light armour', an idea which was seen to be absurd when the soldiers landed among the trackless waterlogged hills of the territory. Still, the missiles were to find other targets. Seeking a defensive weapon for the Gazelle on 7 April, geniuses at Wilton and Middle Wallop seized upon a novel solution, the French MATRA SNEB 68 mm rocket, in service with the Royal Air Force Harrier.

None were held in Britain; no specification or clearance for their fitment existed. Major Frank Esson flew a Beaver to France to collect pods and ammunition which were fitted by Westland Aircraft to outriggers on a Gazelle. A 'rudimentary' sight was devised and fitted. On Easter Monday single and ripple firing trials were completed. A contract was made with MATRA. REME technicians began modifications on 17 April. Operational necessity had procured a new system from articulation of an operational requirement to delivery in ten days.

Landings began early on 21 May 1982. As the assault craft began an unopposed landing, a Royal Marine Gazelle escorting a Sea King helicopter to the north was hit by small arms fire. The pilot, Sergeant A.P. Evans, ditched successfully in the icy sea, though mortally wounded. His crewman, Sergeant E.R. Candlish, dragged him ashore. Just a few minutes later, the same Argentine post hit a second Royal Marine Gazelle, which crashed, killing the crew, Lieutenant K. Francis and Lance-Corporal B. Griffin. A third Gazelle was damaged but managed to recover to a landing ship.

While the lodgement was being secured, the Royal Marine and AAC helicopters operated from their sea transports, and were thus often under fire from the locally based Pucaras or the Argentine Skyhawks and Mirages sweeping in daily from the mainland. Initially, the AAC Scouts supported the two parachute battalions as they occupied the heights commanding the beach-head but were soon being diverted to random tasks, and were for a time split as the sea transports moved to evade air attack. At the end of the first week the commandos and parachute battalions began to march east and south to seize intermediate tactical positions essential to closure with the main Argentine force.

The infantry columns marched over soft, rolling, windswept ground, featureless except for sheep

Scout picking up a Special Air Service patrol in the Falklands (*Museum of Army Flying*)

fences. Between the scattered settlements the land was deserted. The marching men relied absolutely upon helicopters – mostly the light helicopters – for supply and casualty evacuation. These were the tasks of Royal Marine Gazelles and Scouts on 27 and 28 May as 2 Para, striking south for Goose Green, broke into the enemy positions. But Pucaras were active. A pair attacked two Royal Marine Scouts, killing one pilot, Lieutenant R.J. Nunn. His crewman, Sergeant A.R. Belcher was gravely wounded but survived the crash.

Captain J.G. Greenhalgh and Sergeant R.J. Walker, flying 656 Squadron Scouts, took over from the Royal Marines and continued casualty evacuation, flying, as a parachutist described it, 'through Argy fire – wherever they were wanted, they went'.

Goose Green was captured. Within a few days all four Scouts with a highly overloaded Chinook were supporting 2 Para in a daring advance to Fitzroy and Bluff Cove, 40 miles to the east.

More light aircraft were coming. The remainder of the squadron arrived at the end of May, with 70 Aircraft Workshops and 1 Aircraft [Stores] Support Unit essentially close behind. Major C.S. Sibun, the squadron commander, was glad to avail himself of the Goose Green airstrip shortly after arrival, and settlement buildings. The squadron headquarters was not sorry to leave its waterlogged site on San Carlos Water.

To the east the Royal Marine helicopters had been supporting 3 Para and the commandos during their extensive advance on the Argentine force massed to hold Port Stanley, the Falklands' capital. This force was to be attacked in mid-June.

Scout in company with a Wessex 'support helicopter' of the Royal Navy in the Falklands, 1982. This picture manifests the bare and trackless nature of the landscape (*Museum of Army Flying*)

As the date approached, the Scouts and Gazelles, and the naval Wessex and Sea King support helicopters, were engaged in these preparations. The artillery, ammunition and other necessaries had to be advanced. Radio rebroadcast stations were to be posted on high features across the front to ensure communications. Intelligence had to be gathered by aerial reconnaissance. A continuous trickle of casualties had to be lifted by air to the hospitals at sea.

There was a grievous accident in this period. Staff Sergeant C.A. Griffin and Lance-Corporal S.J. Cockton were carrying by night a Royal Signals command party to investigate difficulties at a rebroadcast station. The Gazelle was mistaken for an enemy aircraft and shot down by a British weapon. All were killed.

There were several similar errors at night or in poor visibility. A 656 Scout was narrowly missed by a Blowpipe missile, and a Gazelle by a long burst of machine-gun fire from a British post. But battlefields are dangerous places and when the enemy is employing identical or similar equipment, errors of engagement will occur.

When 5 Infantry Brigade arrived it suffered an early and heavy loss. The landing craft moving the Welsh Guards and part of brigade headquarters to Fitzroy were attacked by Argentine aircraft, the former suffering severely. Air Trooper Price, in charge of 656 Squadron command post vehicle was wounded by shrapnel. For the remainder of the day the RAF Chinook, naval support helicopters, and a mixed party of Gazelles and Scouts, were involved in casualty evacuation.

For a time Sergeant R. Kalinski was an unhappy onlooker. Observing the approaching raiders he wisely decided to hide on the ground and was landing when his Scout's transmission failed. It was recovered later by a Sea King, another task for the REME aircraft technicians, between air raids, and battles against the pervasive surface water.

On 10 and 11 June the two brigades made ready for the offensive designed to end the campaign. The Commando Brigade and 3 Para were to attack from the west on 12 June, 5 Infantry Brigade from the south on the 13th, delayed until 14 June. The wind force increased from the 11th, driving snow and sleet showers.

These were principally night engagements involving infantry advances along broken ridges, taking some posts necessarily head on, encircling them where possible. On both nights Argentine mines caused early casualties; thereafter, the stretchers were returning with men wounded in the mêlée. The Royal Marine helicopters were using night vision goggles to aid night landings but, unfamiliar with their use, 656 employed the longstanding method of torch signals. However, some pick-up points were too far forward for this; light displays attracted fire. Captain S.M. Drennan lifted sixteen casualties from Tumbledown mountain early on 14 June, three from forward slopes, a triumph of skill and nerve. Pilots not engaged with wounded were hauling ammunition and equipment forward into the forward unit lines.

Shortly after daylight on the 14th, the Argentine force collapsed. The British brigades pressed in, and the Scouts found targets, guns and bunkers, for their SS11 missiles. A cease-fire was arranged. In effect, the campaign was over. One officer of 656 Squadron was asked on his return home if he had been engaged in 'hot' war? He was about to respond that it was quite hot enough for him when he realized that war in Europe would be hotter still.

'Not boiling hot,' he said. 'More like the bath temperature before you put the cold water in; too hot for comfort.'

In 1982, following the successful end of the Falklands campaign, the Army Air Corps celebrated its twenty-fifth birthday with an air show incorporating a reunion of its constituent members, from the wartime AOP and Glider Pilot squadrons to those who entered to fly helicopters. Some two thousand former pilots and ground crews attended besides many members of the public. Brigadier Maurice Sutcliffe laid the foundations for such gatherings in 1957 when he organized an officers' dinner club, and followed this by sponsoring a corps association. It was not – is not now – an easy matter for a body small in number with members scattered across the country to maintain regional branches, but the high numbers gathering at Middle Wallop for the air show manifested a wish among past members to congregate and enjoy the company of old friends. Much credit is due to those who have devoted time to maintaining the register of members past and present.

On this occasion all those who had lost their lives in Army flying were commemorated in a new memorial and book of remembrance. The preservation of the aircraft flown in past times was assured by the decision to move the Museum of Army Flying to greatly enlarged, purpose built accommodation at the edge of the Middle Wallop complex. King Hussein of Jordan, an accomplished pilot himself, laid the foundation stone in 1982. The generosity of Sir Jack Hayward, a former Royal Air Force pilot, and glider pilot, brought the project to completion on a grand scale.

In the professional field that year, there were hopes that the Lynx had passed through the worst of its teething troubles and was ready for battle. Actually, it was far from ready, but it was such an excellent aircraft when all its parts were in kilter that it humoured its operators.

Gazelle over the Brandenburg Tor on a routine 'Berlin Wall' patrol in the late 1980s (*Museum of Army Flying*)

Three regiments had been formed from the resources of five on the old model. Specialized equipment for their aircraft included the gyro-stabilized sighting gear for TOW in the Lynx, a Doppler-based navigation fit and roof-mounted optical sight in the Gazelle, and night vision aids for all aircrew. Equipment and tactics had been comprehensively tested. This success raised a number of new questions.

The divisional regiment in Germany would, from January 1983, field two attack squadrons and one for reconnaissance. Armoured reconnaissance apart, the helicopter was thus no longer available to armoured, infantry, artillery or engineer regimental commanders, and only on a concessionary basis to brigade commanders. The new organization was a divisional resource, perhaps even a corps resource. This made for misgivings at and below the brigade level, not least among the armoured regiments. Was this development moving towards displacement of the tank, while lacking the tank's ability to win and hold ground in attack?

Internally the question of aircraft command in the new organization was perplexing. Traditionally the senior man flew it while gunners or missile-operators did their work. Although these specialists received training to land the helicopter in emergency this made the point that once the weapon had been employed, the prime requirement was to recover the helicopter. But strong views were expressed at theatre and director's conventions that weapons and equipment advances might lead to the pilot

Lynx armed for tank-destroying (*Museum of Army Flying*)

Lynx firing TOW missiles (*Westland Helicopters*)

Lynx refuelling during ground operations. Note TOW tubes on mountings and the waist general purpose machine-gun (*AAC GLF 938, Museum of Army Flying*)

becoming subordinate to the weapon operator. Surely the senior member of the crew should 'fight' the aircraft. The 'CREST' scheme – crew restructuring – proposed to solve the problem by introducing a second pilot into the aircrew of the specialized Lynx.

Meanwhile, 'out of area' aviators, and indeed many who were not, became apprehensive that the Army Air Corps was advancing to such a level of specialization for armoured warfare that it would forget how much it continued to be in demand in traditional roles. This view militated sufficiently to sustain the concept basic to the 3rd Division trials, refined by Major-General J.A. Ward-Booth during his tour as Director in the late 1970s, whereby AAC helicopters were widely used to deploy and recover infantry equipped with portable anti-tank guided weapons. Comparisons were made with the cost of a utility as distinct from a specialized Lynx in this role, which suggested its advantages in viability and economy. Similarly, a Lynx was cheaper to use in this way than a support helicopter. The deployment of the Chinook medium lift helicopter for Army use, albeit under Royal Air Force control, upset these calculations.

Undaunted, those who supported further specialization of Army aircraft made the case for procurement of a dedicated 'attack' helicopter. It received sufficient support to be adopted as an operational requirement in 1983, but made little progress due to conceptual opposition by the Royal Armoured Corps and Royal Air Force, and unremitting pressures on defence funds. Major-General David Goodman, Director in 1983, hoped to overcome the first by 'preaching the complementary nature of the tank and helicopter'.

Suddenly, in 1990, an armoured campaign was thrust upon some of the NATO allies when Saddam Hussein occupied Kuwait. Slowly, through the autumn into January 1991, strong United States naval, air, and ground forces joined the local forces of Saudi Arabia and the Gulf states. To these were added a reinforced British air wing and an army formation formed by the subscription of many units and detachments, to provide at full strength an armoured division – 1st Division. Among European allies, France sent a light division containing numerous helicopters and a tactical air wing.

'Last vehicles depart for Emden', was among the entries in 4th Regiment Army Air Corps diary for 4 December 1990. On the 7th,

10 Lynx, 4 Gazelle to [United States Air Force Base] Ramstein [to be conveyed in American C–5 aircraft to the Gulf]
15 personnel and 4 Gazelle depart [RAF Station] Gutersloh in 2 C–130 for Gulf.
Warrant Officers' & Sergeants' Xmas Ball.

8th December. 4 Lynx to Ramstein
Cpls' Mess Xmas Draw.

Lieutenant-Colonel F.M. Wawn was moving 654, 659 and 661 Squadrons, his headquarters and administration to the Gulf from Germany just before Christmas. It was not the happiest of seasons for a parting. As ever in soldiers' families the burden of anxiety and separation fell principally upon those left at home. Husbands and fathers, cast down by their farewells, departed, distracted in some measure by apprehension of the campaign in prospect.

Suddenly, after breaking into aircraft loads, they were all together on the Gulf shore at Al Jubayl, one of several bases established for the build-up of the allied force, surprised to find themselves in cool, clear weather. Shortly, helicopters, vehicles, weapons, ammunition, radios and other stores arrived, were unloaded and distributed. The regiment came to operational life and moved into the interior.

Ascending, they moved through plains of grit and dust, sand seas, low ridges of broken rocks, and stream beds, mostly dry but occasionaly filled by rains in this winter season. The main pipeline road runs north west into Iraq, otherwise movement depends largely on tracks. There are a few scattered villages, scarcely a town, along the border marches of Saudi Arabia. Bedouin groups drift in and out. Otherwise it is empty.

By the middle of January 1991, however, the allied divisions had spread across a huge tract of the desert. Tents, vehicles, sandbagged enclosures, and supply dumps formed a series of hamlets and villages on either side of the pipeline road. At night, careless drivers sometimes passed their vehicles through sub-units or detachments, breaking tent guys and causing the inmates to rush out, protesting.

Although at first it seemed to some of 4 Regiment that they were simply taking part in another major exercise, all came quickly to realize that they were moving towards a battle, and that they were operating in a climate of advanced military technology. American resources seemed endless and were often opened generously to their British and French allies – 4 Regiment acquired invaluable transport in this way. They also imposed their systems of command and control down to divisional level, irrespective of national origin, and the control of air space. The regimental pilots were required to know:

US Army Weekly Special Instructions (SPINS)
US Army Airspace Control Order
Meteorology
Danger areas
Air test areas
IFF [Indicator: Friend or Foe] transponder codes
Authentication codes
Tactical and aviation airspace control maps
Tactical frequencies [own divisional radio nets] and Airspace control frequencies [route allocation, air defence authentication]
Forward Air Control information.

Much of this information changed daily. Those engaged in briefing duties had to identify and display what was new so that individuals flying on that day could copy it into their personal information packs, adding some forty minutes to preparatory work. If a helicopter was to enter the United States Marine Corps' air space, employing its own system, additional information was required.

4 Regiment brought 23 Lynx and 24 Gazelle into operations, all fitted with the observation aids and weapons developed for the anti-tank role. Major-General Rupert Smith, Commander, 1st Armoured Division grouped them with his artillery and ground reconnaissance unit to form the 'Depth' Fire Group. This force was to be responsible for striking targets behind the foremost enemy defences. It was a bold and imaginative use of helicopters, but the regiment would have preferred a more independent role; at any rate, one which would have given them an immediate objective.

There were good reasons for Major-General Smith's decision, however. Helicopter operations would involve movement into the area controlled by the Royal Artillery, whether British or allied guns were involved. On that basis there would be no danger of the helicopters being hit by friendly fire. Equally, the commander, Royal Artillery – the CRA – would be able to apply his guns or rockets, or the helicopters, to targets in the area as circumstances demanded. Air Observation Posts would be required in all circumstances.

Though all this was true, it did not entirely satisfy 4 Regiment. They also began to discover that the two brigades, 4th and 7th Armoured, were dissatisfied with their isolation from a share of helicopter resources and warmed to the idea of developing cooperation; but training time was running out. Major-General Smith was receptive to a proposal which satisfied both parties, the provision of combat reconnaissance patrols comprising a mix of Lynx and Gazelles, on call by the two brigades.

Very early on 17 January 1991 allied air operations began. Intelligence was pouring in from aerial sources. The allied soldiers and marines completed their preparations to destroy the Iraqi ground forces in and around Kuwait. The REME teams supporting 4 Regiment continued to fit sand filters to the aircraft engines, and complete other modifications. At what seemed the eleventh hour, the 1:100,000 maps of the operational area arrived on 14 February.

Actually, they had to wait ten more days in the slips before G for Go day arrived. Then at last the leading columns of the division entered Iraq. The weather was poor. Heavy rain settled the dust but softened road verges. All three squadrons moved forward to selected sites on the 25th, G+1 day, in a 50 knot wind. Corporal Rex Butt of Headquarters Squadron was driving back to regimental headquarters that evening when his driver noticed several men walking across the desert with a white flag. They investigated and found they were Iraqi soldiers who wished to surrender with 178 others nearby. The problem was finding someone to take charge of them as the force was rolling forward.

On 26 February a combat patrol of 654 Squadron was tasked to clear the first bound of the Queen's Royal Irish Hussars battle group. Lacking other commitments, Colonel Wawn ordered another to shadow them and, perhaps by chance, Major Eustace, the squadron commander, entered the rally as a second shadow.

The advance was delayed, which suited the two patrols; the weather was poor. But when the QRIH were ready to move at 11.00 visibility had improved to some 4 miles, and Sergeant M. Thompson commanding Alpha, the first patrol, reported that the way forward was clear. Just after this message was passed, Major Eustace observed Iraqi T–55 tanks with other vehicles. He brought forward Bravo patrol under Captain C. Morley. Two Lynx on the move began to engage the targets, missing initially due to turbulence. Captain Morley opened fire, running the helicopter onto the ground while the TOW was tracked onto its target, and a second was fired from the ground. Both hit their targets. Alpha and Bravo joined forces to destroy a total of four tanks and an armoured personnel carrier.

The patrols drew back as the wind blew up more sand curtains. Their job was in any case done. Indeed, the regiment was hard put to find another as 1st Armoured Division pushed on to cut the highway between Kuwait City and Basra, clearing a path without serious challenge from the enemy. On the last morning [29 February 1991], 659 Squadron expected to support 7th Armoured Brigade from 07.00 but during the preceding night the time was advanced by an hour. The AAC liaison officer at brigade headquarters was 60 kilometres from squadron headquarters and was unable to enter the operations net to relay details of the change of time.

Keen to contribute, the squadron was fortunately on the move early and caught up with the brigade column, seen by Staff Sergeant 'Jeep' Smith as,

> . . . a long snake of white dots clearly visible through Thermal Imaging. Just then the OC gave us a new RV to support the QRIH who were still going east. . . . By this time a few targets were visible, but were obviously abandoned. I then observed a moving target slowly going to right to left about 5 kilometres distant. . . . Corporal Bennet [aircrewman] quickly gave me launch pre-launch restraints. The vehicle stopped and one person got out and ran away. I fired and the missile struck dead centre . . . a Gaz 69 Jeep.

This may have been the last shot of the campaign. A few minutes later, the cease-fire was notified.

The members of 4 Regiment returned to Germany knowing a good deal more about themselves personally and professionally. For while the Arabian desert was, in climate and crust, scarcely comparable to the north German plain, and the Iraqui forces did not match those of the Warsaw Pact, every component of the regimental structure had been tested and tried.

It was not the fault of the regiment that the operational task for which it had been organized

Regimental Tactical Headquarters and HQ, 654 Squadron, inside Iraq (*AAC GLF series, Museum of Army Flying*)

was just then falling away as the Soviet Union broke up, leaving intact only its core, Russia, in a loose confederation with some of its neighbours. And while the notion of a war in north-west or central Europe cannot be dismissed, the Warsaw Pact is defunct. The highly specialized anti-tank regiment of the Army Air Corps is thus inevitably under review.

What is not in doubt, however, is the future of the corps as far as professional military eyes can see. An ascent from Netheravon airfield may assist the process of looking out and on. Rising in a helicopter, we shall soon see below country familiar to generations of soldiers who have served in the air: there is Larkhill, its airfield site pre-dating the founding of the Royal Flying Corps, and used to good effect by Charles Bazeley twenty-five years later. Netheravon, too, an early base for Army flying, was taken into use by 38 Wing and the Glider Pilot Regiment in the Second World War. Its remaining hutments do good service to 7 Regiment at the end of the twentieth century; the camp provides a base for 666 Squadron of the Territorial Army.

On the eastern side of the plain we may see Middle Wallop, for so long the home of Army flying. A Chipmunk is in the circuit. Piece by piece the estate has passed into Army possession. Across the airfield the Sioux of the Blue Eagles once rose to dazzle crowds with rotary aerobatics. And crowds will no doubt continue to gather as the International Air Show flourishes, supported by military, diplomatic, and commercial interests.

Since 1945 successive governments have felt themselves obliged, every year or so, to adopt unexpected military commitments. It is on this account that the Army has nurtured and enhanced its

Back to the future? Sport ballooning, 1990 (*Museum of Army Flying*)

air arm. As long as men are indispensable to campaigning there will be a requirement for reconnaissance, tactical movement of troops including casualty evacuation, supply and communications. But the capability and the wish of the Army pilots, indeed, of all its aircrew, to operate fighting aircraft will also be maintained. The Lynx and TOW combination will be replaced by an attack helicopter built specifically for that task; an aircraft flown by soldiers operating in the third dimension of the ground battle.

Soldiers have been engaged in flying for more than a hundred years as pilots, observers, and gunners in balloons, gliders, and light aircraft, based as often as not among the fighting men on the ground. Soldiers first, they have earned distinction as airmen, and on both accounts have now been declared a Fighting Arm. Thus the Army Air Corps has been awarded a guidon by Her Majesty the Queen. Emblazoned with their battle honours, it enters service in 1994 from the hands of its Colonel-in-Chief, His Royal Highness, The Prince of Wales.

# Appendices

# Squadrons in Service: Air Observation Post to Army Air Corps

| | | |
|---|---|---|
| *651 Squadron* | Formed at Old Sarum (RAF unit) | 1 August 1941 |
| AOP | North Africa, Sicily, Italy, and Palestine | 1942–8 |
| | Disbanded in Egypt | 1 November 1955 |
| | Reformed from 657 Squadron at Middle Wallop | 1 November 1955 |
| AAC | Transferred to AAC (at Feltwell) | 1 September 1957 |
| | From Debden to Middle Wallop | 1 March 1961 |
| | Employed as 3 Div Army Aviation HQ | 1966–9 |
| | Remustered and in Germany from | 1 November 1971 |
| | | |
| *652 Squadron* | Formed at Old Sarum (RAF unit) | 1 May 1942 |
| AOP | France, Holland, and Germany | 1944–5 |
| AAC | Transferred to AAC in Germany | 1 September 1957 |
| | Employed as 1 Div Army Aviation HQ | 1966–9 |
| | Remustered in Germany | October 1969 |
| | | |
| *653 Squadron* | Formed at Old Sarum (RAF unit) | 20 June 1942 |
| AOP | France, Holland, and Germany | 1944–5 |
| | Disbanded in Germany | 15 September 1945 |
| AAC | Reformed in Cyprus | 11 May 1958 |
| | Moves to Aden | 9 March 1961 |
| | Employed as HQ 3 Wing | 1965 |
| | Disbanded | 19 October 1967 |
| | Reformed at Netheravon | 1 November 1971 |
| | Remustered from 660 Squadron | December 1977 |
| | In Germany | 1 November 1978 |
| | | |
| *654 Squadron* | Formed at Old Sarum (RAF unit) | 15 July 1942 |
| AOP | North Africa and Italy | 1942–5 |
| | Disbanded in Italy | 24 June 1947 |
| AAC | Reformed in Germany | 1 September 1958 |
| | Employed as 2 Div Aviation HQ | 1964–9 |
| | Remustered in Germany | October 1969 |

| | | |
|---|---|---|
| *655 Squadron* | Formed at Old Sarum (RAF unit) | 30 November 1942 |
| AOP | North Africa and Italy | 1943–5 |
| | Disbanded in Italy | 31 August 1945 |
| AAC | Reformed in Germany | 1 April 1962 |
| | Employed as 4 Div Aviation HQ | 1964–9 |
| | Reformed at Topcliffe from 666 Sqn | 1 November 1978 |
| | Northern Ireland squadron | 2 March 1983 |
| | | |
| *656 Squadron* | Formed at Westley (RAF unit) | 31 December 1942 |
| AOP | In India, Burma, Dutch East Indies | 1943–6 |
| | Reduced in Malaya to 1914 Flt | 15 January 1947 |
| | Reformed in Malaya from 1914 Flt | 29 June 1948 |
| AAC | Transferred to AAC | 1 September 1957 |
| | Employed as HQ 4 Wing AAC in Singapore and HQ Army Aviation in Borneo operations | 1 October 1965 |
| | Disbanded/reformed in Hong Kong and Seria | 18 December 1969–1 November 1971 |
| | Disbanded (flights retained in Hong Kong and Seria) | June 1977 |
| | Reformed in Farnborough from 664 Sqn | April 1978 |
| | In Operation Agila (Rhodesia) | December 1980–January 1981 |
| | In Operation Corporate (Falklands) returning to England | April–June 1982 |
| | (Army Air Corps Falklands Squadron formed and operated on a contingency basis) | June 1982–June 1987 |
| | | |
| *657 Squadron* | Formed at Ouston (RAF unit) | 31 January 1943 |
| AOP | North Africa, Italy, Holland and Germany | 1943–5 |
| | Disbanded at Middle Wallop (renumbered as 651 Squadron) | 1 November 1955 |
| | Reformed in Germany | 1 November 1971 |
| AAC | To England from | 1 May 1976 |
| | Reformed in Colchester from 665 Sqn | April 1978 |
| | | |
| *658 Squadron* | Formed at Old Sarum (RAF unit) | 30 April 1943 |
| AOP | In France, Belgium, Holland, and Germany | 1944–5 |
| | Disbanded in India | 15 October 1946 |
| AAC | Reformed in Germany | 1 November 1971 |
| | Reformed in Netheravon incorporating 6 and 14 Flights | April 1978 |
| | | |
| *659 Squadron* | Formed at Old Sarum (RAF unit) | 30 April 1943 |
| AOP | France, Holland, and Germany | 1944–5 |

|  |  |  |
|---|---|---|
|  | Disbanded in Pakistan | 14 August 1947 |
| AAC | Reformed in Germany | 1 November 1971 |
|  |  |  |
| *660 Squadron* | Formed at Old Sarum (RAF unit) | 31 July 1943 |
| AOP | France, Holland, and Germany | 1944–5 |
|  | Disbanded in Germany | 31 May 1946 |
| AAC | Reformed in England – Netheravon | 10 November 1969 |
|  | To Ulster returning to Topcliffe | December to April 1970 |
|  | Disbanded to reform as 653 Squadron | December 1977 |
|  | Reformed in Hong Kong | 21 August 1978 |
|  |  |  |
| *661 Squadron* | Formed at Old Sarum (RAF unit) | 31 August 1943 |
| AOP | France and Holland | 1944–5 |
|  | Disbanded in Holland | 31 October 1945 |
|  | Reformed at Kenley as RAuxAF unit | 1 May 1949 |
|  | Disbanded | 10 March 1957 |
| AAC | Reformed in Germany | 1 November 1978 |
|  |  |  |
| *662 Squadron* | Formed at Old Sarum (RAF unit) | 30 September 1943 |
| AOP | France, Holland, and Germany | 1944–5 |
|  | Disbanded in Germany | 15 December 1945 |
|  | Reformed at Colerne as RAuxF unit | 1 February 1949 |
|  | Disbanded | 11 March 1957 |
| AAC | Reformed in Germany | 1 November 1971 |
|  |  |  |
| *663 Squadron* | Formed at San Basilio in Italy | 14 August 1944 |
| AOP | (manned by Polish Army) Disbanded | 29 October 1946 |
|  | Reformed at Hooton Park as RAuxF unit | 1st July 1949 |
|  | Disbanded | 10 March 1957 |
| AAC | Reformed at Netheravon | 2 March 1970 |
|  | In Germany | 1 Novenber 1978 |
|  |  |  |
| *664 Squadron* | Formed at Andover (RAF unit) | 1 December 1944 |
| AOP | (Royal Canadian Air Force) Holland | 1945 |
|  | Disbanded in Germany | 31 May 1946 |
|  | Reformed at Hucknall as RAuxF unit | 1 September 1949 |
|  | Disbanded | 10 March 1957 |
| AAC | Reformed – to Farnborough | 1 November 1971 |
|  | Title transferred to Germany | April 1978 |
|  |  |  |
| *665 Squadron* | Formed at Andover (RAF unit) | 22 January 1945 |
| AOP | (Royal Canadian Air Force) Holland | 1945 |
|  | Disbanded in Holland | 10 July 1945 |
| AAC | Reformed in England – at Colchester | 1 November 1971 |
|  | Disbanded on renumbering as 657 Sqn | April 1978 |
|  | Reformed in Northern Ireland | 1 April 1986 |

| *666 Squadron* | Formed at Andover (RAF unit) | 5 March 1945 |
| AOP | (Royal Canadian Air Force) Holland | 1945 |
| | Disbanded in Holland | 30 September 1945 |
| | Reformed at Perth as RAuxF unit | 1 May 1949 |
| | Disbanded | 10 March 1957 |
| AAC | Reformed at Plymouth | 19 August 1969 |
| | To Topcliffe | November 1970 |
| | Disbanded to form 655 Squadron | April 1978 |
| | Reformed at Netheravon as TA Squadron | 1 April 1986 |
| | | |
| *667 Squadron* | Formed at Netheravon | 1 June 1969 |
| AAC | Redesignated as 7th Regiment | 1 June 1971 |
| | | |
| *668 Squadron* | Formed for Land Forces, Persian Gulf | December 1969 |
| AAC | Disbanded in Persian Gulf | 12 December 1971 |
| | | |
| *669 Squadron* | Formed from 131 Flight in Germany | 1 June 1971 |
| AAC | | |
| | | |
| *672 Squadron* | Formed at Dishforth | 1991 |
| AAC | Amalgamated with 656 Squadron | 1994 |

## Notes

1. Until 5 (Northern Ireland) Regiment was formed in 1979, 3 Flight and subsequently the sixteen squadrons extant served in the province regularly, some as many as seven times in ten years. The regiment continues to be manned by the remainder of the corps on a periodic basis.

2. A number of independent flight detachments have been maintained continuously over twenty years, notably:

7 Flight – Berlin
UNFICYP Flight – in Cyprus
16 Flight – in Sovereign Base Area, Cyprus

AAC detachment – Belize
AAC detachment – Suffield (Canada)
'C' Flight – detached to Brunei from Hong Kong

*Colonel-in-Chief*
His Royal Highness, The Prince of Wales

*Colonels-Commandant*
General Sir Hugh Stockwell, 1957–63
General Sir John Mogg, 1963–74
General Sir Frank King, 1974–9
General Sir Martin Farndale, 1979–88
General Sir John Learmont, 1988–94
Major-General M.J.D. Walker (designate)

*Directors of Air*
Major K.N. Crawford, 1942–6
Major-General M. Chilton, 1946–8

*Directors of Land/Air Warfare*
Major-General A.J.H. Cassels, 1948–9
Major-General R.H. Bower, 1949–52
Major-General G.S. Thompson, 1952–6
Major-General R.N.H.C. Bray, 1954–7
Major-General R.K. Exham, 1957–60
Major-General P. Weston, 1960–4
Major-General N. Crookenden, 1964–6
Major-General F.D.King, 1966–8
Major-General R.D. Wilson, 1968–9

*Directors of Army Aviation*
Major-General R.D. Wilson, 1970–1
Major-General T.A. Richardson, 1971–4

*Directors, Army Air Corps*
Major-General R.L.C. Dixon, 1974–6
Major-General J.A. Ward-Booth, 1976–9
Major-General W.N.J. Withall, 1979–83
Major-General J.D.W. Goodman, 1983–7
Major-General L.F.H. Busk, 1987–9
Major-General R.D. Grist, 1989–92
Major-General S.W.St.J. Lytle, 1992–

# Maps

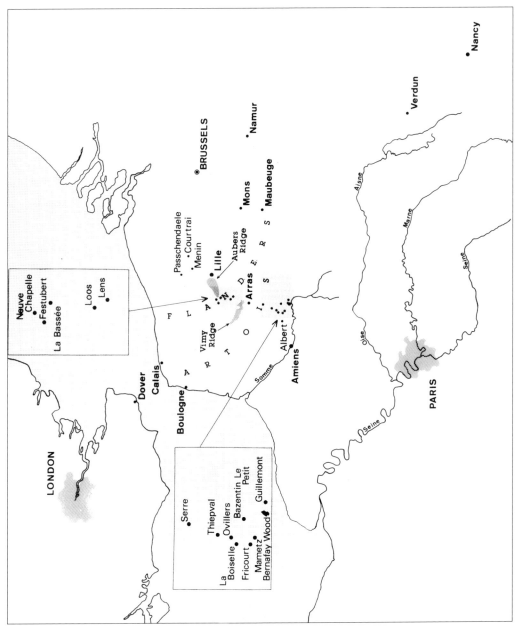

North-west Europe – First World War

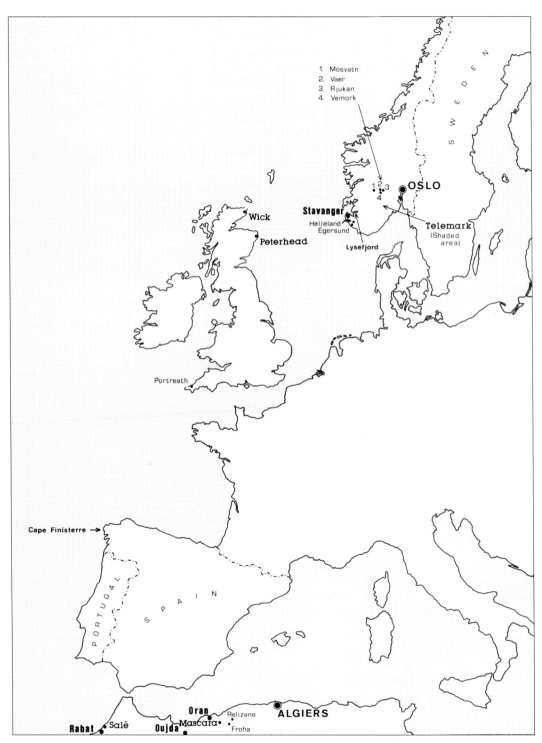

Europe and North Africa – events during 1942–5

1. La Motte
2. Le Muy
3. St Raphael
4. Frejus
5. St Tropez

RHONE

PO

PO

JUGOSLAVIA

SAVA

UNA

ITALY

GOTHIC LINE

Bosanska Petrovac

Split

NICE

TOULON

CORSICA

ROME

Ostia

Anzio
Terracina

LA MAIELLA

VOLTURNO

Termoli

Bari

Naples

Salerno

Gioia

Taranto

Brindisi

Manduria

San Pancrazio

SARDINIA

Messina

ETNA

Catania

Gela

Comiso

C. MURRO DE PORCO

C. PASSERO

Bone

Mateur

Djedeida

Medjez el Bab

Constantine

Bou Arada

Kairouan

Sousse

Msaken

TUNIS

TRIPOLITANIA

PANTELLERIA

MALTA

50    0    50    100

miles

North-west Europe – Market Garden and Varsity, 1944–5

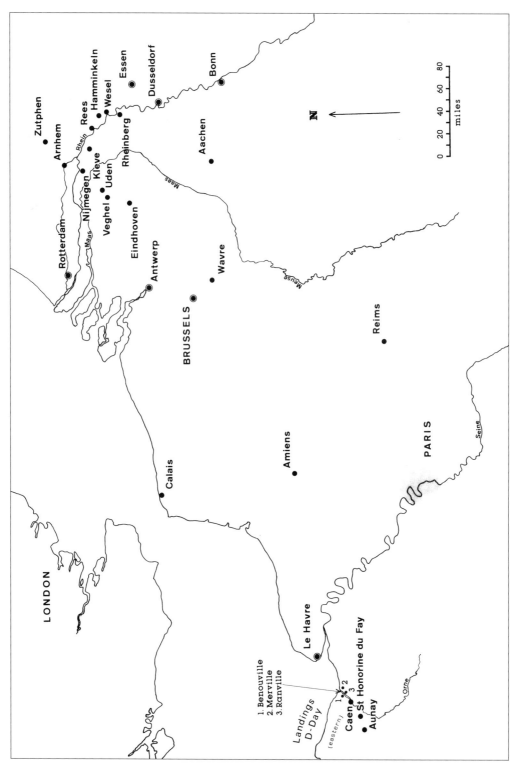

LONDON

Calais

Le Havre

Landings
D-Day
(eastern)
1. Benouville
2. Merville
3. Ranville
Caen
1
2
3
St Honorine du Fay
Aunay
Orne

Amiens

PARIS

Seine

Rotterdam
Zutphen
Arnhem
Rhein
Rees
Hamminkeln
Wesel
Rheinberg
Essen
Dusseldorf
Bonn
Aachen
Nijmegen
Maas
Kleve
Uden
Veghel
Maas
Eindhoven
Antwerp
Wavre
Meuse
BRUSSELS
Reims

N

0   20   40   60   80
miles

North-west Europe – Market Garden and Varsity, 1944-5

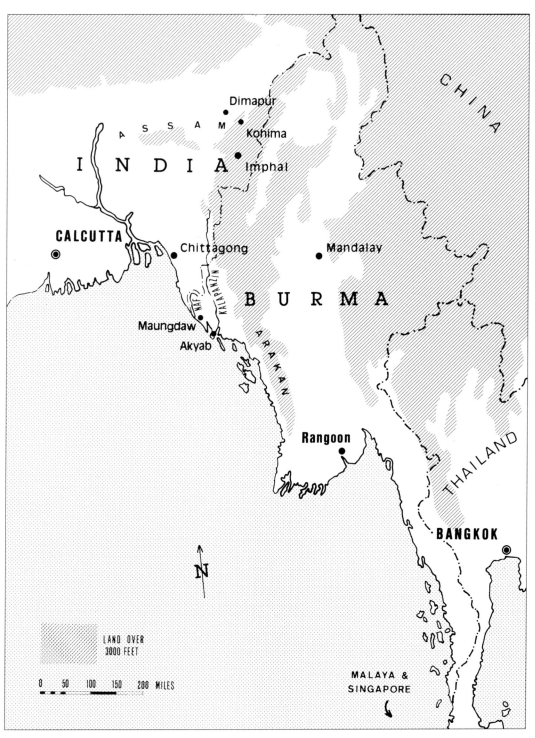

Burma – 651 Squadron operations, 1943–5

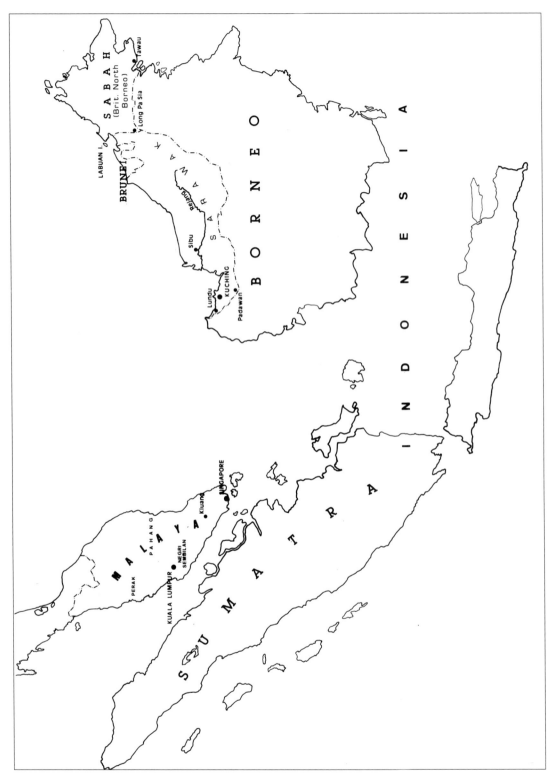

Malaya and Borneo – events during 1948–65

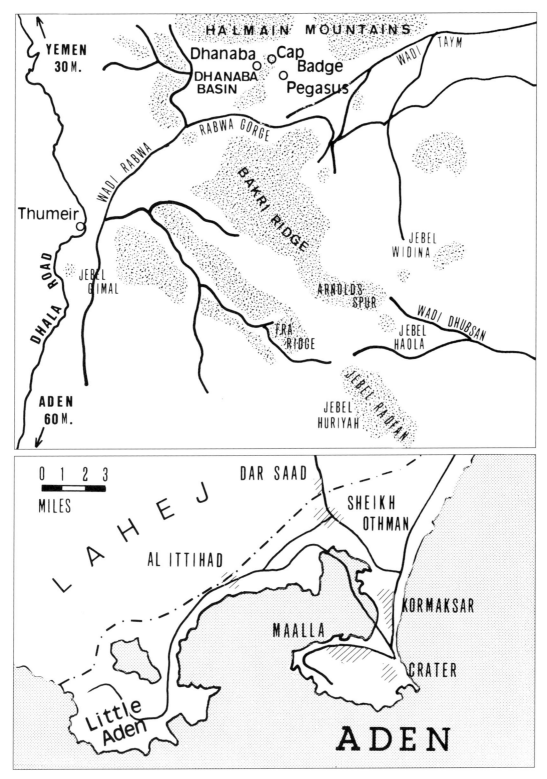

Aden and the Radfan, 1964–5

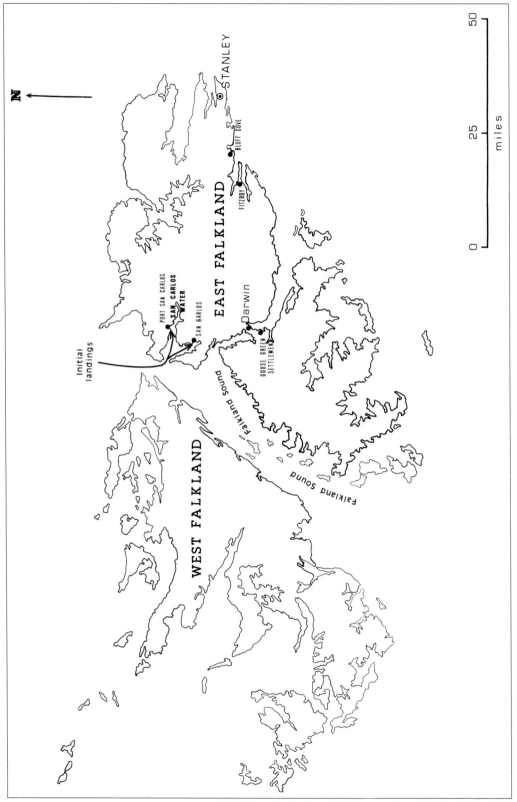

N

WEST FALKLAND

EAST FALKLAND

Falkland Sound

Falkland Sound

Initial
landings

PORT SAN CARLOS

SAN CARLOS
WATER

SAN CARLOS

Darwin

GOOSE GREEN
SETTLEMENT

FITZROY

BLUFF COVE

STANLEY

0       25       50
        miles

Falklands – 1982

Gulf operations – 1991

# Sources and Bibliography

I have written this book on the basis of information from four main areas: official records; private papers and studies; published works, including periodicals; personal interviews and discussions. The following gives some detail of written sources.

## Primary sources

*Cabinet and Ministry of Defence*
War Cabinet Minutes and memoranda, CAB 23, 24 and 65–8
Cabinet Committees, CAB 16/6, 21, 69–70, 78, 83, 85, 92–8
Chiefs of Staff Committee (and sub-committees), CAB 79–82; DEFE 04, 05, and 08
Prime Minister as Minister of Defence (1940–5), PREM 3
Defence Secretariat and Staff papers, CAB 23, 24, 120; DEFE 26
Defence Council Instructions (Army), DEFE 46
Combined Operations, DEFE 02

*Army*
Secretary of State, private office papers, WO 259
Army Council minutes, WO 32 and 163
CIGS (and CGS) papers, WO 216
Home Forces (1939–45), WO 199; war diaries, WO 166
Allied Forces in North Africa, Italy and France, WO 204; war diaries (1942–5), WO 169, 170, and 175
21 Army Group in north-west Europe (1944–5), WO 205; war diaries WO 171
Far East Forces (1942–5), WO 203; war diaries, WO 172
Directorate of Artillery, WO 196
Directorate of Military Training, WO 231
Directorate of Air, WO 233
Directorate of Staff Duties, WO 260
6th Airborne Division papers, WO 191 and 275
AAC Records, WO 295
RAF Glider Pilot Logbooks, WO 900
Falklands Islands campaign 1982, DEFE 14

*Air Ministry*
Secretary of State, private office papers, AIR 19
Air Council minutes, AIR 1, 2, 6 and 8
Bomber Command, AIR 8
Flying Training Command (including airborne forces), AIR 32
Army Cooperation Command, AIR 39
Squadron record books, AIR 27

*Ministry of Aviation and Supply*
Transportation and delivery of airborne forces, AVIA 21
Supply: air division, AVIA 63

*Private papers and studies*
Williams, George K. 'Statistics and Strategic Bombardment: Operations and Records of the British Long Range Bombing Force during World War I and their implications for the development of the post-war Royal Air Force, 1917–1923.' Thesis submitted to the Modern History Faculty, Oxford, 1988; copies in the British and Bodleian Libraries

**Secondary works**

*Air Committee, First and Second Reports by*, AC22 – Cmd 6695
Allen, H.R., *The Legacy of Lord Trenchard* (London, 1972)
Arden-Close, Sir Charles, *The Use of Balloons in War 1784–1902* (Royal Engineers Journal, March 1942)
Baring, Maurice, *Flying Corps Headquarters, 1914–1918* (London, 1920)
Barnett, Corelli, *Britain and her Army, 1509–1970* (London, 1970)
Bird, W.D., *One Air Force or Three?*, Army Quarterly, January, 1923
*British Military Aircraft of World War One*, (HMSO, 1976)
Chatterton, George, *The Wings of Pegasus* (London, 1962)
Cierva, J. de la, *Wings of To-morrow; the Story of the Autogiro* (New York, 1931)
Crookenden, *Napier Drop Zone, Normandy* (London, 1976)
Everett-Heath, John, *Helicopters in Combat, the First Fifty Years* (London, 1992)
Gardner, Richard, and Longstaff, Reginald, *British Service Helicopters, a Pictorial History* (London, 1985)
Gibbs-Smith, C.H., *A Brief History of Flying – from Myths to Space Travel* (London, 1953)
Hart, C., *Kites: an Historical Survey* (London, 1967)
Henniker, Sir Mark, *An Image of War* (London, 1987)
Hickey, Michael, *Out of the Sky* (Chippenham, 1979)
Maclean, Fitzroy, *Disputed Barricade* (London, 1957)
Mead, Peter, *Soldiers in the Air* (London, 1967)
Otway, T.B., *Airborne Forces* (HMSO, 1947)
Parham, H.J., and Belfield, E.M.G., *Unarmed into Battle* (Chippenham, 1956)
Pollard, A.O., *The Royal Air Force, a Concise History* (London, 1934)
Pritchard, J.L., *Sir George Cayley: the Inventor of the Aeroplane* (London, 1960)
*Proceedings of the Third Air Conference Held on 6th and 7th February 1923*, Cmd 1848
Raleigh, Sir Walter and H.A. Jones, *The War in the Air, Being the Story of the Part Played in the Great War by the Royal Air Force*, six volumes (Oxford, 1922–37)
Saunders, H. St.G., *Per Ardua: the Rise of British Air Power, 1911–39* (London, 1944)
Seth, Ronald, *Lion with Blue Wings* (London, 1956)
*A Short History of the Royal Air Force*, AP 125
Slessor, Sir John, *The Central Blue* (London, 1956)
Weyl, A.R., *Fokker: the Creative Years* (London, 1965)
Wood, Alan, *The Glider Soldiers* (Tunbridge Wells, 1992)

The following have also been consulted: Air Observation Post newsletters and brief squadron histories (contained in the Museum of Army Flying archive); The Army Air Corps and Air Observation Post journals; and *The Eagle* (journal of the Glider Pilot Regiment).

# Index

Mateur, 139
MATRA SNEB, rockets, 222
Matthews, Brigadier 'Hammer', 172
Maubeuge, 23–4,
Maungdaw, 148
Maxim, Sir Hiram, 7, 14
Maxim machine-gun, 33, 38
McCardie, Lieutenant-Colonel W.D.H., 121–2
McCorry, Charles, 159
McCulloch, Colonel, 205
McCulloch, Staff Sergeant, 107
McKenna, R., First Lord of the Admiralty, 14
McMillen, Major J.L., 110
McMillen, Staff Sergeant, 107
McNinch, Major (later, Colonel) W., 195
Mead, Major (later Brigadier) Peter, 184–5, 189–90, 194
Medjez el Bab, 140
Megara, 111
Memorandum on Naval and Military Aviation, 1912, 18
Merville, 97, 99
Methven, Lieutenant D.A. (GM), 73
Meuse, River, 113
Middle Wallop, 187, 189, 191, 193–4, 205–6, 207, 209, 210–11, 225, 233
Milan anti-tank missile, 216
Miley, Major-General W.M., 128
Ministry of Aircraft Production, 62, 71, 137
Ministry of Aviation, 205
Ministry of Defence (MOD), 205
Ministry of Supply, 189, 191
Mockeridge, Lieutenant (later Major) John, 82, 110-11
Model, Field Marshal Walter, 118, 122
Mogg, General Sir John, 208
Mons, 24, 113
Montauban, 35, 36
Montgolfier brothers, E. and J., 4–5
Montgomery, Field Marshal Sir Bernard (later Viscount, of Alamein), 76, 78–9, 82, 87, 91, 94, 96, 113, 114, 119, 123, 126, 129, 142, 162
Moore-Brabazon, Lieutenant J.T.C., (later Baron) 27–8
Morley, Captain C., 232
Morocco, 81, 139
Morrison, Staff Sergeant, 107
Moselle, River, 113
Mosvatn lake, 71–2
Mount Etna, 144
M'saken, 81

Mulberry Harbours, 113
Munro, Captain R.L., 155
Murdoch, Captain B., 100
Murray, Major (later Lieutenant-Colonel) Iain, 69, 99, 104, 121, 123–4, 130, 134
Muscat and Oman, 208

Naf estuary, 148
Nancy, 113
Nasser, President of Egypt, 186
Nathan, Major R.S., 221
NATO, 206, 208, 230
Near East Land Forces, 209
Neathercoat, Major R.W.V, 141
Negri Sembilan, 108
Neilson, Captain, 99
Netheravon, 21, 22, 69, 78, 233
Nettuno, 152
Neuve Chappelle, 29–30
Newall, Chief of the Air Staff Sir Cyril, 44–5
Newman, Staff Sergeant, 107
New Zealand, 200
Nice, 109
Nicholson, General Sir W., 14
Nicosia, 186
Nijmegen, 114, 116, 119, 120, 159
Norman, Wing Commander Sir Nigel (later Air Commodore), 61, 63, 65, 70–2, 80–1
Norman-Walker, Major (later Brigadier) R.A., 187, 189, 190
Norsk Hydro, 70
Northern Ireland, 214–15, 217–18
Norway and Norwegians, 70, 71–3
Nunn, Major J., 196
Nunn, Lieutenant R.J., 223

O'Gorman, Mervyn, 22
Oldman, Major (later, Lieutenant-Colonel) D.B., 151, 153
Old Sarum, 51
Oman – see Muscat
Operations: Agila, 221; Anvil, 105; Beggar, 81; Blockbuster, 160; Bunghole, 107–8; Comet, 114; Corporate, 221–5; Deadstick, 99; Dragoon, 107–9; Freshman, 70–3, 81; Fustian, 90, 98, 106; Granby (Gulf), 230–2; Husky series, 74, 76–9, 82, 92, 93, 96, 105–6, 108, 116; Ladbroke, 83, 90–1, 98, 106; Mallard, 103; Manna, 110; Market Garden, 114–16, 124–8; Musketeer, 186; Neptune, 98, 103, 114, 116, 120, 126; Overlord, 91, 93, 107, 114; Roundup, 77, 91; Shingle, 152;